Crich Parish and the Great War 1914 – 1918

Those who went to war

Peter Patilla

&

Brian Gibbons

Published by Crich Area Community News
Crich, Derbyshire

ISBN 978-0-9562271-2-6

British Library Cataloguing-in-Publication Data
A catalogue record for this book is available from the British Library

First published August 2014

Designed and typeset in Minion Pro by Peter Patilla

Edited by Louise Maskill
http://lmaskill.com

Printed and bound in Great Britain by 4edge Ltd., Hockley, Essex

Supported by The National Lottery® through the Heritage Lottery Fund

Crich Parish

The First Volunteers

Postcard courtesy Sue Worboys

In Loving Memory

— OF THE —

MEN OF THIS DISTRICT

Who fell in the Great War, 1914-18.

What does it matter now the war is o'er
What sea shall contain them or on what
shore,
They shall be sleeping afar from their
home,
Not there will we look but to God's great
dome ;
Where the quiet moon and each shining
star
Will tell us that they are not very far ;
God's love shall enfold them all to His
breast
And shall safeguard them wherever
they rest.

"Greater love hath no man than this
that he lay down his life for his friends."

Rest in Peace.

Composed by Corporal Simms,
Late 3rd Reserve Cavalry.

Please buy a copy in Remembrance of our Gallant Dead.

CONTENTS

Crich Parish Boundary

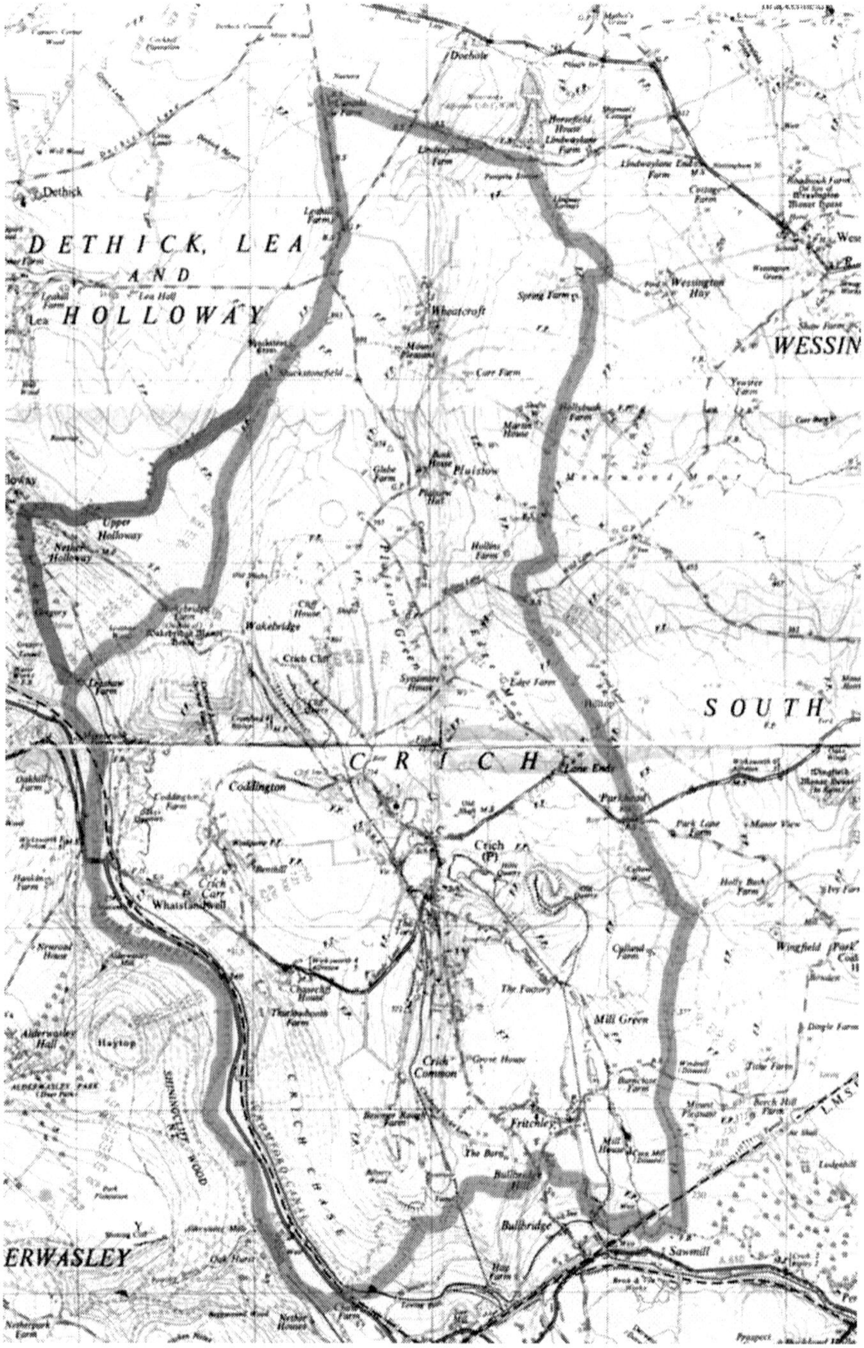

Map reproduced from 1949 Ordnance Survey map; Sheet 43/35 with the kind permission of Ordnance Survey

The map shows both the pre-1897 and post-1897 boundaries. The Nether Holloway area was annexed after a dispute.

FOREWORD

Nothing we do to honour those who served and died in the two World Wars or subsequent conflicts ever seems adequate. As regards World War 1, that has been brought home very emphatically by this book, and especially by the letters sent to the people back home. These provide a vivid illustration of the patriotism and selflessness of our armed forces and the stoicism of those who had to endure the most appalling circumstances and living conditions. They also bring to life what it must have been like to live through those times.

Every year, on Remembrance Sunday, we hear the names of the men from our parish who died in World War 1 when these are read out in St Mary's Church. We now have pen portraits of many of these men which will make our act of remembrance even more meaningful and poignant, especially as we realise how many of those who served came from the same families.

This book is the product of painstaking research by its authors, assisted by many local people who have contributed information and documents which tell a compelling story. It is a fitting tribute from our community that helps to illustrate why the events of a century ago are still relevant to our lives today.

Councillor Margaret Lane
Chair of Crich Parish Council

Acknowledgements

Research undertaken by:

Prunella Bradshaw
Dennis Brook
Brian Gibbons
Rosemary Hall
Simon Johnson
Andy Micklethwaite
Jane Middleton-Smith
John Mumby
Nivard Ovington
Peter Patilla

Photographs courtesy of:

Brenda Adderson
Debbie Bailey
Carol Beadle
John Beresford
Prunella Bradshaw
Nellie Brumwell
David Bull
Elizabeth Bunting
Beryl Calladine
Kathryn Campbell
Margaret Charboneau
Michelle Curzon
Terry Daniels
Michael Davies
Stephen Dawes
Joyce Denton
Alan Flint
Keith Fretwell
Ruby Gould
Mrs E Gratton
Elizabeth Griffiths
Rosemary Hall
Colleen Hardwick
John Hardwick
Barbara Haslam
Christine Hearne
Glynne Hickman
Tony Holmes
Ken Jackson
Pauline Laughlin
Betty Nadin
Stephen Peet
Alan Perry
Michael Porter
Frank Priestley
Ken Pykett
Clifford Raven
Carole Rayner
Kath Rhodes
Fred Sayles
Roy Siddons
R.H. Smith
Stan Smith
Margaret Suddes
Graham Swift
Aileen Taylor
Jennifer Teague
Kathryn Teeter
G. Thompson
Hilda Turner
Nigel Turner
Jim Walker
Hilary Welby
Margery Whitham
Irene Wilkinson
Sylvia Winson
Peter Woolley
Sue Worboys
Roger Worthy
Stu Wykes

Heritage Lottery Fund Grant

This research and its publications would not have been possible without the grant provided by the Heritage Lottery Fund.

Supported by The National Lottery® through the Heritage Lottery Fund

heritage lottery fund

Biographical details with photographs and documents were courtesy of:
David Brown for the letters to Annie Porter.
Family of John Thomas and William Roe for photographs, postcards and memorabilia.
Joy Goodall for biographical details of her grandfather Joseph Goodall.
Linda Hardy for biographical details of her grandfather Oscar Snow.
Gina Hewitt and Sue Taylor for biographical details of their grand-uncle James Hughes.
Simon Johnson for biographical details of his great grand-uncle William Taylor and his great great grand-uncle Arthur Walker Harrison.
Sheila Lockie and Maureen Austick for biographical details of their father Norman Henson.
Trevor Mason for biographical details of his father Arthur Mason.
Louis Sheldon for biographical details of his grandfather William Sheldon.
Jean Smith for biographical details of her step-grandfather George Ernest Watts.
Jenny Smith for biographical details of her grandfather John William Taylor.
Neta Stone for biographical details of her father George Henry Henson.
James Mervyn Taylor and Christine Taylor for biographical details of their father/grandfather Herbert Taylor.
Sylvia Winson and Irene Hallsworth for biographical details of their father/grandfather Harold Greenwood.
British Red Cross for information relating to VAD hospitals and Red Cross nurses.
South Wingfield Local History Society for photographs and documents relating to South Wingfield VAD Hospital.
Crich Heritage Partnership and their donors for access to their photo archives.
Derbyshire Record Office, Matlock for their resources and assistance.
Cliff Housley, Regimental Historian of the Sherwood Foresters.
Peter Donelly, curator, King's Own Royal Lancaster Regiment.
Potter & Co. Solicitors, Matlock for access to their historical collection of the High Peak News.
John Smedley Ltd. for access to their archive and Jane Middleton Smith, archivist.
Stan Smith for permission to use photographs from the George Smith Collection.
Scott Hamilton webmaster of www.aerodrome.com for information on Herbert Victor Rowley

We have tried to acknowledge all our contributors, but if through an oversight we have omitted a name please accept our apology and notify us so that this can be rectified in any reprint.

Sources and references

"The Bath At War: A Derbyshire Community and the Great War" by Charles Beresford – COUNTRY BOOKS/ASHRIDGE PRESS 2007 (ISBN 978 1 901214 91 8)
"The Quakers of Fritchley" by Walter Lowndes 1986 (ISBN 0-9511295-0-3)
Commonwealth War Graves Commission (www.cwgc.org)
The Long, Long Trail: The British Army in the Great War of 1914–1918 (www.1914-1918.net)
The National Archives (www.nationalarchives.gov.uk)
'Struggle for Survival in the Cardiganshire Hills: Story of the Settlement of the Mountains of Llanfair and Llanddewi' by Alan and Sally Leech. 2009 (ISBN: 978-0956111616).

INTRODUCTION

There are two known Rolls of Honour in Crich: one in St Mary's Church (which is still there) and one in the Baptist Chapel (which has disappeared).

The Church Roll of Honour lists the names of men who served. It does not always give the full name, and no regiments are stated. It has been our intention through this research to produce a new Roll of Honour, this Memorial Book and a website to ensure that all these men are "more than just a name".

It has not been possible to discover the criteria by which the names were originally recorded on the Rolls of Honour. Some of the men were born and always lived in the parish, some were born in the parish but had moved away, some had moved into the parish, and some had relatives in the parish. However, for some men it has been difficult to discover any links to the parish whatsoever.

The Roll of Honour in the church has some errors and omissions which hopefully have been corrected in this book and will be corrected in the new Roll of Honour which will be placed in the Glebe Field Centre, Crich. The website will also show the corrected records.

This memorial includes all the names on the original Roll of Honour, corrected where appropriate, plus omissions which have been unearthed during the research.

This book is a memorial both to those who lost their lives and to those who returned. It contains a mini biography of each man (and one woman). After the memorials is a collection of records which complement those of the individuals and add to the knowledge of events which occurred.

Sadly, we were unable to discover regimental details for some men because these were lost when the buildings housing the records were bombed during World War II and almost two-thirds of the records were destroyed.

It is important to remember the support given to our armed services during the Great War by the Commonwealth Countries and our allies. Several Crich men returned from Canada and Australia to serve in the conflict with their "new" country's army. They are also remembered in this book and in the new Roll of Honour.

The men of the parish served in seventy-seven different regiments and services. Elsie Sayles, from Crich served with the Red Cross in military hospitals; she is also remembered. We have a photograph of Harriet Self wearing a Red Cross nurses' uniform but she has been omitted because no proof was found of her involvement at the time of the war. Men from the parish served in the Army, the Royal Navy, Royal Naval Flying Service and the Royal Flying Corps (the RNAS and RFC to become the Royal Air Force).

The ages of the men who volunteered or who were called into service varied widely. There were fifteen-year-old youths trying to enlist and men in their forties (even one aged fifty) were called to serve. Crich youths as young as seventeen and eighteen lost their lives. Brothers joined (often at the same time), fathers and sons served. Their stories are very moving.

Wherever conflict was taking place, whether in Europe, the Mediterranean, Egypt or Salonika, the men of Crich Parish could be found serving their country. They could also be found in India and modern-day Pakistan. Men of the Royal Navy were serving in many different places across the globe. Sometimes soldiers served nearer home. The troubles in Ireland are often overlooked at this time, yet men of the parish were serving there.

Some of the men did not serve abroad but were nonetheless actively fulfilling a vital role in the necessary work keeping the forces supplied with their needs.

Our research found men who wanted to serve but were denied the opportunity because of their work in a reserved occupation, or because of their state of health. Some men were taken from the trenches to return to their occupation or to undertake necessary war work at home, particularly in the mines, on the railways or in munitions works.

We became aware that some men had disciplinary punishments recorded on their service record. The usual punishment was either to be confined to barracks for a few days or the loss of a few days' pay, or both. The "crimes" were typically being late on parade, equipment faults, answering back to non-commissioned officers (NCOs) and returning late from a period of leave. Often they indicated the harshness and sometimes unkind nature of army discipline. In the main we have not included disciplinary records in the men's records.

If the records stated any money awarded we have left the amounts in their original form and not converted them into current decimal values.

We have had challenges trying to track down information on some of the men and continue our research. The website www.crichparish-ww1.co.uk will be updated as we discover more. The records in this book are what we have discovered up to the time of printing.

We have felt it an honour to record a little about these men (and woman) and we appreciate the help given to us by many of their descendents. Whatever else we may have achieved, we feel the vast majority are now much more than "just a name".

Peter Patilla and Brian Gibbons

British Army Regiments and other services in which those of the parish served

Naming the regiments and services in which people served proved to be an interesting task. Many of the regiments were known by their initials, or abbreviated title or "familiar" name. For instance – the King's Own Yorkshire Light Infantry were known as KOYLI; the Sherwood Foresters (Nottinghamshire and Derbyshire Regiment) were recorded variously as the Sherwood Foresters, Notts & Derby or just the Foresters; the Gloucestershire Regiment were often the Gloucesters.

Some regiments and services changed their names during the course of the war. In 1918 the Army Service Corps (ASC) became the Royal Army Service Corps (RASC). and the Royal Flying Corps (RFC) combined with the Royal Naval Air Service (RNAS) to become the Royal Air Force (RAF).

The key below gives the full regimental title, but in the records abbreviated names are sometimes used, especially in the narrative reports.

ACC	Army Cyclist Corps
AIF	Australian Imperial Forces
APC	Army Pay Corps
ASC	Army Service Corps
BR	Border Regiment
CEF	Canadian Expeditionary Force
CG	Coldstream Guards
CoR	Connaught Rangers
CR	Cheshire Regiment
DCLI	Duke of Cornwall's Light Infantry
DLI	Durham Light Infantry
DoW	Duke of Wellington's (West Riding) Regiment
DoR	Dorsetshire Regiment
DeR	Devonshire Regiment
DY	Derbyshire Yeomanry
EL	East Lancashire Regiment
ER	Essex Regiment
EY	East Yorkshire Regiment
GG	Grenadier Guards
GR	Gloucestershire Regiment
HeR	Herefordshire Regiment
HLI	Highland Light Infantry
HC	Household Cavalry Composite Regiment
KLR	King's (Liverpool Regiment)
KORLR	King's Own (Royal Lancaster Regiment)
KOSB	King's Own Scottish Borderers
KOYLI	King's Own Yorkshire Light Infantry
KRRC	King's Royal Rifle Corps
KSLI	King's Shropshire Light Infantry
LC	Labour Corps
LeR	Leicestershire Regiment

LeY	Leicestershire Yeomanry (Prince Albert's Own)
LF	Lancashire Fusiliers
LiR	Lincolnshire Regiment
LR	London Regiment
MFP	Corps of Military Foot Police
MiR	Duke of Cambridgeshire's Own (Middlesex Regiment)
MGC	Machine Gun Corps
MMP	Corps of Military Mounted Police
MR	Manchester Regiment
NF	Northumberland Fusiliers
NoR	Northamptonshire Regiment
NS	Prince of Wales's (North Staffordshire Regiment)
NY	Nottinghamshire (Sherwood Rangers) Yeomanry
QOH	7th (Queen's Own) Hussars
QRS	Queen's (Royal West Surrey) Regiment
RAF	Royal Air Force
RAMC	Royal Army Medical Corps
RASC	Royal Army Service Corps
RAVC	Royal Army Veterinary Corps
RDC	Royal Defence Corps
RE	Royal Engineers
RF	Royal Fusiliers (City of London Regiment)
RFA	Royal Field Artillery
RFC	Royal Flying Corps
RGA	Royal Garrison Artillery
RHA	Royal Horse Artillery
RIR	Royal Irish Rifles
RM	Royal Marines
RMA	Royal Marines Artillery
RN	Royal Navy
RNAS	Royal Naval Air Service
RNVR	Royal Naval Volunteer Reserve
RoB	Princess Charlotte of Wales's (Royal Berkshire Regiment)
RoS	Royal Sussex Regiment
RoW	Royal Warwickshire Regiment
RSF	Royal Scots Fusiliers
SF	Sherwood Foresters (Nottinghamshire and Derbyshire Regiment)
SG	Scots Guards
SR	Suffolk Regiment
SRY	Sherwood Rangers Yeomanry
SS	South Staffordshire Regiment
SH	Seaforth Highlanders (Ross-Shire Buffs, The Duke of Albany's)
SWB	South Wales Borderers
TR	Training Reserve
WYR	Prince of Wales's Own (West Yorkshire Regiment)
Y&L	York and Lancaster Regiment
RC	Red Cross

Crich Roll of Honour 2014

The Roll of Honour was designed by Stephen Furguson-Swain (the bees knees design bureau) and the frame made by Keith Fretwell (Ram Furniture).

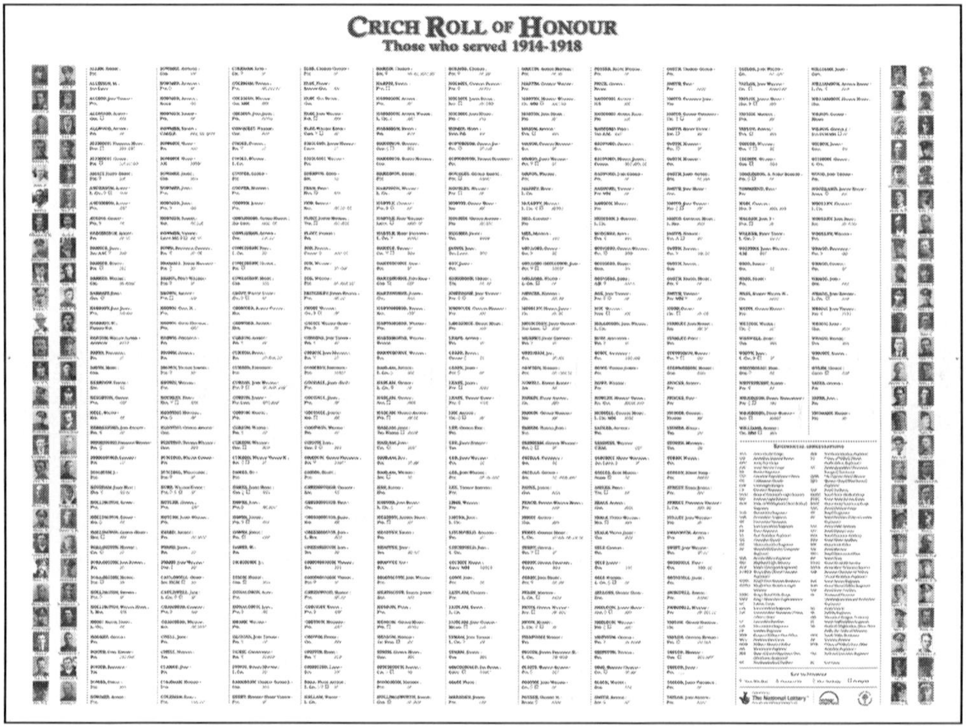

To mark the centenary of the start of the Great War there is a new Roll of Honour situated inside the Glebe Field Centre, Crich. This contains (where known) full name, rank, regiment and photograph for each person. It corrects errors and includes names omitted from the original.

The following records are intended to ensure that those on the Roll are more than "just a name".

Records of those who served in the Great War 1914 – 1918

ALLEN, Private – Ernest

Regiment unknown

Ernest was born in Crich in about 1887 to James and Elizabeth Allen who lived in the Bullbridge area. Before he went to war he worked as a wood turner in Sawmills and married May Smith. They had a son, Francis Humphrey.

ALLISTON, Second Lieutenant – M.

Regiment unsure

It has not been possible to identify a definite candidate for the 'Second Lieutenant M. Alliston' listed on the original Roll of Honour in Crich Parish Church. Public records show that Alliston was a very rare surname in Derbyshire during the nineteenth and twentieth centuries and no individual named Alliston has been identified with links, familial or otherwise, to the parish of Crich or the surrounding area.

The 'Medal Rolls Index Cards', created by the Army Medal Office near the close of the First World War, provide the most complete listing of soldiers who served during the war, containing approximately 90% of their names. Only one individual named Alliston was located who matched the name and rank and that was Montague James Alliston. He was a London man who initially served with The London Regiment, then the Royal Flying Corps. He was promoted from Second Lieutenant to Lieutenant. We are unsure as to whether his is the name on the Roll as he has no obvious link to Crich or Derbyshire. However, fuller details of him have been included on the *www.crichparish-ww1.co.uk* website.

ALLSOP, Private – John Thomas

Regiment unknown

John Thomas was born in Crich Carr in about 1881; his parents were John and Ellen Allsop. Before the war he married Mary Elizabeth Smith and they had two children, Harry and Essie. In 1911 he worked at Lea Mills but had left by 1914 because he is not recorded in the Mill's records at that time.

ALLWOOD BROTHERS

Albert and George were the sons of William and Elizabeth Allwood, who lived at Wakebridge. It seems that all the family, apart from Elizabeth, worked at Lea Mills.

Arthur and Frederick were the sons of Herbert and Mary Ann Allwood. They both worked at Lea Mills, as did their father and sisters. The family lived at Wakebridge.

ALLWOOD, Gunner – Albert

Royal Field Artillery

Photo Roy Siddons

Albert was born about 1898. Before the war he worked in the warehouse at Lea Mills as a packer. He joined the forces on 12th May 1916, serving in France during 1916 and 1917, but he was wounded and returned to England where he was in hospital. Records at the mill show he received food and hosiery parcels on four occasions. Addresses included Trafalgar Hospital in Greenwich and the Battery Band Room, Charlton Park, London. The reference to the band room at Charlton Park suggests that he was a bandsman at some time. He acknowledged receipt of all the parcels he received, with some letters including descriptions of what life was like. He was back at work in Lea Mills by 28th August 1919. His brother George is also on the Roll of Honour.

Cards sent by Albert to his mother and sisters

Photo Nellie Brumwell

Albert Allwood (marked with a cross) with some of his RFA regiment

Photo Nellie Brumwell

Thursday 16/11/16

Dear Sir,

I received your parcel safely that you sent through Austins on 26th Oct, and your letter on Nov. 6th for which I thank you the contents were very good, and was gladly welcomed, for we were in action at a place were it was not possible to buy anything. I hope you will excuse me not writing sooner, but we have been on the move from 31st Oct. until 12th Nov, and during that time no letters could be sent. The place we're in action now is not so hot fighting as the last, and we have also got good dug-outs, and a bed each. I thank you very much for the offer of under clothing we have had new underclothing issued this morning. There is better conditions here for keeping yourself clean, and can wash your clothes there was no chance of washing clothes before you had to wear them as long as possible and then throw them away. I am thankful to say I am in good health although we have had some very wet weather. Shall now have to close, thanking you once more for your parcel.

Yours truly, A. Allwood

Wednesday 27/12/16

Dear Sirs,

Just a few lines in acknowledgement of parcels, which I received on the 25th and 26th. The one with eatables in had been broken, but I don't think anything was missing. We have had a very decent Xmas here, we had salmon, sweets, and plum pudding on Xmas day, and I passed away the night in one of the dug-outs with a gramaphone. The weather I think is more like spring, than winter, we have had a little snow, but it soon melted away with the rain, which we have had pretty well of lately. I have not got much news, one day is same as another, only you work Sundays. I am very pleased to say I am in the best of health and hope to keep so. I must now conclude, thanking you for your kindness, which I am sure all out here will appreciate.

Yours truly, A. Allwood

Photo Nellie Brumwell

Albert Allwood's family taken c 1905 at Wakebridge.
Right to Left: William Snr, William, Elizabeth, Fred, Sarah Hannah, Albert, George

ALLWOOD, Private – Arthur

Sherwood Foresters (Nottinghamshire and Derbyshire Regiment)

Arthur, born about 1893, attested at Lea on 21 October 1914. The Magistrate who signed was J. B. Marsden-Smedley, Managing Director, of Lea Mills where Arthur once worked. When he enlisted he was working as a quarryman.

On 4th December 1914, after a short two months in the Army, he was discharged as being medically unfit for War Service. His brother Frederick is also on the Roll of Honour.

ALLWOOD, Driver – Frederick Henry

Royal Field Artillery
Army Service Corps

Before the war Fred worked at Lea Mills. He joined the forces in January 1915 and was in France during 1916. He received several food and hosiery parcels from the management at Lea Mills to which he replied. Some of his letters were very informative.

Sunday, November 12th 1916, France

Dear Sir;

Thank you very much for the kind letter I received from you about a

fortnight ago. I was very pleased with the contents of the parcel you so kindly sent to me, as I told you, in a letter I sent you thanking you for sending it. I asked several of my pals to have a taste of the Camp-Pie, & they all said it was "tres bon", & it was. I have been up at the guns for 10 or 11 days, making new positions & have not had any chance to write, or I should have answered your letter before now. Where we are now is a long way from either a Y.M.C.A, or a shop or any other place that is occupied by any one only troops. We are on a much quieter part of the line now, than what we were in July and August, although it is "lively" enough occasionally as "Fritz" keeps sending a few big shells over daily. About a fortnight ago a party of us were getting bricks for some stables, & we had been having a look round some houses that had been shelled a few days before, & we had only just got out of the houses when "Fritz" commenced to shell the place, & he put some big shells in the same house that we had just left & knocked it all to bits. Luckily, no one of our party was hit. I am writing this in a dug-out in which we are living at the present time. We have made a stove out of an old oil-drum, as of course we have to make ourselves as comfortable as possible. It is a "little bit" different to going to church on Sunday evening. Of course, I am not grumbling, as I know all these things happen in war. It is a great deal better being in a dug-out with a decent roof over your head than lying out in the open for 3 nights in the open, in the rain with nothing over you only a great coat. We have just been unloading wagons that have come up with material, one of them has got stuck in the mud down the road, the other teams have gone to pull them out. Again thanking you for the nice letter, I am pleased to say I am in the best of health at present, & hope to keep so.
Yours respectfully, Drv F.H. Allwood

December 30th 1916, B.E.F.
Dear Sir,
Thank you very much for the splendid parcel of good things I received from you a few days ago. I was very pleased indeed with it, & I have enjoyed the contents very much. It is very nice to know that the people at Home think about us out here, & I for one (& I am sure all the other boys as well) appreciate very much, any such kindness. It was a very different Xmas here, to what it used to be in good old 'Blighty' before the war. Of course, when we awoke on Christmas morning, we sang "Christians Awake", & several other Carols etc, before we went on parade, just to remind us that it was really Xmas. Again, thanking you very much for your Kindness, & wishing you a Prosperous New Year.
Yours respectfully, Dr F.H. Allwood R.F.A

Lea Mills offered him a job on his return from service but he declined the offer.

ALLWOOD, Private – George

Leicestershire Yeomanry
Labour Corps
Gloucestershire Regiment

Photo Kathryn Campbell

George was born in about 1894 and like his father and brother Albert he worked at Lea Mills. He joined the forces on 24th November 1916 and received a regular supply of parcels from J. B. Marsden-Smedley of Lea Mills. He trained in East Yorkshire before going to France with the British Expeditionary Force (B.E.F.). He landed in France in April 1917 and an extract from a letter published in the Dethick, Lea and Holloway Parish Magazine dated April 22nd 1917 noted that '*I have landed back in army life*'. This was followed by another dated August/September 1917 which says, '*A few lines to let you know I am in Hospital. I have had a fortnight of it now*'. The reasons for his time in hospital did not become clear until he wrote a letter on 21st October 1918 thanking the Company for the parcel sent earlier that month. The letter also contains information about his medical condition: '*I wrote to you last Friday regarding my low grade and hope that you will put in an application for me being released from the army to come back to work as I am B now which is next to discharge*'. The Company recorded on 28th August 1919 that he had returned from the war and had been re-employed, but he was left suffering from trench fever. It is not known whether he also suffered wounding. Trench fever is a disease causing pain in the joints and muscles that was prevalent among soldiers living in the trenches, caused by rickettsia and transmitted by lice. Rickettsia is a micro organism found in lice and ticks, and when it is transferred to man by lice causes typhus and other serious diseases.

18/12/16
Dear Sir
Just a few lines to let you know that I received your most welcome parcel this morning, which I thank you very much for, me and my pal have had the sardines for tea to day they went down better than the bread and dripping that we should have had to have had again thanking you I remain yours sincerely
George Allwood

11/2/18
Dear Sir
Just a few lines to let you know that I have received your parcel dated 9/1/18 yesterday For which I thank you for, but am sorry to say that it was all broken up so I only received the remains of it, but what little I did get was very much appreciated as things are out here: we are having some very icy weather at present, so again thanking you for parcel and wishing you the best of health and the best of prosperity I remain yours
Pte Geo Allwood

Photos Kathryn Campbell

George Allwood and his wife Lily May (née Key) on their wedding day, just prior to enlistment.

Lea Mills commemorative certificate presented to George Allwood

George's brother Albert is also on the Roll of Honour.

AMATT, Private – Joseph Ernest ✝

Leicestershire Regiment

Joseph was born in Fritchley, although at some time before 1901 the family moved to Leicestershire. His parents were Ernest and Martha Amatt of Crich. He attested in Leicester on 14th October 1914 aged twenty, working as a "clicker". He joined the British Expeditionary Force to France on 29th July 1915 and was killed in action four months later on 11th November 1915. He is buried at the Bienvillers Military Cemetery.

ANDERSON BROTHERS

Albert and Alfred were the sons of Alfred and Annie Anderson who lived most of their married life in Holloway, Derbyshire.

ANDERSON, Lance Corporal – Albert ✝

Duke of Wellington's (West Riding Regiment)

Albert was born at Holloway and was living in Crich as a Co-op shop assistant during 1911.

When he attested on 28th November 1915, aged twenty-two, he was living in Sheffield and working as a grocer's assistant. He was killed in action on 28th August 1917 and is remembered at the Tyne Cot 'Memorial to the Missing' in Belgium.

Albert had eight siblings and he lived for a while in Crich with his married sister Annie Roe. His brother, named Alfred after their father, is also on the Crich Roll of Honour.

Albert's death was reported in the Derbyshire Times.

Derbyshire Times 22 Sept 1917

CRICH SOLDIER KILLED

Albert Anderson, Lance-Corpl. West Riding Regiment, of Crich, has been killed in action on the Western Front. The sad news was received on Friday last week and caused profound sorrow and regret amongst the inhabitants of Crich, at which place the deceased soldier was well known and universally liked. Lance Corporal Anderson resided with his brother-in-law and sister, Mr and Mrs Abram Roe, of Crich Common, and they received the official intimation on Tuesday. The officer in charge, Infantry Record Office, York, wrote saying that Lance-Corpl. Anderson was killed in France on August 27th 28th, and Lord Derby also wrote conveying to Mr and Mrs Roe the sympathy of their Majesties the King and Queen. Lance-Corpl. Anderson enlisted in November 1915. He was 24 years of age on April 28th last, and was single. Before the war he was employed by the Sheffield Cooperative Society at their Eccleshall Branch. Previous to taking up duties at Eccleshall he was for about six years employed at the Ripley Cooperative Society's Crich branch. He was educated at the Crich British School, and was a member of the Crich Baptist Church and Sunday School. He is the second member of the Baptist Church at Crich to make the supreme sacrifice, and the second to be likewise recorded on the Roll of Honour at the Council School. Lance-Corpl. Anderson was wounded last year and on returning to France after recovery received his promotion. His loss will be felt keenly at Crich and Eccleshall, and the sympathy of all is extended to the bereaved relatives.

ANDERSON, Private – Alfred

Army Service Corps
Royal Army Service Corps (M.T.)

Alfred was born in Holloway and was living with his married sister, Annie Roe, during 1911 – as was his brother Albert and sister May. He attested on 16th May 1916 in Derby, aged twenty-five; he was a hosiery hand employed at the Derwent Mills, Belper. At the time he was married to Rosetta Ludlam and they had a daughter Florence May. He was demobbed on 19th February 1919 with a disability allowance of 30% for neurasthenia. For this he was awarded a pension of 8s 3d which was increased to 12s 0d in 1920. His demob address was Millgreen, Fritchley.

ATKINS, Private – Gilbert ✝

Training Reserve

Gilbert was born in 1899 in Fritchley; his parents were William and Alice Atkins. He died in hospital with cerebro spinal fever on 25th May 1917 aged eighteen and was buried in St Mary's churchyard, Crich. He has a commemorative headstone on his grave.

BAINBRIDGE, Private – Albert

Sherwood Foresters (Nottinghamshire and Derbyshire Regiment)
Labour Corps

Albert was born in about 1874 in Chesterfield, his parents were Silas and Ann Bainbridge. Shortly after Albert was born the family moved to Crich. He worked as a limestone quarryman and married Emily Brooks in 1906.

BARBER, Air Mechanic 2nd class – James ✝

Royal Flying Corps
Royal Air Force

Handley Page O/400 bomber D8345 of 207th Sqn RAF

James was born at Church View, Crich in 1894; his parents were James and Margaret Barber. When he enrolled he was a wagon oiler on the Midland Railway. He enlisted on 3rd August 1917 and the RAF Muster Roll gives his rate of pay as 1s 8d. The RAF was formed on 1 April 1918. He served with 207th Squadron. James died on 7th February 1919, some three months after the Armistice, and he is buried at Cologne Southern Cemetery. More than one thousand Allied prisoners and dozens of German servicemen were buried in Cologne Southern Cemetery during the First World War. Commonwealth forces entered Cologne on 6th December 1918, less than a month after the Armistice, and the city was occupied under the terms of the Treaty of Versailles.

James's squadron moved to Germany as part of the Army of Occupation in January 1919, serving there until the August.

BARBER, Private – Robert

Durham Light Infantry

Robert was born at Starkholmes in 1900; his parents were Robert and Mabel Barber. Shortly afterwards the family moved to Sawmills and then to Crich Carr, where both Robert and his father worked at Dawbarns joinery firm. He attested aged eighteen on 25th May 1918 at Derby, giving his address as Bents Hill Cottage, Crich Carr. He was posted overseas on 12th October 1918 and received a gunshot wound to his right shoulder on 23rd October 1918. He was demobbed on 26th January 1919. After the war he played for Whatstandwell Football Club along with several other returning servicemen; see the photo on page 243.

BARBER, Corporal – William

South Staffordshire Regiment
Royal Army Medical Corps

William was born in 1888 at Crich; his parents were Samuel and Fanny Barber. He married Tansley-born Mary Booth in 1914; she worked at Lea Mills, while he was a farm labourer. They had a daughter, Marion.

He attested on 15th July 1916, aged twenty-seven, at Bakewell, giving his address as Stable Yard, Scotland, Tansley. His occupation was horseman and nurseryman. He was transferred from the South Staffordshire Regiment to the RAMC and appointed Acting Corporal, with pay, on 12th May 1919. He reverted to Private on 27th July 1919 but seems to have been promoted to full Corporal after that. William was demobbed on 11th January 1920.

BARRATT, Gunner – Jesse

Regiment unknown

Jesse was born in about 1890 in Eckington and was named after his grandfather. From 1900 he was living in Fritchley where he married Sarah Ann Perry in 1913. He was a wireworker at Johnson and Nephew, Ambergate before the war but afterwards he farmed at South Wingfield. Jesse played football for one of the Crich teams. He died at Tansley in 1949 aged fifty-nine.

BARRATT, Private – John James ◊

North Staffordshire Regiment

Royal Sussex Regiment

John was born in 1896 at Fritchley; his parents were John and Mahala Barratt. Before the war he was a wood-turner before becoming a gardener.

He attested on 10th December 1915 at Derby aged nineteen, and his address was listed as Hill Top, Fritchley. He was transferred to the Royal Sussex Regiment on 6th September 1916. On 18th November 1917 he was discharged suffering from a post-combat disorder called Disordered Action of the Heart with a weekly pension of 27s 6d for thirteen weeks, which then reverted to 22s 0d. per week. He was awarded the Silver War Badge.

BARRATT, Farrier Sergeant – W.

Regiment unknown

There is some uncertainty about this record. The Roll of Honour named W. Barratt and this is the only one found with Crich connections.

William Barratt was born in about 1874, and was a coal miner living in Fritchley. His mother was Hannah Barratt, a farmer and widow. Army records show a Sergeant William Barratt of the Army Veterinary Corps who enlisted in June 1915 and was discharged in May 1918.

BARTON, Artificer – William Alfred

Royal Navy Volunteer Reserve

William was born in about 1895 in Gorton, Manchester and his parents were William Alfred and Marion Barton. The family moved to Ambergate when his father became a clerk at the wireworks. William engaged in the RNVR aged twenty-three. Standing at over six feet he was tall for the time. During the war he served as an Engine Room Artificer (ERA) aboard the minesweeper HMS *Tedworth*. After the war he married Florence Mountney.

BATES, Private – Frederick

Sherwood Foresters (Nottinghamshire and Derbyshire Regiment)

Fred was born at Whatstandwell in 1893; his parents were Fred and Hannah Bates. At the start of the war the family were living at Hill Top, Fritchley.

He enlisted before the start of the war on 29th April 1912 at Belper. He was a general labourer aged nineteen who lived at Crich Carr. On 21st November 1914 he transferred to the Reserves. Two weeks after his transfer to the Reserves he was discharged as being medically unfit for further military service.

BATES, Gunner – Henry

Regiment unknown

Henry was born in about 1892 at Ambergate; his parents were Joseph and Eliza Bates. Before the war he was employed as a horse driver in the Ambergate wireworks. His cousin, Richard Cyril Tatham, became a prisoner of war in Holland.

Ripley & Heanor News 16 April 1915

A PRISONER IN HOLLAND

> Mr J. Bates of Canal-side, Bull Bridge, has received a letter from his nephew, Seaman R. C. Tatham, who is a prisoner in Holland, giving an interesting account of his experiences since he left the old country. He was in the defence of Antwerp, and was one of the 1500 men who in the retreat got onto Dutch soil, and there has had to remain a prisoner of war. He points out that Holland is in rather a perilous position at present and if things turned the wrong way they may find themselves in the trenches again. "The sooner the better," he concludes

BEARDOW, Sapper – Samuel

Royal Engineers

Born about 1879 at Wheatcroft, Samuel was the son of John and Hannah Beardow. He worked as a stonemason before joining the Army.

BEIGHTON, Private – George

Canadian Expeditionary Force

George was born on 3rd February 1876 at Fritchley. He became the adopted son of John and Dorothy Ollerenshaw who lived on Chapel Lane, Crich. He joined the Royal Garrison Artillery in July 1900 aged twenty-three, while working as a wire trimmer. He served with the army for nearly eight years.

Records show that a George Beighton left Liverpool on SS *Sardinian* for Halifax, Nova Scotia, arriving there on 15th August 1912. He then joined the Royal Canadian

Garrison Artillery and was stationed at Sandwich Battery in Halifax, where he served for six years before attesting for the Canadian Expeditionary Force in March 1918, aged forty-two. The next of kin was his brother Thomas Beighton, Station House, Gloucester Central, England. George had blue eyes and dark hair and was five foot nine inches tall. Interestingly he refused to sign the declaration on his attestation papers.

BELL, Sapper – Walter

Royal Engineers

He is on the original Crich Roll of Honour but little further information has been found. He appears on the 1918 Electoral Roll as an Absent Voter. His wife Elizabeth is also registered. Walter married Elizabeth Phillips in 1912.

BERRESFORD, Private – John Stanley Harrison ✞

Seaforth Highlanders

John Stanley Harrison Berresford was born in 1899; his parents were John Harrison and Mary Alice Beresford. He must have enrolled at an early age because he died 20th July 1918 aged seventeen and is listed at the Ploegsteert Memorial, which commemorates more than 11,000 servicemen of the United Kingdom and South African forces who died in this sector during the First World War and have no known grave. He enlisted with another young Crich volunteer, Nelson Martin Bollington, who had previously tried to enlist with the Sherwood Foresters in 1914 when he was only fifteen. John and Nelson had adjacent regimental numbers throughout their service.

BERRISFORD, Private – Frederick William ◊

Sherwood Foresters (Nottinghamshire and Derbyshire Regiment)

Frederick was born in 1897, the son of Frederick and Ellen Berrisford. The spelling of their surname varied and even changed to Collins for a time. His army records show him as Frederick William Beresford. Before the war he worked for Joseph Yeomans, who was a well-known local shop-keeper. His medal index card records him with an address of Town End, Crich, enlisting on 19th October 1915 and being discharged 14th December 1918. He was awarded the Silver War Badge, the record giving his age as twenty-one on discharge after serving abroad.

BERRISFORD, Private – Leonard

Coldstream Guards

Leonard was born at Crich in 1899; his parents were Leonard and Elizabeth Berrisford. He enlisted at Derby on 29th April 1918, although he was deemed to have enlisted on 18th December 1916 because he was working as a miner. On enlisting he was aged nineteen. He was demobbed on 30th April 1918. The address for his pay was the Cliff Inn, Crich.

BINGHAM, Private – J.

Regiment unknown

He is on the original Crich Roll of Honour but no further information has been found for him.

BINGHAM, Driver – James Hunt ✝

Royal Engineers
Labour Corps

James was born in about 1886 at Crich. Before marrying Annie Cowlishaw in 1903 he was living with his grandparents. In the 1918 register of electors James and Annie were recorded as living on the Dimple, Crich; James was marked as absent. He died in Canterbury Hospital on 14th November 1918 of wounds received in action and is buried in St Mary's churchyard, Crich, where a military memorial headstone marks his grave.

BOLLINGTON BROTHERS

Alfred, Nelson and William Henry were the sons of Sarah Bollington and William Martin who married in 1913 after having had at least nine children. The children were also known by their father's surname, Martin, as well as Bollington.

Herbert, John Edward and Stephen were the sons of Edward and Amy Bollington. The family moved from Crich to Heage in about 1900. They all served in the Sherwood Foresters. Their father Edward Bollington also served during the war.

BOLLINGTON, Private – Alfred

Regiment unknown

Alfred was born in 1896 at Heage; he was a limestone quarryman before he joined the Army. His brothers Nelson and William Henry Bollington are also on the Roll of Honour.

BOLLINGTON, Sapper – Edward ◊

Royal Engineers

Edward was born in about 1867 at Crich. He was a married coal miner whose sons John Edward, Herbert and Steven Bollington also served in the forces. He enlisted in 1915 and entered France on the 14 August 1915. He was with the 175th Tunnelling Coy of the Royal Engineers. On the 15 November 1915 he was admitted to hospital with severe hearing difficulties and was discharged with chronic deafness on 25 February 1916. He was awarded the Silver War Badge.

BOLLINGTON, Driver – George Henry

Royal Field Artillery

George was born in 1892 at Crich. He enlisted at Ripley Drill Hall on 17th September 1914 (although elsewhere on his records it states that he enlisted at Newcastle under Lyme). He was a quarryman, aged twenty-two and living at North View, Crich. His army record showed he initially signed for the Sherwood Foresters but this was deleted and R.F.A. added. He served in France for two months in 1915 before being transferred to Salonika, where he remained until April 1919.

In his file is a letter from his mother, Mrs Mary Heappey, to the Army asking for information as to his whereabouts:

6 November 1918 – Mrs R Heappey, 2 North View, Crich, Nr Matlock

Dear Sir,

Could you kindly give me any information of my son who is in Salonika it is 8 weeks since I heard from him any news would be greatfully received.

Driver Geo H Bollington, 81132 R F A, D115 Howitzer Battery, Med Expdy Force

George Bollington was finally demobbed on 30th May 1919.

BOLLINGTON, Corporal – Herbert

Sherwood Foresters (Nottinghamshire and Derbyshire Regiment)

Herbert was born in 1897 and worked in the coal mining industry as a pony driver. The photograph shows him seated with his friend Jack Cauldwell. Jack is also on the Crich Roll of Honour. We could only find one Herbert Bollington in the records and he was listed as a Corporal, however, on the original Roll of Honour he was recorded as being a Private. His brothers John Edward and Stephen Bollington are also on the Roll of Honour as is his father Edward.

BOLLINGTON, Private – John Edward

Sherwood Foresters (Nottinghamshire and Derbyshire Regiment)

John Edward was born in 1892, and prior to enlistment he worked in the coal mining industry. He entered France in August 1915 and was discharged in January 1919. His brothers Herbert and Stephen Bollington are also on the Roll of Honour as is his father Edward.

BOLLINGTON, Private – Nelson Martin

Seaforth Highlanders

Nelson was born in September 1899 at Heage, and was taught at Alderwasley school between 1910 and 1913. He is on the photograph of Crich recruits to the Foresters dated December 1914 (see page 237) when Nelson would have been just fifteen. It would appear that his ineligibility was discovered as he later served with the Seaforth Highlanders, having enlisted with John Stanley Berresford, a friend from Crich. They had adjacent regimental numbers throughout their service. John Berresford was killed in September 1918, aged seventeen, and is on the Crich Roll of Honour. Nelson Martin Bollington is listed on the 1918 absent voters list as serving in the forces. His brothers Alfred and William Henry are also on the Roll of Honour.

BOLLINGTON, Private – Stephen ◊

Sherwood Foresters (Nottinghamshire and Derbyshire Regiment)

Stephen was born in 1894 and worked in the coal mining industry as a "trammer". He enlisted in September 1914, entered France in March 1915 and was discharged in May 1919 aged twenty-five, having been awarded the Silver War Badge. In some records he is named as Steven not Stephen. His brothers Herbert and John Edward Bollington are also on the Roll of Honour as is his father Edward.

BOLLINGTON, Lance Bombardier – William Henry

Royal Field Artillery

William was born at Belper in 1878. In 1891 he and his brother Arthur were at the Stockport Industrial School where William was a knitting machinist and Arthur was in the sewing room.

On 1st March 1900 William joined the Army at Derby. In 1901 he was a driver with the Royal Field Artillery and then served in South Africa until 1906 when he was posted to India. There he remained until the start of the war. On the 7th December 1910 he fractured his little finger and spent fifteen days in hospital. The report stated: *On the 23rd Nov 1910 at Kirkee (India) the soldier was on parade when the accident occurred owing to his horse getting restive. He was not to blame.* Then on 11th April 1911 he developed pyrixia (fever), spending twenty-four days in hospital. In 1914 he went to France before moving to Mesopotamia in 1915. Then in 1918 he was in Egypt and Palestine, where he remained until February 1919. He was finally discharged on 24th January 1920 suffering from dermatitis, when he was granted a 20% disability pension for six months. His army record stated that he was a good hard-working man who was good with horses.

His brothers Alfred and Nelson Bollington are also on the Roll of Honour.

BOND, Lance Corporal – Samuel Doxey

Royal Engineers

Samuel was born at Bonsall in 1881, the son of Jacob Doxey Bond and Emily Richards. When he joined the army he was married to Emma and was a quarryman. He embarked to France on the 10th December 1915.

BOOKER, Private – George

Regiment unknown

The only George Booker with Crich connections found in the records is George Francis Booker who was born in 1874, the son of George and Kezia Booker. He would have been towards the upper age limit so some caution is needed.

He married Hannah Hunt in the Belper area during 1895. Hannah died 16th January 1943 aged sixty-eight while living at the Cross, Crich. George died in Crich in 1952 aged seventy-eight.

BOOTH BROTHERS

Cyril Edward and Frederick were born at Ambergate, the sons of Lawrence and Clara Booth.

BOOTH, Private – Cyril Edward

Durham Light Infantry
Dorsetshire Regiment

Cyril enlisted at Derby on 24th May 1918. He was aged eighteen years, a miner at Hartshay Colliery, living at Fritchley. He served in Ireland, and while there, on 14th August 1918, he was attached to the 4th Dorsetshire Regiment. On 5th September 1918, in Londonderry, he was made up to unpaid acting Lance Corporal. Some six days later on the 11th September 1918 he returned to Private at his own request. His record shows that he was of good character.

His brother Frederick is also on the Roll of Honour.

BOOTH, Trooper – Frederick

Regiment unknown

Frederick was born in about 1896 and worked as a grocer's assistant before the war. He married Edith Lilian Mather in 1918 and died aged forty-one in 1937.

His brother Cyril Edward is also on the Roll of Honour.

BOWER, Private – Oswald

Royal Field Artillery

Oswald was born in 1895, the son of Charles and Harriet Bower. The family lived near the Cross, Crich, and Oswald worked in the Cooperative shop.

BOWMER BROTHERS

Alfred, Arthur, Ernest and Vernon were the sons of John and Mary Ann Bowmer, originally from Park Head; they moved to live near the Cross at Crich where they remained for many years. A fifth brother, John James, was ineligible for service having lost a limb in an accident.

John and Hannah Bowmer lived near the church in Crich. They had five sons, William (1891), John (1893), Samuel (1895), Harry (1897) and Ernest (1898). The records show that John, Ernest and Harry are on the Roll of Honour but there is some ambiguity over whether Samuel is also on the memorial. There are several men called Samuel Bowmer who have Crich connections. Hannah died in 1907 aged thirty-nine and her husband John died in 1908 aged forty-three. Their children went to live with relatives or adoptive parents

Anthony and Harry were the sons of Joseph and Harriet Bowmer.

BOWMER, Private – Alfred

Regiment unknown

Alfred was born in 1886 and worked as a carpenter.
His brothers Arthur, Ernest and Vernon are also on the Roll of Honour.

BOWMER, Private – Anthony ◊

Sherwood Foresters (Nottinghamshire and Derbyshire Regiment)

Anthony was born in 1890 at Crich, the son of Joseph and Harriet Bowmer. He enlisted 17th November 1915 and was discharged on 19th October 1917 having been wounded and awarded the Silver War Badge.

He had a brother, Harry Bowmer, who also served in the army and is on the Roll of Honour.

BOWMER, Gunner – Anthony

Royal Navy

Anthony Bowmer was born on 20th February 1895 at Crich, the son of Thomas and Lucinda Bowmer. In 1913, on his eighteenth birthday, he engaged in the Royal Navy for twelve years; at the time he was a farm servant.

His naval record reports that his conduct was very good throughout his service, which ended on 8th February 1922 owing to invalidity. Anthony served on many ships during his time in the Royal Navy. He was aboard HMS *Warspite* when it was involved in the Battle of Jutland on 31st May 1916. Early newspaper reports stated that HMS *Warspite* had been lost in the battle and that Anthony Bowmer had gone down with it.

Derbyshire Times 10 June 1916

CRICH MEN LOST

Anthony Bowmer of Crich Carr , who has been in the Navy for about five years, and whose age was 22, is reported as having gone down in the North Sea fight on the 31st of May; also Jim Rodgers, son of Mr William Rodgers of Bull Bridge, who joined the Navy since the war broke out, went down in the "Black Prince".

HMS *Warspite*

HMS *Warspite* fought at the Battle of Jutland,which was the largest fleet action since the Battle of Trafalgar in 1805. During the action her steering gear jammed, and as she circled in front of the German fleet was pummelled with large shells. Although there were many casualties Anthony was not one of them.

BOWMER, Signaller – Arthur

Grenadier Guards

Arthur was born in 1888 and worked as a grocer in Macclesfield, Cheshire. He attested at Buxton on 3rd March 1916, aged twenty-eight, working as a grocery manager and with a second class Certificate of Education. His address was the Cross, Crich. Arthur was appointed acting, unpaid Corporal on 2nd February 1918, although he relinquished this rank on 19th April 1918 when he transferred to the 5th Reserve Battalion. He suffered during a mustard gas attack on the 12th April 1918 and was hospitalized. He was discharged from the 3rd Western General Hospital some three months later with burn marks on his leg. He was demobbed on 7th February 1919.

Arthur's brothers Alfred, Ernest and Vernon are also on the Roll of Honour.

BOWMER, Private – Ernest

Sherwood Foresters (Nottinghamshire and Derbyshire Regiment)

Ernest was born in 1898 at Crich. Sometime between 1901 and 1911 he was adopted by William and Lizzie Piggin. He worked as a stone delver in the quarries.

BOWMER, Company Quarter Master Sergeant – Ernest

Royal Field Artillery

Royal Engineers

Queen's Own Hussars

Ernest was born in 1890. He worked as a locomotive fitter before the war.

Ripley & Heanor News 12 March 1915

WAR ITEMS

> Lance Cpl Ernest Bowmer of Crich, who is now stationed at Curragh, with 4th Queen's Own Hussars, has sustained a fracture of his right arm.

Ernest's brothers Albert, Arthur and Vernon are also on the Roll of Honour.

BOWMER, Able Seaman – Harry

Royal Naval Volunteer Reserve

Harry was the son of John and Hannah Bowmer and was adopted by Charles and Elizabeth Stocks.

From his service record Harry was born on 21st January 1897 and engaged with the Royal Naval Volunteer Reserve on the 25th September 1916. His height was 5ft 6¾in and he had fair hair, grey eyes, a fresh complexion and a scar on his left cheek. He served aboard HMS *Victory VI*, *Vivid III*, *President III* and the *Devonshire*. His character throughout was recorded as good and very good. HMS *Victory*, *Vivid* and *President* were shore-based establishments whilst HMS *Devonshire* was an armoured cruiser.

HMS *Devonshire*

BOWMER, Private – Harry

Army Service Corps

Harry was the son Joseph and Harriet Bowmer.

BOWMER, Private – James

Royal Garrison Artillery

James married Gertrude Willgoose in 1901 whilst a limestone quarryman at Crich. By 1911 he was the landlord at the Jovial Dutchman, Crich before moving to the Three Horseshoes at Ripley from where he enlisted in November 1915 aged thirty-seven. Previously he had been in the Territorials serving with the 5th Battalions Sherwood Foresters.

BOWMER, Private – John

Regiment unknown

John Bowmer was one of two on the original Roll of Honour. No further information has been found on one of them. A possible candidate was John Bowmer son of farmers Thomas and Hannah born in about 1890 at Fritchley.

BOWMER, Private – John ✝

Grenadier Guards

John's medal record shows he went to France on 20th October 1915. He was killed sometime between the 14th and 17th of September 1916 and is remembered on the Thiepval Memorial – which is the Memorial to the Missing of the Somme. It bears the names of more than 72,000 officers and men who died in the Somme sector before 20th March 1918 and have no known grave. Over 90% of those commemorated died between July and November 1916.

He was the son of John and Hannah Bowmer, of Crich. His mother died in 1907 aged thirty-nine and his father died in 1908 aged forty-three. In 1911 the family had become separated with the children being looked after by grandparents and adoptive parents. John's brothers Ernest and Harry are also on the Roll of Honour.

BOWMER, Sergeant – Samuel

Leicestershire Regiment

Sherwood Foresters (Nottinghamshire and Derbyshire Regiment)

Samuel entered France in November 1914. However, there are two possible Samuel Bowmers with Crich connections, the son of John and Hannah Bowmer (born about 1895), and Samuel Bowmer (born about 1877), a wood sawyer, the husband of Mary.

BOWMER, Lieutenant – Vernon **MC** ✝

Royal Fusiliers (City of London Regiment)
Sherwood Foresters (Nottinghamshire and Derbyshire Regiment)

Vernon, a skilled footballer who played for Chesterfield Town and local Crich football clubs, was born in 1896. He served with the 21st Royal Fusiliers before being transferred to the Sherwood Foresters where he was promoted to Second Lieutenant, commissioned on 4th August 1916. He was posted to France on 14th August 1915.

Before his death Vernon had been awarded the Military Cross. This was reported in the London Gazette and in local newspapers.

SUPPLEMENT to the LONDON GAZETTE
26 January 1917

His Majesty the KING has been graciously pleased to confer the Military Cross on the undermentioned Officers and Warrant Officers, in recognition of their gallantry. Temp. 2nd Lt. Vernon Bowmer, Notts. & Derby. R. For conspicuous gallantry in action. He led his platoon with great dash and showed marked initiative and ability. He organised bombing parties and accounted for a large number of Germans.

Derbyshire Times 3 February 1917
CRICH OFFICER HONOURED

It was announced in the "London Gazette" on the 26th January that His Majesty the King had been graciously pleased to confer the Military Cross on Second Lieutenant Vernon Bowmer, of the Sherwood Foresters. The official account was a follows: – "For conspicuous gallantry in action. He led his platoon with great dash and showed marked initiative and ability. He organised bombing parties and accounted for a large number of Germans." Lieutenant Bowmer is the fifth son

Second-Lieutenant V. BOWMER.

of Mr and Mrs John Bowmer of White House, Crich. He enlisted in the Public Schoolboy's Corps in the early stages of the War, and earned his commission whilst fighting on the Western Front. On his promotion he was attached to the Sherwoods. Since he won the distinction referred to above he has been severely wounded by machine-gun fire, and has unfortunately lost his left eye, but we are glad to hear that he is now making satisfactory progress at St Mark's College, Chelsea, which is now a hospital. Lieut. Bowmer was educated at Crich British and Wirksworth Grammar Schools, and on leaving the latter he elected to enter the Civil Service, and was some considerable time in London. He however left the Metropolis to take up a position at the Derby establishment of Messrs Bemrose and Sons, where he was engaged at the time War broke out. He is a member of the Crich Baptist Church, and in pre-war days took an interest in Sunday School work. An all-round athlete he is a worthy representative of the renowned "Bowmer" family of Crich sportsmen. He was the popular outside-right of the Crich Town Football Club, and is also experienced at cricket, tennis, running, etc., and at billiards knows how to handle a cue. Four of Mr and Mrs Bowmer's sons are in the Army, the other being ineligible owing to loss of a limb in an accident years ago. Lieut. Bowmer is 21 years of age and single. His success is particularly gratifying to the inhabitants of the parish of Crich.

Vernon married Dorothy Phillipa Perrett in 1918. He died in a military hospital at Bournemouth on 9th October 1919 and is buried in St Mary's churchyard at Crich.

Derby Telegraph 11 October 1919

CRICH LIEUTENANT'S DEATH

The death has taken place at Bournemouth of Lieut. Vernon Bowmer, of The Cross, Crich. An operation took place on Wednesday for an internal complaint, following a severe attack of dysentery, contacted on foreign service. Lieut. Bowmer was awarded the M.C. for leading his men, and also losing an eye in the same engagement. He was widely known in football and cricket circles in the locality.

Vernon's brothers Albert, Arthur and Ernest are also on the Roll of Honour.

Vernon's memorial stone in St Mary's churchyard, Crich

BOWN, Private – Frederick Charles ✝

Sherwood Foresters (Nottinghamshire and Derbyshire Regiment)
Cheshire Regiment

Photo: Derbyshire Times 12 August 1916

He was born in 1897 at Fritchley to Christopher and Mary Ann Bown. He worked as a wood-turning machinist. He attested at Derby, aged nineteen, on 1st February 1915. Although initially with the Sherwood Foresters he was quickly transferred to the Cheshire Regiment. He joined the B.E.F. in France on 17th July 1915. In July 1916 he suffered a gunshot wound to his right knee and then in September a gunshot wound to his right hand. This was followed in February 1917 by admission to hospital with bronchitis. During August 1918 he was wounded by a gas shell, resulting in hospitalization at Lichfield until September 1918. He was discharged from the Army as being fit on 6th February 1919. However, he died in Leicester hospital a few weeks later. He was buried, aged twenty-two, in St Mary's churchyard, Crich.

BRAMALL, Private – Joseph Baggaley ◊

Royal Fusiliers (City of London Regiment)

He was born in about 1875 in the Ockbrook area of Derby to John and Ellen Bramall. Before the war he worked as a bait stable keeper, then as a school attendance officer. In 1898 he married Ada Carline Wass and had two children, Ellen and Joseph, but it appears the marriage broke up, his wife returning to Nottingham to live with her mother.

Joseph attested on 18th September 1915 at Perham Down, Wiltshire, aged forty-two, listed as a retired butcher living at The Sycamores in Crich. He had previously served seven years in the Derbyshire Yeomanry. Although he was posted with the rank of Acting Sergeant on 18th September 1915 he was discharged on 3rd June 1916 a Private, no longer physically fit for active service. He received his Silver War Badge on 30th November 1916 at the Sycamores in Crich. He made a request for a weekly pension which was rejected.

BRANN, Private – Percy William ✝

Sherwood Foresters (Nottinghamshire and Derbyshire Regiment)

Percy was born in about 1888 in Wittersham, the son of William and Minnie Brann. Before the war he worked as a gardener, and perhaps this is what brought him to Derbyshire as records indicate that he enlisted at Crich. He died on 5th March 1917 aged twenty-nine and is buried at Foncquevillers Military Cemetery, near Arras.

BROWN BROTHERS

David and Cyril were the sons of David and Catherine Brown. In 1911 their father was the inn keeper at the Black Swan in Crich.

George and William were the sons of William and Harriet Brown of Fritchley.

BROWN, Private – Arthur

Australian Imperial Forces

Arthur was born in about 1880 at Shirland, the son of George and Elizabeth Brown. Just after his birth the family moved to live in Crich. Both Arthur and his father were boot makers. In 1889 he married Louisa Jane McCreery and continued to live in Crich. They had two children, Harold Spencer Brown and Dorothy Brown. The middle name "Spencer" ran in the Brown family. Arthur's first cousin was called Arthur Spencer Brown and he is on the Lea Mills Roll of Honour – he was killed during the war. This Brown family, from Holloway, were also boot makers.

Arthur emigrated to Western Australia, leaving London on 9th July 1909 on SS *Otway* with his wife and family, and it was there on 24th May 1916 that he joined the Australian Imperial Forces, aged thirty-six – still working as a boot-maker. His address was recorded as Chapel Street, Burwood. The 27th Battalion was an infantry battalion of the Australian Army. It was initially raised in 1915 as part of the First Australian Imperial Force for service during World War I. During the conflict the battalion saw action briefly at Gallipoli before later fighting on the Western Front between 1916 and 1918, which is where Arthur served.

Photos Christine Hearne

Arthur with his wife Louisa in Australia after the war

Arthur, on the right, with his wife and family

Arthur Brown died aged seventy-five in August 1955.

BROWN, Private – Cyril Harry

Regiment unknown

Cyril was born in 1899 in London. His brother David is also on the Roll of Honour.

BROWN, Private – David Douglas

Queen's (Royal West Surrey) Regiment

David was born in 1896 at Tunstall and attended the Herbert Strutt School in Belper. His brother Cyril is also on the Roll of Honour.

Belper News 18th June 1915

STRUTT SCHOOL OLD BOY WOUNDED

PRIVATE DAVID BROWN, CRICH

The first old boy of the Belper Strutt school to be wounded at the front is Pte. David Brown, of the Queen's Royal Surreys. After being in four battles he took part in a bayonet charge and was stunned by the premature explosion of a star shell in the hands of one of his own officers. He is now in hospital at Boulogne. Altogether 30 old boys from the Strutt Schools are serving with the colours.

Black Swan, Crich– once home to Cyril and David Brown

BROWN, Private – Frederick

Regiment unknown

Frederick was born in about 1886, the son of George and Elizabeth Brown. He worked as a mill hand and he married Louisa Otterwell in 1909. During the 1911 census they were living in Holbrook.

BROWN, Private – George

Regiment unknown

George was born in about 1889 at Fritchley and worked in the Ambergate wireworks.

BROWN, Private – Thomas Samuel †

Royal Fusiliers (City of London Regiment)

Thomas was born at Derby in about 1899, the son of George and Mary Brown. Some time after 1911 the family moved to Woodbank, Crich.

He died of his wounds on 28th August 1918 aged nineteen and was buried at Daours Communal Cemetery Extension, which is near Amiens.

Monday 16 September 1918

Derby Daily Telegraph

> **BROWN** – Thomas S. Brown, aged 19, private in the 3rd Royal Fusiliers, on Aug. 28, at one of the casualty clearing stations, from wounds received in action, beloved and eldest son of Mr and Mrs G. H. Brown, of Crich. One of the best.

BROWN, Private – William

Regiment unknown

William was born in about 1891 and he worked as a coal miner.

BUCKLEY, Driver – Fred ✝

Royal Field Artillery

Fred was born in about 1885 in Crich, the son of Anthony and Annie Buckley. He married Annie Harrison in 1903 and enlisted at Mansfield. He was posted to France on 24th September 1915 and died aged thirty-two on 30th July 1916. He was buried at Becourt Military Cemetery, Becordel-Becourt on the Somme.

BUNTING BROTHERS

Douglas, Thomas William and Willoughby were the sons of Joseph Job and Lizzie Bunting of Crich Carr.

George Arnold and Walter were the sons of George and Ellen Bunting. Their father was a Crich-born blacksmith and the family lived at Whatstandwell.

BUNTING, Private – Douglas ◊

Sherwood Foresters (Nottinghamshire and Derbyshire Regiment)

Douglas was born in about 1895. He enlisted on 4th November 1915 before being discharged on 21st January 1919 as a result of his wounds, for which he received the Silver War Badge. Douglas's brothers Thomas William and Willoughby are also on the Roll of Honour.

In September 1917 there was a newspaper report of him being wounded.

Derby Daily Telegraph – *Monday 3 September 1917*

THE ROLL OF HONOUR

Wounded 32129 D. Bunting

(Whatstandwell)

BUNTING, Gunner – George Arnold

Regiment unknown

George was born in about 1887 at Wirksworth and worked as a stonemason before the war. He died aged fifty-two in 1939. His brother Walter is also on the Roll of Honour. No further information has been discovered about George or Walter.

BUNTING, Gunner – Thomas William

Royal Field Artillery

Thomas was born at Crich Carr in about 1885 and he attested in Mansfield on 7th September 1914, aged twenty-seven, working as an unmarried plate-layer. His address was Coddington House, Whatstandwell. He was posted to France in May 1915. He was awarded home leave in January 1917 and should have returned by the 16th January. However, he took a few extra days leave returning 25th January. This resulted in him forfeiting ten days pay. In 1918 he received a shell gas wound. He was demobbed 31st March 1920. His brothers Douglas and Willoughby are also on the Roll of Honour.

BUNTING, Private – Walter Edward

Regiment unknown

Walter was born in about 1888 at Wirksworth. He worked as a wood machinist before enlistment. His brother George Arnold is also on the Roll of Honour. No further information has been discovered about Walter or George.

BUNTING, Private – Willoughby ✝

Sherwood Foresters (Nottinghamshire and Derbyshire Regiment)

Willoughby was born in 1885 and he married Martha Ann Turner in 1908. He enlisted at Matlock, and on 18th October 1917 died of his wounds. He was buried at Dozinghem Military Cemetery, in Belgium. His brothers Douglas and Thomas William are also on the Roll of Honour.

BURR, Private – William Enoch ◊ Δ

Sherwood Foresters (Nottinghamshire and Derbyshire Regiment)

William was born in 1894 at Ashby de la Launde, Lincolnshire the son of William and Mary Jane Burr. He came to Crich to work for Mrs Vaughan Taylor at the "Mount" in Crich. On the Roll of Honour in St Mary's Church, Crich he is marked as "killed in action". This is an error, in fact he had been taken as a prisoner-of-war.

William enlisted aged twenty 20th October 1914 at Belper. He embarked from Southampton for Rouen on 25th June 1915 and was reported missing in the field on 8th July 1916. In October 1916 he was a prisoner of war at camp K33, Munster, Germany. Whilst engaged in blasting in a mine a stone fell on his left knee. He reported sick but was not allowed to see a doctor and he continued at work until sent to hospital at Munster. Four months later he was working in a power station at Duisburg. Eventually, on 23rd November 1916, his knee was operated on at a Munster hospital. William served in France for thirteen months and was a prisoner of war in Germany for two years four months. He was demobilised at Grantham on 19th February 1919 with a 20% disability allowance due to his knee injury. He was discharged, single, aged twenty-five, and awarded a Silver War Badge in 1919.

See the photograph on page 237 of the 1914 Crich Recruits taken at "Roskeen", the home of the village doctor. Billy Burr was recorded as one of the men.

BUTLER, Private – James William

Regiment unknown

James was born in about 1883, at Crich, the son of George and Ann Butler. The family lived in Fritchley. Sadly no further information has been found about him.

BYARD: Private – Arthur

Sherwood Foresters (Nottinghamshire and Derbyshire Regiment)
Machine Gun Corps

Arthur was born in about 1897 at Fritchley, his parents were Horatio and Hannah Byard. They had at least eleven children.

He attested aged eighteen on the 15th November 1915, at Derby, where he was working as a labourer. In 1916 he was transferred into the Machine Gun Corps before being posted to Alexandria. In November 1916 he was hospitalised with an injured right thigh. During November 1917 he was wounded but stayed on duty and in December 1917 he was wounded with a gunshot to his right arm and admitted to Kantara hospital. On his discharge, in February 1918, he was posted to Abbassia, Cairo.

Abbassia Military Hospital 1916

While there he was again hospitalised. He returned from Egypt aboard the *Canberra* and was demobbed on 8th April 1919.

His Army record described him as being sober, reliable, intelligent with a mechanical aptitude. A very steady conscientious worker.

BYARD, Private – James
Sherwood Foresters (Nottinghamshire and Derbyshire Regiment)

James was born in about 1883 at Bolehill in Wirksworth, son of William Henry and Mary Ann Byard. He married Ellen Jones in 1905, was posted to the Balkans on 31st December 1915 and was demobbed 23rd July 1919.

BYARD, Driver – John William ✝
Royal Engineers

John was born in Alfreton in about 1895, the son of Francis and Thirza Ann Byard. He married Hannah Bowmer in 1914. They lived at Rock Terrace in Crich. He died aged twenty-three on 14th January 1918 and is buried at the Metz-en-Couture Communal Cemetery British Extension, near Calais.

Derbyshire Times: 26 January 1918

CRICH SOLDIER KILLED

The sad news has been received by Mrs J. W. Byard, of Park Head, Crich, that her husband Driver Jno. Wm. Byard was accidentally killed in France. The following letter dated the 16th inst. was received from Capt. J. Strachen, R.E. : – "Dear Mrs Byard, It is my sad duty to have to inform you of the death of your husband, Driver J. W. Byard. He was engaged along with four others in collecting bricks from ruined buildings for the construction of stables for his horses, when part of the wall of the building suddenly collapsed. He ran back to clear himself but tripped and fell. As he fell he was struck in the back by a part of the falling brickwork, which threw him to the ground with great force and must have killed him instantly because there were no signs of life left when his companions went to his rescue. The men who were working along with him took him on a stretcher to a field ambulance near by, but it was, unfortunately, no use. His body was brought back to camp and we buried him the next day, January 15th at the English Cemetery here. The Church of England Chaplain performed the service. The funeral was attended by the Drivers of the Mounted Section who have been his comrades for the past three and a half years and with whom he was most popular. They formed a firing party and the bugler blew "The Last Post" and so paid the last military respects to one who had served his country so well and given his life for the great cause for which we are fighting. Driver Byard was a splendid driver and a fine soldier, with a great sense of duty. He is greatly missed by all in this Company and especially by the men of the Mounted Section and myself, their officer. We all join in sending you and your family our most sincere sympathy in your very great loss." Driver Byard was the third son of Mr and Mrs Francis Byard of Park Head Crich, and would have been 24 years of age next July. He leaves a widow and two children. He joined the Army at the commencement of war and was previously employed as a miner at the Wingfield Manor Colliery.

CAULDWELL BROTHERS

Henry and Jack were the sons of John and Charlotte Cauldwell.

CAULDWELL, Sapper – Henry **DCM**

Royal Engineers

Photo Ken Jackson

Henry, born in about 1886 at Crich, entered France on 15th October 1915 as part of the 176 Tunnelling Coy of the Royal Engineers. He was awarded the Distinguished Conduct Medal on 27th July 1916.

London Gazette: 27 July 1916

Medal Citation for D.C.M.

132003 Spr H. Cauldwell, 176 Tunnelling Coy, R.E, For conspicuous gallantry. When the enemy exploded a camouflet, he rescued from the foul gas a sergeant and a corporal without any rescue apparatus, at imminent personal risk. He was himself only saved by the rescue party.

Note: A 'camouflet' is a countermine dug by defenders as a measure against undermining. The defenders would dig a tunnel under the attackers' tunnel and then an explosive charge would be set off to create a camouflet that would collapse the attackers' tunnel.

Photo Ken Jackson

Henry seated with unknown friend

Henry's brother Jack is also on the Roll of Honour.

CAULDWELL, Lance Corporal – Jack ◊
Sherwood Foresters (Nottinghamshire and Derbyshire Regiment)

Jack was born in about 1896 in Heage and was one of the first Crich volunteers, enlisting on 17th October 1914; see the photograph on page 237. He entered France on 26th June 1915 and was discharged owing to wounds on 29th January 1919. He was awarded the Silver War Badge,

The photograph shows Jack standing with his friend Herbert Bollington, who is seated.

CHAMBERS, Private – Charles ✝
Leicestershire Regiment

Charles was born at Market Harborough in 1892, the son of George and Jane Elizabeth Chambers. Sometime between 1901 and 1911 his parents moved to live on the Common, Crich. Charles enlisted in the Leicestershire Regiment in June 1908, aged eighteen, when he was working as a shoe-hand. He spent some time in the UK with his regiment before leaving for India in March 1910 aboard RIMS *Dufferin.*

RIMS *Dufferin*

Charles returned from India four years later in March 1914. He then entered France in March 1915. After suffering gas poisoning the following September he received treatment at Boulogne Military Hospital. In November the Regiment left Marseilles for Basra, stopping off in Egypt en route. Arriving in Basra in November 1915, he died of wounds received in action on 7th January 1916. His personal effects of a belt and Princess Mary's gift box were sent to his mother in Crich.

Princess Mary's gift box was sent out at Christmas 1914

On the Leicestershire County Council War Memorial website there is a record for Charles Chambers which lists his death and an extract from the Battalion War Diary.

> The War Diary for today records. At 11.12am orders were received that the attack would shortly be renewed on both banks. In the meantime enemy's line was subjected to bombardment from 28th Bty ROYAL FIELD ARTILLERY. Orders were received to renew the attack at 2.00pm, the Battn moving forward as soon as 53rd SIKHS were seen to leave their trenches. The 92nd PUNJABIS had now been attached to the Bde to support the attack on the left of the Battn. A and B Coys advanced in short sharp rushes, supported by C Coy, D Coy being kept close up in reserve under cover. The advance progressed in spite of very strong opposition and D Coy was thrown in, the whole Battn finally carrying out the assault successfully over about 300 yards. Two of the Battn machine guns pushed along the nullah X Y towards X, greatly assisted the advance in first enfilading Turkish trench P and later distributing their fire along trench Q. The Battn was splendidly supported throughout by one section of the 28th Bty ROYAL FIELD ARTILLERY, the F.O.O. advancing with his telephone immediately in rear of the Battn. The enemy's trenches were occupied and quickly put in a state of defence, while, from both ends of these trenches a line of entrenchments was extended for some considerable distance, the left flank being well turned back. About 80 prisoners were taken by the Battn, and a large quantity of rifles, ammunition, equipment etc. Many dead and wounded Turks were found in the trenches. The Battn buried 62 enemy dead on its section of trenches. Enemy sniped to some extent during the night from our left flank. The following casualties among officers occurred during this days operations. Officers killed Lt DOWDING and Lt ROYCE. Wounded Capt SUTHERLAND, 2nd Lt BILLINGS, 2nd Lt BELLE and 2nd Lt BUCKINGHAM. Other ranks killed and wounded on operations of the 6th and 7th January totalled 303.

Charles Chambers is buried and remembered on the Basra Memorial, Iraq.

CHELL BROTHERS

John and Norman were the sons of John and Catherine Chell of Woodbine Cottage, Fritchley.

CHELL: Private – John

Regiment unknown

John was born in 1896 at Fritchley and worked in the Ambergate wireworks before joining the army. No further information has yet been found. His brother Norman is also on the Roll of Honour.

CHELL: Trooper – Norman

Regiment unknown

Norman was born in 1898 at Fritchley. No further information has yet been found. His brother John is also on the Roll of Honour.

CLARKE, Private – John

Regiment unknown

John was born in 1890 at Crich, the son of William and Ellen Clarke. In different records his name was spelt Clark and Clarke. Before the war he worked at the Ambergate wireworks, as did his father. His mother, Ellen, was the daughter of George and Mary Ann Curzon, a well known Crich family.

Johnson and Nephew Wireworks at Ambergate where many men from Crich Parish worked.

COLEMAN BROTHERS

Isaac, Luke, Thomas and William were the sons of Aaron and Elizabeth Coleman of Crich. Isaac was born 1881, Luke 1888, William 1890 and Thomas 1895.

COLEMAN, Driver – Edward

Regiment unknown

Edward was born in 1888, the son of framework knitter John Coleman and his wife Rebecca. Before the war Edward had moved to Marylebone, London, where he was working as a night watchman.

COLEMAN, Private – Isaac

York and Lancaster Regiment
Labour Corps

Before Isaac enlisted he worked as a builder's mason. He was named Isaac after his uncle. After the war his masonry skills came to the fore as he worked on the War Memorial outside St Mary's Church, Crich. His brother, Luke, was one of the named men on the memorial.

Isaac Coleman on the left with Walter Fantom on the right

COLEMAN: Corporal – Luke ✝

Sherwood Foresters (Nottinghamshire and Derbyshire Regiment)

Photo Colleen Hardwick

Luke attested on 29th October 1914 at Crich, aged twenty-six. He was living at Hilts Cottages, working in the quarries and was about six foot tall. He entered into France 25th June 1915, was promoted to Corporal on 1st November 1915, and on 1st July 1916 was reported missing, killed in action. The painting shown here was a "Battlefield Portrait". His personal effects returned to the family were a pocket book, piece of chalk, a souvenir and brush. He was buried at Gommecourt Wood New Cemetery, Foncquevillers, just south-west of Arras. Nearly two-thirds of the men buried were unidentified.

COLEMAN, Private – Thomas ◊

Sherwood Foresters (Nottinghamshire and Derbyshire Regiment)
Durham Light Infantry
Labour Corps

Thomas enlisted on 20th October 1914 aged nineteen, a stone quarryman. His record stated he was a Primitive Methodist living on Surgery Lane, Crich. During his training period Tom was stationed at the Hayes in Swanwick and wrote many letters to his girlfriend, Annie Porter (who worked at Lea Mills and was sister to his friend John (Jack) Porter). The letters refer to several of his Crich friends also training with him and give an insight into Army life while training. What follows are edited extracts from some of the letters.

3 November 1914
Dear Annie, just a line to let you know that I have not forgotten you altogether it is very near as bad as being in Derby jail here but its no good bothering, me and your Jack is in the cook-house today so we shall know how to go on when we come home. We are coming home on Sunday. If we are not in the cook-house we shall be home by 4 o'clock and we shall have to be in at 9.30. There's a lot of men here, 210, and by this weekend there will be 12 hundred. I went to Somercotes Palace on Monday night it was very good. A Belgian man was speaking in his own language and a very nice girl came and shook hands with all the soldiers that were in. She said we were a nice lot of boys only she said it in her language. We had some fun I can tell you but it's not like being at home same as the Gramophone says. Jack Cauldwell got drunk the other night but don't tell Flo or she might tell him about it. W Curzon and our Luke went out to tea with two girls on Sunday and they wanted me to go but I thought about you and I did not go. It is taking me a lot of writing this letter is, they are all singing like mad. Tell your mother that she must not be surprised if she gets some money because Jack's allowed her 4d a day out of his money and they allow so much it will amount to about 7/6 or 8/- a week. Well Annie I can't say a deal more because I have not got time and the seargent says I have been long enough to write a B news paper but I take no notice of him. Yours ever, Tom

In a letter dated 5th November 1914 he mentioned Percy Brann and Alfred Curzon being among a hundred men going to France. Both were killed in action.

On 26th November 1914 he bemoaned the fact that Duncan Cooke and himself had been denied leave as they had been chosen to play football. He threatened to send his football kit home in case it happened again. Duncan Cooke was later killed in France.

3 December 1914
Annie just a line hoping to find you very well as it leaves me the same at present. I feel just like upsetting somebody because I have not got my leave this week and there many a lot of men got leave that hasn't been here half as long as me. I have asked the Sergent about it and he says he forgot to put my name down and I told him what I thought about him. He lets all the Belper lot go home about every week and he says if I don't keep my mouth shut he shall stop me from coming at all. But I am afraid he will have to keep me under lock and key if he means keeping me away from Crich. I hear that J Davis has got leave this week but I don't know for shure, it seems that anybody can get it besides me. There isn't one Crich got it this week. We should have got it if William Curzon would have opened his mouth but he doesn't care now he has had his. Our Luke and Duncan Cooke has had their photos taken and they are very good ones too. I don't think mine will be half as good but I shall see when I go for them, if they are.
Tom

7 December 1914
Annie we are having a holiday on Thursday afternoon to play a football match for medals and I have refused to play but they say that they shall make me play because they can't manage without me and I don't want to play now I am better again. I will write towards the weekend and let you know if I get my leave, and if any one would like to come and see us on Wednesday they could do so. Tell your Fred to come and bring W Perry with him if nobody else is coming. The Officers have allowed us to have friends visiters every month and it is our turn on Wednesday. We shall have a half days holiday and anybody that comes will be able to look through The Hayes and all the grounds for 2 hours so just let them know at home. Them that comes will be under the Military Police and they take them round they will be able to get a good tea in the canteen and we shall be pleased to see anybody from Crich. It will be a month after Wednesday before anyone can come again so please make it known to all Crich folk. There is 8 companys here and they are allowing 2 companys to have visitors one week and 2 more Companys next week and so on and it just brings it one month between so them that wants to come had better come on Wednesday because I don't expect we shall be here many months. J Curzon has written for W Perry to come and I hope he will bring some more.
Tom

John Curzon was later killed in action.

28 December 1914
Dear Annie, Duncan Cooke and Jack Kneebone is going to go with me through the Mill either Thursday or Friday so tell Elsie to tell her mother that if she cares to go with us she can. Me and Arthur Tomlinson is going to ask the Col if we can get transfered into the RFA. We are tired of being here I hope it won't bother you I know you can't help but bother a bit but you will soon get over it, I am not shure wether we shall be able to get into the RFA or not but we are determined to try.
Tom

Jack Kneebone was later killed in action.

Dear Annie I shall be coming home on Thurs and we will come through the Mill on Friday so ask for us. There will be 4 or 5 I don't know for shure because George Wragg and William Frost wants to come with us if they can and Duncan Cooke is coming through as well so don't be surprised to see all of us. I am in a hurry to catch the post and have not had my tea yet so good bye till Thurs night.

24 February 1915
Dear Annie, I am sorry I could not write before but I have been very busy ever since we left Luton to go to Hoddesdon in Hertfordshire. The 5th Battalion are going to France tonight and we are in the first Reinforcements so we are expecting to have to follow them on although we shall have to go to Luton first for firing. I am staying in the next house to your Jack [Porter] and its not above twenty yards from where one of those bombs dropped on Sunday night. The people here are about going mad they have all insured their property and it was only last night that we had orders to get under cover because a Zepellin was flying about and a wire came from Colchester to say it had been there but it had not dropped anything. Well Annie its just awful here no lights at night and everything is in darkness if we go out at night we have a puzzle to get back at night and I knocked a kid down the other night because it was so dark I could not see it. I have had a good place at Hoddesdon I was of living with a gentleman and we had everything I wanted I never used to go out at night because he found us a billiard table and we used to play till 11 o'clock at night. It was just like being in a palace. We had a room to ourselves me and D Cooke, J Kneebone & W Curzon and we did enjoy ourselves, but its all over now. We have got a poor place to what the last was and it was worse than leaving home when we left it, but we shall have to put up with it. You know everything doesn't run smooth in the Army, they say we are going to be enoculated in a few days but we don't know if its right or not, we shall not be long before we are shifting from here, but if we do go to France I shall think of you. Please remember me to Florrie, Jack Cauldwell is just writing a letter perhaps it is to her, I have been with him ever since we came here he is living next door to me.
Tom

No date

> *Dear Annie, thanks very much for those cigerretts which you sent me I am very glad to know that you have not forgotten me altogether. I have asked for a transfer into the RFA and they tell me that if I get transfered I shall have to sign for 4 years on and 7 years in the reserve but that won't bother me because I never felt better in my life than I have done since I joined the army. Don't tell anyone about it because I don't know for sure wether I shall get it or not but I am having a good try. I have asked to go to Colchester to Bill.*
> *Tom*

His brother Bill was in the Royal Field Artillery stationed at Colchester.

> *29 March 1915, Luton*
> *Dear Annie, just a line in answer to your letter which I have just received it has been lost it has been to 4 different Battallions 6th 7th 8th Sherwood Foresters & now it has been undone and you can bet someone has read it. I have not got that transfer that I told you about but I am not bothering now I know we are going away. I have refused to be enoculated and I mean to stick to it. I told the officer this morning that they can do as they like with me as long as they keep that needle out of my arm. He says I am very silly for not being done but I know best & they are not going to do me. He says that I shall probabley have to go into the home service lot & then I shan't go to France at all, but I think he is only having me on a bit. I think every one will have to go yet, home service men as well.*
> *Tom*

Many of the men mentioned in Tom's letters are on the 1914 Crich Recruits photograph on page 237.

In April 1915 he had his left clavicle broken while playing football for his Regiment. The subsequent Court of Enquiry stated he was not on duty and was not to blame for his accident. Lance Corporal Hill who was a witness gave evidence as to what happened.

> 3576 L.Cpl Hill 1/5 Sherwood Foresters "*I was watching a football match between 1/5 and 1/8 Sherwood Foresters on April 27th and I saw Pte Coleman charged by two other players and that he was hurt. I helped to take him to the hospital when he was detained*"

Thomas entered France in April 1917 where he was posted to serve with the Durham Light Infantry. The following May he was transferred to the Labour Corps. In March 1918 he was posted to serve at Derby with the Agricultural Coy of the Labour Corps before being discharged, with the Silver War Badge, in April 1919 having a good character reference.

COLEMAN, Gunner – William **MM**

Royal Field Artillery

William enlisted with the colours for three years at Ripley, aged twenty-three, on 18th September 1914. He was a quarryman and a Wesleyan. He was sent to France on 25th July 1915 and awarded the Military Medal in January 1917. This was reported in the *London Gazette* dated 22nd January 1917.

Like his brother Tom he wrote to Annie Porter.

12 October 1914, Colchester
Dear Annie, I wish from the bottom of my heart they would send us to the Front to have a go at Kaiser Bills men. I do not think we shall stop here long we have been told we are shortly going to Scotland I wish we were going to morrow. The sport we have it is in barracks. There is nothing in the town. It is as bad as Crich.
Your Dear Old Friend Will

29 November 1914, Colchester
Dear Friend, How are they all going on at Crich. I had a letter from Tom last week he said he might only get off for an hour or two I hope and trust they will give them a day or two. We are having 7 days we expect going to Foreign parts when we get back. The Sergeant-Major told us 3 week ago we were going to Egypt. I hope so I want to have a ride across the herring pond. I have not much fresh news as there not much going off in Colchester it is almost as dead as Crich.
From your friend Will

COLMAN, Private – John James

King's Own Yorkshire Light Infantry

John was born in Crich during 1880 to Thomas and Mary Ann Colman but they moved away to Doncaster between 1881 and 1891. He enlisted as a regular soldier attesting at Pontefract in July 1898, aged eighteen, a Crich-born labourer, who had previously served with the 3rd Derbyshire Regiment. He served in South Africa and Ireland. In 1905 he extended his army service by eight years and was described as being a good soldier. He was discharged a Private on the termination of his engagement on 17th July 1910 and attested to the Reserves between 30th November 1910 and 4th August 1914.

He entered France on 8th November 1914 but was discharged, in January 1915, owing to asthma and on the termination of his second period of engagement.

He had previously married Elizabeth (née Henry) at Hasland on 8th April 1907.

CONQUEST, Gunner – William
Royal Garrison Artillery

William was born 12th June 1878 in Holloway, the son of Thomas and Hannah Conquest. He married Sylvia Bradley in 1902 at Belper Salem Church and they had two daughters, Ivy, born 1903, and Sarah Hannah, born in 1910. His younger brother Joshua worked at Lea Mills and also served in the forces in the Northumberland Regiment.

He enrolled in the RGA on 11th December 1915 aged thirty-five, listed as married and a miller's waggoner living at Bullbridge. He was posted to a siege battery on 26th June 1917. On 8th August 1918 he was suffering from trench fever and was hospitalised in Rouen until he was sent to England on HS *Western Australia*. He was then admitted to the War Hospital at Nantwich. He was demobbed in March 1919.

HS *Western Australia*

COOKE BROTHERS

Duncan, born about 1894, and William, born about 1890, were two of the six children of George and Hannah Cooke. In 1911 the family were living at Dial Farm, Crich.

COOKE, Private – Duncan ✝
Sherwood Foresters (Nottinghamshire and Derbyshire Regiment)

Duncan attested at Crich on 28th October 1914. He was aged twenty-one and was six foot tall, living at Tor View, Crich Common. He was posted to France on 25th June 1915 and died of bronchial pneumonia on 7th November 1918. He was buried at St. Sever Cemetery Extension, Rouen.

As well as being recorded on the Crich Church Memorial he is also remembered on the War Memorial plaque in the Wesleyan Chapel at Crich; see page 228.

COOKE, Lance Corporal – William
Regiment unknown

In the 1911 census, before he joined the Army, William lived at Dial Farm, Crich and worked as a blacksmith.

COOPER BROTHERS

George, Joseph and Herbert were the sons of Philip and Elizabeth Cooper who lived at "The Poplars" in Fritchley. It is believed that all three are on the Roll of Honour but there is another possibility for Herbert Cooper.

COOPER, Private – George

Regiment unknown

George was born in about 1887 and worked as a labourer, with his father, at the Ambergate wireworks.

COOPER: Private – Herbert

Regiment unknown

There are two possible Fritchley-born Herbert Coopers. One was the son of Philip and Elizabeth, born in about 1897, who worked at Glossop's bobbin mill before the war. The other was born about 1879, a limestone burner (husband of Gertrude) who would have been thirty-five with three children when the war broke out.

COOPER: Private – Joseph

Regiment unknown

Joseph was born about 1890 and worked as a colliery dataller. A 'dataller' was a man employed to do service work in the mine and paid by the day.

COWLISHAW BROTHERS

Alfred Ranson and Fred were the sons of Frederick and Mary Cowlishaw. Their father was chief clerk at the Crich gritstone quarry.

COWLISHAW, 2nd Lieutenant – Alfred Ranson

London Regiment (Queen's Westminster Rifles)
Machine Gun Corps

Alfred enlisted into the London Regiment as a Private and was demobbed from the Machine Gun Corps as a Second Lieutenant.

He was born on 27th September 1894 at Crich and attended Wirksworth Grammar School. After leaving school he worked for the General Post Office then in 1911 he was a boy clerk in the Civil Service working at Holborn in London. Later when he enlisted, he was employed as a Chemical Engineer's Clerk.

Alfred attested on 6th December 1915 aged twenty-one, a Baptist who suffered from a slight stammer. His army record listed his father as manager of stone quarries and his mother as Mary Cowlishaw (née Ranson) who lived at Derwent Terrace in Whatstandwell. In July 1916 he was called to the Colours from the Reserves but his employer tried to claim some exemption from this call-up.

South Metropolitan Gas Company
Chemical Works
PHOENIX WHARF
East Greenwich, S.E.
July 5, 1916

To the Recruiting Officer
Town Hall,
Greenwich.
Dear Sir
Your Notice Paper warning A. R. Cowlishaw of 42 Honeybrook Road, Balham S. W. to present himself for service with the Colours on the 18th inst. has been handed to me for attention. This young man is engaged on Munitions Work and is in possession of Badge No. 2473 T. He cannot be reasonably dispensed with, and I take it that the notice in question does not apply in this case. Would you please let me have confirmation of this and greatly oblige.
Yours faithfully,
Chemical Works Manager

He had a six-month exemption and was posted to the London Regiment as a Rifleman in January 1917. During May 1917 he was transferred to the Machine Gun Corps Officer Cadet Battalion at Grantham and in November 1917 was promoted to Second Lieutenant. During May 1918 he was posted to France but very shortly afterwards was admitted to hospital suffering from neurasthenia. In September 1918 he was returned to England and was demobbed on grounds of ill health in March 1919. Alfred's brother Fred is also on the Roll of Honour.

COWLISHAW, Driver – Arthur

Lincolnshire Regiment
Labour Corps

Arthur was born in about 1896 in Crich, the son of Thomas and Emma Cowlishaw – his mother was widowed in 1900. Before the war Arthur lived in Fritchley and worked at Glossop's woodyard. He was posted to the Balkans on 1 July 1915 and served in Greece and the Dardanelles where he was twice wounded, as reported in the local press.

Derbyshire Times 15 January 1916

FRITCHLEY MAN WOUNDED

Mrs Emma Cowlishaw, who is a widow, of Fritchley, has received a letter from her son, Arthur, a drummer in the 33rd Infantry Brigade, 6th Service Battalion Lincolnshire Regiment, with the Expeditionary Forces in Greece, stating that he was in the General Hospital at Wandsworth, London, suffering a wound the nature of which was not stated. This is the second time he had been wounded, the first being at the Dardanelles when he was taken to a hospital in Cairo. He enlisted just after the outbreak of war and has been in the fighting line for the past six months. He is 20 years of age and was formerly a member of Crich Brass Band.

COWLISHAW, Lance Corporal– Fred

Royal Engineers

Born in about 1880 in Crich, he worked as a clerk on the Midland Railway before becoming a guard. His wife was Florence (née Smith), whom he married in the Baptist Church at Belper in 1912. Fred was mobilised on 6 February 1917 and he served with the Railway Operations Division of the Royal Engineers in Egypt before being invalided home on the hospital ship *HS Boomah* after suffering with dysentery and malaria. Records indicate that he was an acting, unpaid Sergeant. His brother Alfred is also on the Roll of Honour.

COWLISHAW: Private – George

Regiment unknown

George Cowlishaw was born at Coddington, half a mile to the west of Crich, on 11th May 1899. He was the sixth of the twelve children of George Cowlishaw and Selina Henson. Of the children who survived beyond infancy, George had five brothers and four sisters.

Mick Dagley, his late stepson, recalled that George had served in the army during the First World War, but did not know his regiment. Unfortunately George's army service records have not survived, so it has not been possible to identify his regiment with any certainty. George and his five brothers all suffered, to varying degrees with muscular dystrophy, which affected their mobility. At the time of the First World War George's condition was evidently not severe enough to prevent him from entering the armed forces, though the condition became increasingly debilitating as he grew older.

After the war George returned to live with his parents at Crich Carr. He was involved with Whatstandwell Football Club and was part of their medal-winning team of 1922–23. See the photograph on page 243

Photo: Simon Johnson

George in later life

Some time later he moved to live at Derby where he worked for a number of years at the depot of the Royal Army Ordnance Corps on Sinfin Lane. He married a widow named Vera Mary Dagley (née Broadhurst) in 1941, and from this marriage George became the stepfather of two young boys. George Cowlishaw passed away at Derby in 1978, aged 79 years.

George's cousins Norman Henson and George Henry Henson are also listed on the Roll of Honour, as is George's brother-in-law Arthur Mason.

COWLISHAW, Private – Henry
Royal Field Artillery

In 1881 Henry was in Belper Union Workhouse, aged ten, with his brother John and sister Mary. In 1894 he married Susannah Shore of Heage. He enlisted in 1914, aged forty-four, while working as a coal miner and living in Crich. During 1916 the army transferred him to the Army Reserve – "*so long as it is necessary to retain him in employment at Wingfield Manor Colliery.*" When he was finally discharged in 1918 as surplus to military requirements he was recorded as being "*of good character*".

CROFT, Corporal – Walter Lucas ✝
Royal Fusiliers (City of London Regiment)

Walter was born in Derby in 1893, the son of James and Edith Croft. He died, aged twenty-three, on 17 November 1916 and is buried in Etaples Military Cemetery.

There is an oddity in that his name does not appear on the Crich Roll of Honour but it is on the War Memorial outside St Mary's Church.

Derbyshire Times 9 December 1916

CRICH FUSILIER'S DEATH

The following further particulars regarding the only son of Mr and Mrs James Croft will be of interest to Crich and Fritchley residents: – Corpl. Walter Lucas Croft, of the Royal Fusiliers, P. S. well known in Fritchley, Crich and Ambergate, died on the 17th November at Etaples as the result of wounds from shrapnel. Corporal Croft was wounded twelve days previously and his last letter of a few lines to his parents, written on the 11th, spoke confidently of looking forward to being in England by Christmas. However, complications set in which terminated fatally. Twenty-three years of age in October last, Corporal Croft had spent his 21st birthday as a soldier of the

King. He was educated at the private school of Mr W.A. Watkins, at Crich Common, and was afterwards for 2½ years with the Midland Railway Company at their Locomotive Works in Derby, as a privileged apprentice, subsequently going to Manchester to Messrs Maradon, newspaper manufacturers. He joined the forces in September 1914, arriving in France with his Battalion in November last year. He was back in England wounded in February returning to France in June last. The more technical part of a soldier's career appealed to Corporal Croft and he was proficient as a bomber and a signaller. As a hockey player he showed considerable promise, on several occasions before the War being selected to represent his native county in the Hockey Associations matches.

CROWDER BROTHERS

Albert and Arthur were sons of George and Mary Crowder. In 1911 they lived near The Cross in the village.

CROWDER, Bombardier – Albert Foulds

Regiment unknown

He was born in about 1895 and worked for the Water Board before the war.

CROWDER, Driver – Arthur

Regiment unknown

He was born in about 1892 and worked as a limestone quarryman before the war.

CURZON BROTHERS

Alfred, Francis, Samuel and Walter were the sons of John and Hannah Curzon of Crich. Two of the brothers were killed during the war and one of them died shortly afterwards. It is possible that a fifth brother Frederick is also mentioned on the Roll of Honour.

Joseph and William Thomas Ellis were the sons of Joseph and Emma Curzon. By 1901 their mother was widowed with seven children; the youngest, Joseph was aged one.

CURZON, Private – Alfred ✝

Sherwood Foresters (Nottinghamshire and Derbyshire Regiment)

Alfred was born on 28th July 1884 and was a gritstone quarryman before he joined the Sherwood Foresters. He entered France in March 1915 and was killed on 1st July 1916 aged thirty-two; he is remembered on the Thiepval Memorial.

CURZON, Private – Francis (Frank)

Sherwood Foresters (Nottinghamshire and Derbyshire Regiment)
Royal Berkshire Regiment
Labour Corps

Frank Curzon was born on 3rd April 1888, joining the Notts and Derby Regiment on 25th November 1915 before transferring to the Royal Berkshire Regiment in 1916. He was aged twenty-eight and a lime burner. After being posted to France he was transferred to the Labour Corps looking after prisoners of war. Demobbed in October 1919, he sadly died shortly afterwards in March 1920 aged thirty-two. He is buried in Crich churchyard; his memorial stone bears the regimental crest of the Royal Berkshire Regiment.

CURZON, Private – Frederick

Regiment unknown

On the Roll of Honour is Frederick Curzon, born 31 May 1876. He could be a brother to Alfred, Francis, Samuel and Walter but there is insufficient information to be sure.

CURZON, Private – John William ✝

Sherwood Foresters (Nottinghamshire and Derbyshire Regiment)
Royal Warwickshire Regiment
Machine Gun Corps

Jack Curzon was the son of William and Eliza Curzon of Crich. Born during 1892, a limestone quarryman, he was three times wounded in France before being killed on 1st October 1918 aged twenty-seven. He is buried in the Windmill British Cemetery at Monchy-le-Preux. Before the war he was a keen footballer.

Photo Catherine & Andrew Allsop-Martin

Jack Curzon, second left in the front, playing for the Jovial Dutchman

CURZON, Flight Lieutenant – Joseph

Royal Flying Corps
Royal Air Force

Joseph was born on 27th September 1899 at 'The Mount', Crich. He was educated at Crich Council School and the Herbert Strutt Secondary School, Belper. On leaving school he worked for the Midland Railway Company. On 22 April 1917 he enlisted with the Royal Flying Corps and was called into service the following November. The headmaster of the Herbert Strutt School, William Wright Tunnicliffe, stated that Joseph has attained a standard of education suitable for commissioned rank. Interestingly his record showed that he could ride horses, bicycles and motor cycles. He was declared fit to be a pilot during January 1918 and he served with the No. 4 Squadron who flew R.E.8 aeroplanes. Joseph transferred into the RAF when it was formed on 1 April 1918.

R.E.8 aeroplane WWI

CURZON, Private – Samuel

Regiment unknown

Samuel was born on 31st October 1876 and was a gritstone quarryman before joining the army. He had married Mary Grace Hopson in the Durham area during 1905. Nothing further is known of his army service.

CURZON, Private – Walter ✝

Sherwood Foresters (Nottinghamshire and Derbyshire Regiment)

Walter was born in 1892 enlisting at Matlock, a farm labourer by occupation. He died of his wounds in France on 25th March 1918 aged twenty-six and was buried at Iwuy Cemetery.

Derbyshire Times 21 July 1919

CRICH SOLDIER'S DEATH

> Official notification has been received that Pte. Walter Curzon of the Sherwoods, son of Mrs Hannah Curzon, of Crich Common, has died in hospital in France. He enlisted about three years ago. A brother was killed in France about two years ago and there are two other brothers serving in the Forces.

CURZON, Gunner – William

Royal Garrison Artillery

William joined the army in February 1918 aged thirty-eight. He was Crich-born, the son of William and Harriett Curzon. He married Sarah Brocklehurst in 1903, moving from Crich to Longway Bank, Whatstandwell. He was employed at Lea Mills and, along with all his other employees who were serving, received food and clothing parcels from its managing director J. B. Marsden-Smedley

Photos: Michelle Curzon, granddaughter

Some time during the war he was at Charnwood Forest VAD convalescent hospital.

William is standing third right

Charnwood Forest Convalescent VAD Hospital in Leicestershire

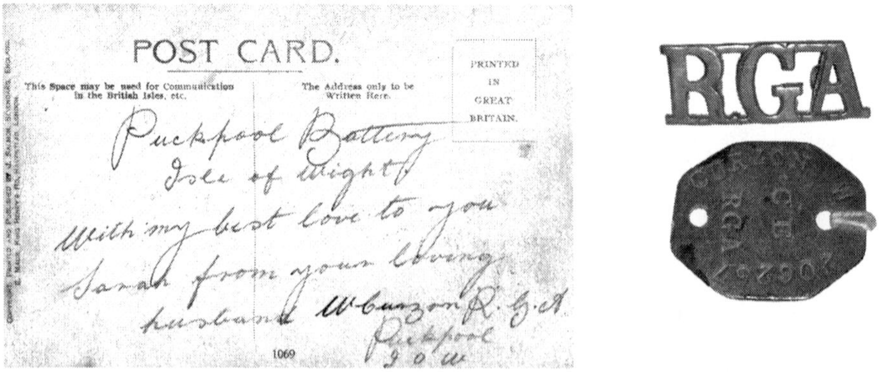

Postcard from William when he was at the Puckpool Battery on the Isle of Wight, and his dog tags

William Curzon's demob certificate

CURZON, Sergeant – William Thomas Ellis ◊
Sherwood Foresters (Nottinghamshire and Derbyshire Regiment)

William was born in 1890, a coal miner hewer before he joined the Foresters in 1914, enlisting at Crich aged twenty-four. He entered France in March 1915 and was discharged wounded in March 1917, receiving the Silver War Badge. He had his left arm amputated as the result of a bullet wound to his elbow. The Sherwood Forester's records show him mentioned as rescuing men buried under sandbags at Kemmel during May 1915. Later he was mentioned as keeping two guns in action at Hooge.

On returning to Crich he became the village postmaster. In 1935 he died of natural causes in the Derby Royal Infirmary aged forty-four.

Ripley & Heanor News 20 April 1917

THE NEW CRICH POSTMASTER

> Ex-Sergt. William T. Curzon, of Crich, has been appointed postmaster for the village. The appointment has given the greatest satisfaction. Curzon was one of the first to volunteer, and for some time was in training at The Hayes, Swanwick. He went to France in February 1915, and was wounded on the Somme, being hit in the left arm with an explosive bullet, which shattered the elbow. The arm has had to be amputated.

See the Crich first volunteers photograph on page 237.

DAWES BROTHERS

Joseph and Josiah were sons of Abraham and Elizabeth Dawes. Their father was a one-time grocer in Crich before becoming a house painter.

DAWES, Private – Harry

Regiment unknown

This soldier is John Henry Dawes, born in about 1895, son of Robert and Elizabeth Dawes.

DAWES, Gunner – James Henry ◊

Royal Garrison Artillery

James was born in 1879, the son of John and Jane Dawes. His father was a well-known general dealer and surveyor of highways. He enlisted in December 1915 and served on the Western Front where he was wounded in the leg by shrapnel and gassed. He was discharged with a Silver War Badge in March 1918 aged thirty-six. He married Elsie Bowyer on 15th June 1918 and died on 8 January 1940 aged sixty-one.

James on returning from the war; his sheepskin was riddled with lice

DAWES, Private – John ◊

Sherwood Foresters (Nottinghamshire and Derbyshire Regiment)
Royal Defence Corps

John was born in 1899, the son of John and Margaret Dawes who were publicans at the Wheatsheaf Inn in Crich. He enlisted with the Sherwood Foresters at Derby in May 1917 and was transferred to the Royal Defence Corps in the September of that year. Six months later in March 1918 he was wounded and discharged, having been awarded the Silver War Badge. When John enlisted aged eighteen, his record stated that he was a voluntary enlisted miner under War Office letter 27/ Gen. No. /6110 dated 12th March 1917.

DAWES, Private – Joseph ✝

Highland Light Infantry

Photo Kathryn Teeter

Joseph, like his father, was a house painter before the start of the war. He was born in Crich in about 1886 and died on 22nd March 1918 aged thirty-two. He is honoured on the Arras Memorial which commemorates almost 35,000 servicemen from the United Kingdom, South Africa and New Zealand who died in the Arras sector between the spring of 1916 and 7 August 1918, the eve of the Advance to Victory, and who have no known grave. His brother Josiah is also on the Roll of Honour.

DAWES, Private – Josiah

Canadian Expeditionary Force

Photo Kathryn Teeter

Josiah Dawes was born on 8th March 1889. Along with his mother, Elizabeth (née Wigley) he emigrated to America, arriving in Ellis Island, New York on 30th September 1905. They went out on the SS *Lucania* having had their passage paid for by Joseph J. Wigley (Elizabeth's father) who had lived in New York State with his wife Ann for about seventeen years. Josiah's brother and sister, Abraham and Mary Ann, also emigrated.

In 1910 Josiah married Florence P. Lemmon and in 1915 they had a son, George F. Dawes. Josiah's American Draft Registration Card dated 5th June 1915 gave his age as twenty-eight, living at Overill Park, New York. He was a married alien with one child, born at Crich, Derbyshire, England and employed at the Faith Knitting Company. He had grey eyes and brown hair. However, he enlisted with the Canadian Expeditionary Forces on 20th April 1918 at Montreal. The Canadian attestation papers named him as Josiah Oakdon Dawes, born 8th March 1889, Crich, Derbyshire. He was a chauffeur, married to Florence, living at Sandlake, USA. His height was 5 feet 5 inches, and he had grey eyes with dark brown hair. According to his granddaughter he had flat feet which is why the American Army would not enlist him.

After serving in the war he returned to the United States during March 1919. He returned from the Canadian Corps Camp at Bramshott aboard the troop ship SS *Carmania,* sailing from Liverpool. Josiah's brother Joseph is also on the Roll of Honour.

DAWES, Private – William

Regiment unknown

William Dawes, born in 1877 to Abraham and Elizabeth Dawes, is the only W. Dawes found with Crich connections. He was born in the village and worked in the local brick yard but he is at the upper age range for serving, so some caution is needed with this record.

If this William Dawes is the W. Dawes on the original Roll of Honour then he is the brother of Josiah and Joseph Dawes, both of whom are on the Roll of Honour.

J DE RIDDER

It is assumed that this person is related to one of the Belgium refugees who came to live in the parish and that he was involved in the war effort. On the Medal Roll Index cards there is a Jules Charles de Ridder, a Belgian Agent who was awarded the British War Medal. Belgian Agents were civilians in British service, but were not with the armed forces. In April 1915 the High Peak News reported that two Belgian refugees from Crich, Mlle Anna De Ridder and M. Joseph Maes, were married by Father Le Roy at St Joseph's Catholic Church in Matlock. Most of the twenty-minute ceremony was in Flemish, but the bride and bridegroom had learned sufficient English to be able to respond to the wedding questions in that language. See the photograph of the Crich Belgium refugees on page 247

DIXON, Gunner – Ernest

Royal Garrison Artillery

Photo Debbie Bailey

Ernest, born on 26th November 1896, was a wireworker at Johnson and Nephew, the son of Robert and Sarah Dixon. His father was a foreman at the works. He enlisted on 11th December 1915 to the Royal Field Artillery but was transferred into the Royal Garrison Artillery 182 Siege Battery. He died on 27 July 1952.

DONALDSON BROTHERS

Alexander and John were the sons of James and Margaret Donaldson. Alex was born in Radnorshire, Wales and John in Scotland. Their father worked for the Water Board and travelled around as a Public Works Inspector. At the time of the war the family were living locally to the Ambergate Reservoir where James was working.

DONALDSON, Private – Alex

Regiment unknown

He was born about 1898 in Radnor.

DONALDSON, Private – John ✝

Scots Guards

John was born about 1895 in Dumbarton. Before joining the Scots Guards in 1914 he worked at Crich for the Water Board. He was one of the early casualties of the war, being killed on 18 December 1914. He is remembered on the Ploegsteert Memorial in Belgium (near Armentières in France).

Derbyshire Advertiser 13 February 1915:

CRICH MAN KILLED

> News was received on Thursday of last week that Private John Donaldson of Crich, had been killed in action, his father, Mr James Donaldson, who is inspector over the Derwent Valley Water Board's property, being notified by the War Office of his son's death. Private Donaldson, who was 20 years of age, enlisted nearly a year ago in the 2nd Battalion Scots Guards, a regiment which has seen much fighting during the war. Private Donaldson fell on December 18th. Prior to joining the Army, he was employed on Derwent Valley Water Board's Works at Crich, and he was extremely popular both at Crich and Belper, having lived at the latter place for several years before removing to Crich, and his death is greatly regretted throughout the district.

DRAKE, Private – William

Regiment unknown

William was born in about 1885 in Burton-on-Trent to Ernest and Caroline Drake. Sometime between 1901 and 1911 he moved to Crich where he worked as a gritstone quarryman and married Annie Elizabeth Allwood.

DUGGAN, Private – John Thomas ✝

Sherwood Foresters (Nottinghamshire and Derbyshire Regiment)

John was born about 1896 in Radnor, Wales to a Water Board civil engineer John Duggan and his wife Sarah. In 1911 John Thomas was still in Radnor working as a cowman, but his parents were in Crich so it is presumed that is why he is remembered on the Crich memorials. He was killed 23 June 1916 and is buried at the Le Touret Military Cemetery, Richebourg-L'Avoue.

Note that there are reporting errors in the newspaper obituary; the name should be John not William Duggan.

Derbyshire Times 8 July 1916

CRICH MAN KILLED

Friends of Mr and Mrs J. Duggan, late of Crich, will be sorry to hear of the death at the Front of their only son William, who was shot through the head by a German sniper on the night of June 22nd. The sad news was conveyed to Mrs Jno Taylor, of "The Fields" Crich on Saturday. He was 23 years of age and enlisted the Army almost a year ago, having previously been employed at Messrs Yelverton Dawbarns joinery works, Whatstandwell. Mr Duggan, whilst at Crich, held the position of valve inspector for the Derwent Valley Water Board, afterwards removing to Little Eaton where he is still serving the above Company in the same capacity.

DURIE, Private – Christopher ✝
King's Own Royal Lancaster Regiment

Christopher was born in about 1898 in Liverpool the son of dock-worker William Durie and his wife Mary. In some records his name seems to have changed from Durie to Drury. He entered France in May 1915 and was killed in action on 26th April 1917 aged nineteen. He is remembered on the Arras Memorial.

Note that there are reporting errors in the newspaper obituary, the name should be Durie not Drury, he was aged nineteen not twenty-four and his regiment was based in Lancaster not Liverpool.

Derbyshire Times, 19 May 1917

Mrs Wright of Park Head, Crich received the news on Monday that Pte Christopher Drury, who was one of the first to enlist from Crich, had been killed at the front. He was a native of Liverpool and joined a Liverpool Regiment. He was about 24 years of age, single and worked at Crich for many years.

DYSON: Lance Corporal – Sydney Newton
Royal Engineers (Railway Troops)

Sydney was born in about 1894 in Crich, the son of the village British School headmaster Heyworth Dyson and his wife Rosamund. Before the war he was a privileged apprentice at the Derby Locomotive Works. He entered France in February 1915 after attesting in London, aged twenty-one, in October 1914. He was demobbed in April 1919 when he returned home to "The Bower", Crich.

EARNSHAW, Gunner – Charles Alfred John ◊
Royal Field Artillery

Charles was born in Sheffield about 1872 to Charles and Maria Earnshaw. His father was an engineers' accountant. The family moved from Romford to Derby and then Whatstandwell, from where he enlisted in May 1916 aged thirty-nine. He had married Minnie Isabel Lovick in November 1906 at Derby. In 1911 he was the chief costs clerk in an engineering works but on joining the army he stated he was an artist. In March 1918 he was discharged from the army, with a Silver War Badge, on health grounds suffering from rheumatism.

EBERT, Private – Herbert Harry Vernon
Sherwood Foresters (Nottinghamshire and Derbyshire Regiment)

Herbert was born at Crich in about 1897. He was the son of Peter Ebert and Rebecca Hannah (née Sims). Peter Ebert was a German engineer. Herbert's service record shows he received a gun shot wound to his neck and received a 20% disability pension. His name on the Medal Roll Index Cards was Bertii Ebert.

ELSE BROTHERS

Charles, Guy and William were the sons of Charles and Hannah Else. Their father was a farmer with private means and the family lived at Fritchley.

ELSE, Private – Charles Glossop
Sherwood Foresters (Nottinghamshire and Derbyshire Regiment)

Charles enlisted at Sutton in Ashfield in December 1915 aged twenty-four; he was an articled surveyor. Previously, while at school, he had served with the Officer Training Corps (OTC), Derbys. His pension record stated that he was discharged as medically unfit almost immediately on his enlistment.

Charles's brothers Guy and William are also on the Roll of Honour.

ELSE, Seaman Gunner – Francis Edward
Royal Navy

Francis was born about 1884 at Lea Bridge, the son of John and Ellen Else. Just before the war he was living and working at Hankin Farm, Whatstandwell with his brothers and sisters.

ELSE, Gunner – Guy Victor

Regiment unknown

Guy was born about 1898. After the war he was a garage proprietor at Ambergate and omnibus proprietor at Heage. His brothers Charles and William are also on the Roll of Honour.

ELSE, Sergeant – John William

Royal Field Artillery

Photo Elizabeth Griffiths

John William was born in 1886 to Samuel and Eliza Else of Crich. Before the war he worked at Lea Mills as a frame minder. He worked in the factory and he joined the forces on 10th April 1917 aged thirty-three. An application had been made for his return to the factory by August 1919. J.B. Marsden-Smedley, the managing director of Lea Mills, had promised all returning servicemen their jobs back when war ended.

He was posted to Kingsway Camp, Delhi, India where he received parcels of hosiery in December 1917 and groceries in January 1918. Distance and duties meant that his replies were delayed. The hosiery was acknowledged in a letter when he wrote of '*a very useful parcel and also thank you for the undershirts and writing paper which was forwarded on to me by my wife.*'

Photo Elizabeth Griffiths

Sergeant Else with his regimental football team; venue unknown

On Crich Roll of Honour and in the Lea Mills parcels book he is listed as "Driver John William Else", but the photograph of him with the footballers indicates that he was a Sergeant.

ELSE, Captain – William Edwin ✝

Royal Fusiliers (City of London Regiment)
Sherwood Foresters (Nottinghamshire and Derbyshire Regiment)

William joined the Royal Fusiliers as a Private in September 1914 and in January 1915 was commissioned as an officer into the Sherwood Foresters. He was killed in action on 3rd January 1918, aged twenty-four, when he was the officer commanding "D" Coy, 17th Battalion, Sherwood Foresters. He is buried at Vlamertinghe New Military Cemetery. He had married Ada Kay during 1916.

In his book 'The Bath at War' Charles Beresford made the following observations about William – he was well-known in Matlock Bath as he worked at Parr's Bank on the Parade. William had joined the Public Schools battalion on the 15th September 1914 and was commissioned to the 10th Sherwood Foresters some four months later. On New Year's Eve he was attached to the 17th Sherwood Foresters in the Ypres area. The battalion's War Diary described everything as being quiet. It was snowing and the Germans could be heard singing. The 17th were due to be relieved by the 16th Foresters on the 3rd January 1918 but it was on this day that William was shot in the head by a German sniper and died instantly. He was just twenty-four years old and had been married but a year. The War Office telegram was sent to William's parents –*"To Else, Park Lodge, Fritchley. Derby. Deeply regret to inform you Lieut W E Else Sherwood Foresters was killed in action January third The Army Council express their sympathy"*. William was an acting Captain when he was killed and although he was recommended for a Military Cross this was not awarded.

Derbyshire Times 12 January 1918

CRICH LIEUTENANT KILLED

The inhabitants of Crich and Fritchley were greatly grieved when they received the sad news that Lieutenant William E. Else of the Sherwood Foresters, son of Coun. Charles J. Else of The Lodge Fritchley had been killed in action on the Western Front on the 3rd inst. Lieutenant Else joined the Army in September 1914 as a private and he was promoted second lieutenant in February 1915, apparently he was promoted whilst in France to the rank of lieutenant. He was over in December 1917 on 14 days leave. The late Mr Else was 24 years of age. He was educated at Dartford Grammar and Derby Schools, and afterwards was engaged on the staff at Parr's Bank, Matlock. On the declaration of war he was one of the most enthusiastic in the district in encouraging recruits for the Army. On December 13th 1916 he married Miss Ada Evelyn Kay, daughter of Mr A. Kay the manager of Messrs Richard Johnson and Nephew's wire mill at Ambergate.

High Peak News 19 January 1918

MATLOCK BATH

> Official intimation has been received of the death in action in France of Lieut. William Else of "Westleigh," Ambergate. He belonged to a well-known and highly respected Ambergate family, and was only 24 years of age. His young widow, for whom much sympathy will be felt, was formerly a Miss A. Kay, of Ambergate, and she is at present assisting in the work at the War Pensions Department at Derby. She has received a letter from the Colonel of Lieut. Else's regiment stating that her husband was shot through the head, and that death was instantaneous. The sad circumstance is that the late lieutenant Else was home on leave only three weeks or a month ago. He will be remembered here as one of the staff of Parr's Bank.

The Commonwealth War Graves Commission records his rank as Captain although the newspaper reports name him as Lieutenant. The fourth bell in St Mary's Church, Crich, which was recast in 1928, is dedicated to William Else. William's brothers Guy and Charles are also on the Roll of Honour.

ENGLAND BROTHERS

Joseph and William were the sons of Samuel and Martha England. Their mother died in 1904 and their father married Mary Ann Haslam, a widow, in 1906.

ENGLAND, Lieutenant – Joseph Harold

Sherwood Foresters (Nottinghamshire and Derbyshire Regiment)

Joseph was born in 1894. He attended Crich Council School and Wirksworth Grammar School before working at Lea Mills as a framework knitter and clerk. When he joined the Army in August 1915 he was no longer employed at Lea Mills. He was posted to France in August 1916, was promoted to Second Lieutenant in March 1918 and to full Lieutenant in September 1919. He married Helen Smith in 1917 and they lived in the Market Place in Crich.

ENGLAND, Private – William

Regiment unknown

William was born in about 1884 and on leaving school worked as a railway surveyors' clerk. He married Lucy Ellen Bower in 1910.

EPERSON, Sapper – Edwin

Royal Engineers

Edwin was born in about 1878 in Ramsbottom, Lancashire where his father (also Edwin) was a licensed victualler. The family soon moved to South Darley and then to Crich. Edwin married Emma Proctor in 1900 and they lived in Fairfield, Buxton where he worked as a stone mason. His parents continued to live in Crich Parish which is why he was remembered on the Crich Roll of Honour.

FERN, Driver – Fred

Royal Field Artillery

Photos Joan Haynes

Fred was born in Bonsall in about 1898; his parents were John and Elizabeth Fern. In some records their name is spelt Fearn. John's father was a ganger on the railway. Fred was untruthful about his age and joined the Royal Field Artillery when aged seventeen. He was posted to France in December 1915 and was wounded during his service but was able to return to his unit after treatment.

In October 1916 he sent his wife-to-be a photo postcard in which he told her not to worry that he looked a little "out of sorts" in the picture.

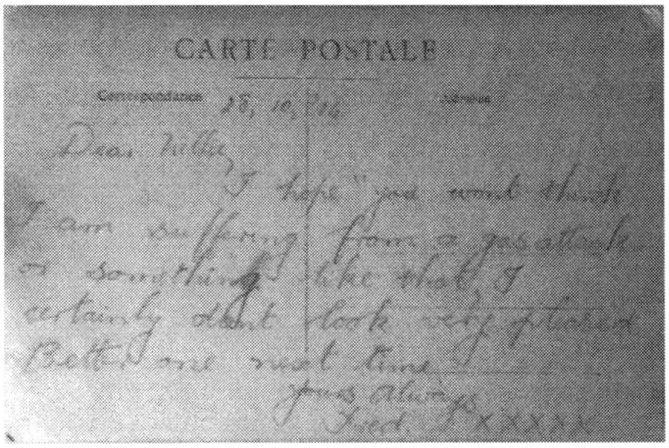

CARTE POSTALE

Correspondance 28. 10. 16. Adresse

Dear Nellie,
I hope you wont think
I am suffering from a gas attack
or something like that, I
certainly dont look very pleased
Better one next time.
Yours always
Fred xxxxx

28.10.16; Dear Nellie, I hope you wont think I am suffering from a gas attack or something like that I certainly dont look very pleased. Better one next time, Yours always, Fred xxxxx

In December 1917 he sent his parents a regimental Christmas card.

After the war Fred worked as a joiner and in 1923 he married Sarah Ellen Flint whom he called "Nellie". He was secretary to Whatstandwell Football Club – see the photograph on page 243.

Photo Joan Haynes

Fred and Sarah Ellen Flint

FEW, Sergeant – Arthur

Sherwood Foresters (Nottinghamshire and Derbyshire Regiment)
Royal Engineers
Labour Corps,

There are no obvious links with Crich for Arthur Few. His inclusion on Crich Roll of Honour is a bit of a mystery. He entered France on 11th December 1914 so he must have volunteered in the very early stages of the war. The Derby and Chesterfield Recorder dated 23rd July 1915 shows him on a casualty list as wounded.

FLINT, Trooper - Joseph Bertram

Household Cavalry
Royal Garrison Artillery

Photo Mrs E Gratton

Bert was the son of Samuel and Emma Flint, born in about 1895 in Crich Carr. He attested in November 1915, a gritstone quarryman, and was mobilised in May 1917 when he joined the Household Cavalry. In July 1918 he suffered gas poisoning and was admitted to the Military Hospital in Calais. January 1919 found him in the Military Hospital at Frodsham, Cheshire and he was discharged from the army "sick and wounded" in March 1919. After the war he was captain of the successful 1923 Whatstandwell Football Club (see page 243).

FLINT, Private - Stanley

Regiment unknown

Stanley was born in 1900, the son of Thomas and Harriet Flint. His father worked at Lea Mills, as did Stanley, who was employed in the warehouse 'papering'. He joined the services on 9th November 1918 aged eighteen, only two days before the Armistice. He was the last to be recruited and an application was in place for his return to the Mill on 28th August 1919.

FOX BROTHERS

Francis (Frank) and William were the sons of William and Ellen Fox who lived at Bullbridge. In 1894, shortly after William was born in 1893, Ellen died aged thirty-three, leaving husband William with four young children - one a baby only a few months old. His mother Caroline came to live with him. However, the demands of a young baby were great and William was "adopted" by the Redfern family.

FOX, Cyclist – Francis (Frank) ◊

Army Cyclist Corps
Labour Corps

Frank, born in 1889, worked as a coal-getter before joining the Army. He enlisted in August 1914 as a volunteer in the Army Cyclist Corps and at some point was transferred into the Labour Corps. He entered France in July 1915 and was discharged through sickness in March 1919, receiving the Silver War Badge. After the war he lived near Rotherham.

FOX, Private – William

Sherwood Foresters (Nottinghamshire and Derbyshire Regiment)
Connaught Rangers

William Fox was born in 1893 and was adopted by James and Mary Redfern who lived at Buckland Hollow. In 1911 he was an eighteen-year-old miner and boarder with the Throssell family at Upper Hartshay. He had a relationship with their daughter Annie Throssell and they had two daughters, Mary Ellen and Annie. William and Annie married in 1924.

He was an early volunteer, enlisting in 1914 before being posted to France in November 1914.

Ripley & Heanor News 2 April 1915

WAR ITEMS

> Information has been received at Bull Bridge by Mr William Fox that his son, Private William Fox, 1st Notts and Derby Regiment, recently returned from India, has been wounded and is now in hospital, but hoping soon to be discharged.

FOX, Lance Corporal – William

Sherwood Foresters (Nottinghamshire and Derbyshire Regiment)
King's Liverpool Regiment
Labour Corps

William was born at Crich in 1897 to William and Selina Fox. Before enlisting in December 1915 aged eighteen he was living and working in Holloway as a gardener. His Army record shows no evidence of him serving abroad. After a short period with the Sherwood Foresters he was posted to the Infantry Works Coy of the King's Liverpool Regiment and then the Agricultural Coy of the Labour Corps.

The address for his army pay was c/o Mrs Poyser, The Cross, Crich and this was the address given at his demob in March 1919.

FRITCHLEY, Private – Joseph Kelsall

Sherwood Foresters (Nottinghamshire and Derbyshire Regiment)
Labour Corps

Joseph was born in about 1892 to William and Mary Fritchley, who lived in Fritchley. His father was a farmer and young Joseph also worked on the farm. Joseph's medal index card doesn't give any indication that he served abroad.

FROST, Corporal– William (Billy) ✝

Sherwood Foresters (Nottinghamshire and Derbyshire Regiment)

William was born at Crich in 1897; his parents were George and Sarah Hannah Frost. George died in 1904, leaving Sarah Hannah with four young children. Billy was one of the first Crich men to volunteer in 1914. He was killed on 21st November 1917, aged twenty-one, and is buried at Rocquigny-Equancourt Road British Cemetery, Manacourt. At the time of his death his mother was living at Arch Cottages, Market Place, Crich. See the photo of Crich volunteers on page 237.

His sister "Gerty" Frost featured on the front of a popular 1915 postcard of Crich Market Place. She is the girl with the pram. The baby was Kathleen Gaunt whose family lived in Archway Cottages.

Photo Rosemary Hall

GAUNT, Private – William Henry Δ
South Staffordshire Regiment

William attested at Derby in October 1916 aged thirty-five, listed as married and working as a mason for the Haynes Brothers in Crich. His parents were William and Sarah Gaunt, although his father died when he was about ten years old. William married Emma Elizabeth Cooper in 1905 at Nether Heage and they had a son, Robert William, born in 1911. He was awarded compassionate leave in February 1918 as his son was seriously ill. Shortly after his return to the regiment in March 1918 he was captured and became a prisoner of war. He was repatriated on *SS Porto* in November 1918.

In his Army record is the following note:

Haynes brothers Crich hereby declare that William Henry Gaunt was in our employment on August 4 1914 & that we are prepared to offer him employment as mason immediately on his return to civil life.

GIBBONS, Private – John Turner ✞
Sherwood Foresters (Nottinghamshire and Derbyshire Regiment)

John was born in 1883, the son of Wheatcroft farmer Daniel Gibbons and his wife Elizabeth. He married Mabel Annie Alton in December 1916 and was called up to join the Army in January 1917. Sadly, just two months later, in March 1917 he died of cerebro spinal meningitis in Sunderland Sanatorium. He is buried in St Mary's churchyard, Crich.

GIBSON, Private – John Maurice ✞
Sherwood Foresters (Nottinghamshire and Derbyshire Regiment)

John was born in Crich during 1895; his parents were William and Elizabeth Gibson. He attested at Derby aged seventeen in February 1912, two years before the war started. When he enlisted he was working as a moulder with Simpson and Knightons in Derby. In August 1914 he was embodied into the Sherwood Foresters and he entered France in March 1915. During June 1915 he was injured twice with gunshot wounds. In March 1916 he was attached to the machine gun section; the following July he was initially reported as wounded and missing, only to be subsequently recorded killed in action. His burial was reported by the O.C. Graves Registration Units in May 1917. He is buried in Gommecourt Wood New Cemetery, Foncquevillers, Pas de Calais

GODFREY, Private – Frederick

King's Own Yorkshire Light Infantry

Frederick was born in June 1900, the son of Cyril and Jane Godfrey. He enlisted in May 1918. His father was a nurseryman, florist, fruiterer and market gardener of Whatstandwell; Frederick worked for him. He was posted to the King's Own Yorkshire Light Infantry in February 1919, but during training suffered chest pains and palpitations. Rheumatism was also discovered, so he was discharged as being physically unfit in April 1919.

GOODALL, Private – James (Snr)

Regiment unknown

James Goodall (senior), born in about 1871 in Codnor, would have been about forty-four when he joined the Army. He, his wife Annie and their children lived in the Fritchley/Bullbridge area. He worked as a lime burner. His son James Goodall (junior) also served in the Army.

Ripley & Heanor News 12 March 1915

BULL BRIDGE MAN'S GALLANTRY

> We understand that Pte. James Goodall, who was, along with Cpl. Large, responsible for the gallant deed of removing a fire bomb dropped by German aircraft at Braintree recently, is a native of Bull Bridge, and before enlistment worked at the lime kilns.

GOODALL, Private – James (Jnr)

Sherwood Foresters (Nottinghamshire and Derbyshire Regiment)

James was the son of James and Annie Goodall of Fritchley. He joined as a volunteer at Belper in May 1911 aged seventeen, a collier at South Wingfield. As a volunteer he was embodied at the very start of the war in August 1914. He was posted to France in March 1915, returning home in May 1916 to be discharged owing to "*termination of first period of engagement*".

GOODALL, Sapper – Joseph

Royal Engineers

Private Joseph Goodall is on the original Crich Roll of Honour. The only Joseph Goodall found with local connections is this soldier who lived at Homesford, near Whatstandwell, and also at Longway Bank. Other soldiers from Longway Bank are on the Roll of Honour. There is a discrepancy over the rank recorded on the Roll and the rank of this Joseph, but there are many other instances of incorrect ranks for other men on the Roll.

Joseph Goodall was born at Middleton-by-Wirksworth in 1883, the son of James Goodall and Emma Mather. Raised at Middleton, he married Sarah Ann Frost in 1904. They had three children together, two boys and a girl. During his early married life Joseph lived at Wirksworth and Darley Dale before settling at Homesford, near Whatstandwell. During the First World War Joseph served in the Royal Engineers. He was stationed in Egypt, having been posted there in December 1915.

Photos courtesy Joy Goodall

After the war Joseph worked in local quarries as a stone mason, before later finding employment with the Ilkeston and Heanor Water Board, from where he retired in 1948. After the death of his first wife in 1936, Joseph married Alice Taylor in 1940 and moved to live at Longway Bank. Joseph Goodall passed away in 1954 and was laid to rest in Wirksworth Cemetery.

GOODWIN, Private – William ◊

Sherwood Foresters (Nottinghamshire and Derbyshire Regiment)

William was born in about 1897 in Heage, the only child of William and Rachel Ann Goodwin. His father was a colliery worker and he was a farm worker. The family moved from Heage to Park Head, Crich from where William attested in December 1915 at Derby. He was mobilised in August 1916 and entered France in December of that year. In April 1917 he was discharged as being no longer fit for military service and returned to live at Brown Lane Farm in Ashover. He was awarded the Silver War Badge and his army record stated that he was a sober and trustworthy soldier.

GOUGH, Gunner – John ✝

Royal Field Artillery

Photo Michael Davies

John Gough was born at Thurlow Booth, Crich in 1892, the son of John Henry and Sarah Ann Gough. He was in the Royal Field Artillery and entered France in 1915 aged twenty-three. He was killed in action on 4th May 1917 and is buried at Bucquoy Road Cemetery, Ficheux.

Derbyshire Times 19 May 1917

> Mr and Mrs Jno Hy Gough, who lately left Crich Parish to live at Belper, received the sad news on Saturday last that their son Gunner John Gough (R.F.A.) was killed in action. He has been two years in France is 24 years of age, single and previous to enlisting worked at Messrs Yalverton Dawbarns, Whatstandwell.

On a seat at Coddington overlooking the valley towards Holloway (one of the most beautiful views in England) is the plaque shown in the photograph alongside.

J.G. is believed to be John Gough, and E.G. is believed to be Ernest Gregory who is also on the Roll of Honour.

GRATION, Private – George Frederick ✝

Royal Army Medical Corps

George Gration was born in South Normanton during 1893 to Charles and Elizabeth Gration. He attested in December 1915 and was called-up in November 1917. He married Ethel May Fogg in September 1917 and they lived at East View, Crich. Being over six foot, George was unusually tall for the time. He was a horse-hair sorter, wore glasses and was recorded as having a poor physique. The Army Medical Board pronounced him fit for sedentary work and he was posted to the War Hospital in Barnet as part of the Royal Army Medical Corps. During December 1918 he was admitted to Colchester hospital with influenza, dying a few weeks later of pneumonia. He died on 24 December 1918 and was buried in St Mary's churchyard, Crich.

GREEN, Private – Henry

Regiment unknown

On the 1918 Voters' Register for Bullbridge are John Green and his wife Rose Ann. This couple had several children, one of whom was Henry Green, born in 1899 at Alfreton. The H. Green on the original Roll is possibly this Henry.

GREENHOUGH BROTHERS

Charles and James were the sons of William and Sarah Ellen Greenhough of Crich Carr. Their father, William, died in 1900.

Fred and John were the sons of John and Emma Greenhough. John died in 1906.

John, Thomas and Vernon were the sons of William and Elizabeth Greenhough, who lived in the Marketplace area of Crich.

GREENHOUGH, Sapper – Charles

Royal Engineers

Photo Simon Johnson

Charles after the war

Born at Crich Carr in 1886, Charles was a gritstone mason before becoming a steam labourer. After the war he was actively involved with and supported the Whatstandwell football team. See the photograph on page 243. His brother James is also on the Roll of Honour.

GREENHOUGH, Corporal – Fred

Regiment unknown

Fred was born in about 1888 in Crich before moving to Leyburn, working as a labourer just before the start of the war. His brother John is also on the Roll of Honour.

GREENHOUGH, Sapper – James

Royal Engineers

About 1882 James was born at Crich Carr. In 1911 he was living with his sister Emma and brother Charles in Whatstandwell. James worked as a stone mason. No details have been found of his army service.

GREENHOUGH, Sapper – John

Royal Engineers

John, born in 1887, was a plumber by trade. His brother Fred is also on the Roll of Honour.

GREENHOUGH, Lance Bombardier – John (Jack)

Royal Garrison Artillery

Jack, born in 1899, was a clerk when he enlisted in September 1917 aged seventeen. He was mobilised in February 1918 and was posted to France during July 1918. When he was demobbed from his Siege Battery of the Royal Garrison Artillery in October 1919 he was awarded a pension of 5s 6d per week on account of the 10% deafness he had suffered. His brothers Thomas and Vernon are also on the Roll of Honour.

GREENHOUGH, Sergeant – Thomas
Royal Field Artillery

He was born during 1897 and worked at the Dawbarns steam joinery mill before entering France in February 1915. His brothers Jack and Vernon are also on the Roll of Honour.

GREENHOUGH, Private – Vernon ✞
Sherwood Foresters (Nottinghamshire and Derbyshire Regiment)

Vernon was born in 1891 and worked in the wire works and as a collier. He attested at Derby in June 1915 aged twenty-three, and was posted to France in March 1916. In August and September of that year he developed scabies before receiving a gunshot wound in the October. He was hospitalised in Boulogne before being transferred to the VAD hospital at Chipstead aboard the hospital ship HS *St Denis*. Returning to France in July 1917 he suffered trench foot to his right toes before being killed in action on the attack near Poelcappelle, Belgium, on 4 October 1917. He is remembered on the Tyne Cot Memorial. His brothers Thomas and Jack are also on the Roll of Honour.

GREENWOOD, Private – Harold
Sherwood Foresters (Nottinghamshire and Derbyshire Regiment)
North Staffordshire Regiment

Photo Sylvia Winson

Harold Greenwood was born on 3 March 1893 at Chapeltown, Yorkshire. He was a Wesleyan with grey eyes and auburn hair who was working as a blast furnaceman before joining the police force in 1914 aged twenty-one. He was posted to Crich as PC 480 in September 1914, where he served before joining the Sherwood Foresters in July 1915. He served in France and Belgium with the Foresters before being transferred to the North Staffordshire Regiment. He rejoined the police after his demob in January 1919 when he was again posted to Crich.

After serving as a police officer in Crich, Ilkeston and Thorpe he moved to Belper where he served for over twenty-years before retirement in 1946. Harold died in January 1949, aged fifty-six.

Derby Daily Telegraph, Tuesday February 1, 1949

Former Belper Policeman's Death

A funeral Service will be held at Christ Church, Belper, on Thursday at 3 p.m. for Mr Harold Greenwood, a former member of Derbyshire County Constabulary, who died at his home, 118 Kilburn Road, Belper, aged 56. Interment will follow at Belper Cemetery.

Mr Greenwood, whilst in the Police was stationed at Belper for more than 20 years. He had been in poor health since his retirement in 1946.

A native of Sheffield he joined the County Police in 1914 and then served in France and Belgium from 1915 to 1918 with the Sherwood Foresters and then the North Staffordshire Regiment.

On demobilisation he was stationed as constable at Crich, Ilkeston and Thorpe, before moving to Belper in September 1923. He was commended on nine occasions by the Chief Constable.

He leaves a widow, a son and a daughter.

GREGORY, Private – Ernest ✝

Royal Scots Fusiliers

It is believed that this is the Ernest Gregory who is on the Crich Roll of Honour. He was born in Matlock in about 1895 and worked as a cab driver. He had a brother Ezra who was also killed in the war, and he is on Matlock Roll of Honour although Ernest is not. Ernest was killed on 1st October 1918 and is buried at Anneux British Cemetery.

On a seat at Coddington overlooking the valley towards Holloway (one of the most beautiful views in England) is this plaque – E.G. is believed to be Ernest Gregory and J.G. to be John Gough, who is also on the Roll of Honour.

GRETTON, Private – Benjamin

Army Service Corps

Royal Army Service Corps

Benjamin was born in Crich in 1898 and lived at Wheatcoft with his parents Benjamin and Hannah Gretton. He worked at Lea Mills in the spinning department and was twenty-one when he joined the forces on 16th September 1916, serving in the Motor Transport Division of the Army Service Corps. He was attached to 95th Siege Battery Royal Garrison Artillery, British Expeditionary Force, France. Ben received four parcels of groceries between December 1916 and September 1918 and one parcel of hosiery in December 1917. His letters, like so many written from foreign parts, expressed his gratitude for the gifts, his appreciation of the fine condition in which the groceries were received and sent his good wishes to the firm and the family. He had not returned to the Mill by August 1919, although all employees had been promised re-employment.

Pte B Gretton

24.9.18

Mr. JB Marsden- Smedley

Dear Sir

I am pleased to say that I received your welcome parcel two days ago; I wish to thank you so much for it and I hope in your good work that you prosper as I am sure you earn the goodwill of all those lucky enough to get the "tangeable thought" So here's Luck to the "Old Firm" and may fortune smile on it even in these hard times.

I am Sir, Yours Gratefully

B Gretton

GRIFFIN: Corporal – Dennis

Royal Field Artillery

Dennis was born in Crich Carr during 1897 to James and Hannah Griffin. Hannah died in 1910 aged forty-three. Dennis attested in August 1915 at Derby, a farm labourer aged nineteen. He entered France as a gunner in October 1915 and was working as a shoeing-smith in February 1916. April 1916 saw him in hospital with scabies. In February 1918 he was a day late returning from home leave and was fined two days' pay, although this did not stop his promotion to corporal shortly afterwards. He was demobbed in January 1919 and married Jane Allsop early in 1920. Sadly, shortly afterwards he was killed at work on the Midland Railway.

GRIFFIN: Private – Harry ✞

The King's Liverpool Regiment

Harry was born in 1886 at Whatstandwell; his parents were Harry and Mary Griffin. For a short time he worked at Lea Mills before moving to the steam joinery works of Yelverton Dawbarn Brothers. He died on 27th September 1915 and is remembered at the Cambrin Military Cemetery.

Derbyshire Times: 20th November 1915

WHATSTANDWELL NATIVE KILLED

Private Harry Griffin, 1st Kings Liverpools, a son of Mr and Mrs H. Griffin, of New Mills, and formerly of Whatstandwell was killed during the great advance in September. The information was contained in the following letter from Second Lieutenant J.R. Swallow, 1st Liverpools dated November 4th :- "Dear Madam, – In reply to your letter it is my sad duty to inform you that Private H. Griffin 28257 died on September 27th. I am pleased to be able to tell you that your son met an honourable death in action on that day. He received a severe wound in the side, and was able to make his way unaided to the dressing station, but here he died in the doctor's arms. Your son received a Christian burial, and his last resting place is marked with a wooden cross. He has met the fate which has been meted out to thousands of other brave men in this terrible war, and I offer you what consolation I can. – I am, yours truly, J.P. Swallow"

Private Griffin, who was 29 years of age, was born at Whatstandwell, and educated at the Lea Board School, Holloway. Subsequently he started work at the steam joinery works of Yelverton Dawbarn Bros., and held a position there until he removed to New Mills. Both the deceased and his father were well known in the Matlock district as poultry breeders, and they carried off many prizes with their noted Wyandottes. He had completed a course of training in the Territorials before the War, but re-enlisted and went to the Front in May. He was married a week before going abroad, his wife being a native of Newton, Tibshelf.

GRIFFITHS, Steward – Leigh

Royal Navy

In some records his name is recorded as Griffith, but in the 1911 census his father recorded it as Griffiths. Leigh was born in May 1897 at Derby, the son of Thomas and Louisa Amy Griffiths. He joined the Royal Navy in October 1915 aged eighteen. All his postings appear to have been shore-based on HMS *Victory*. When discharged he is recorded as having "a very good character". He married Cromford-born Edith Shaw in 1919.

HALL: Lance Corporal – Frank Arthur ✝ ◊

Sherwood Foresters (Nottinghamshire and Derbyshire Regiment)

Photo Rosemary Hall

Frank Hall was born in 1891 at Longford; his parents were Frank and Minnie Hall. On 18th September 1913, at Crich, he married Hannah Hancock; they had two children Kathleen Mary and John Francis (Frank). He served in Ireland with the Sherwood Foresters but was discharged in October 1918 owing to illness and awarded the Silver War Badge. He died in a flu epidemic at Crich on 27th November 1918, aged twenty-eight, when he was a clerk to the National Service Tribunal Office. He is in an unmarked grave in St Mary's churchyard, Crich, next to James Bingham who had died of wounds two weeks earlier.

Frank Hall kept a small album in which he and friends sketched. It also contained a poem from one of the nurses in the measles ward at Normanton Military Hospital.

Pages from Frank Hall's album, courtesy Rosemary Hall

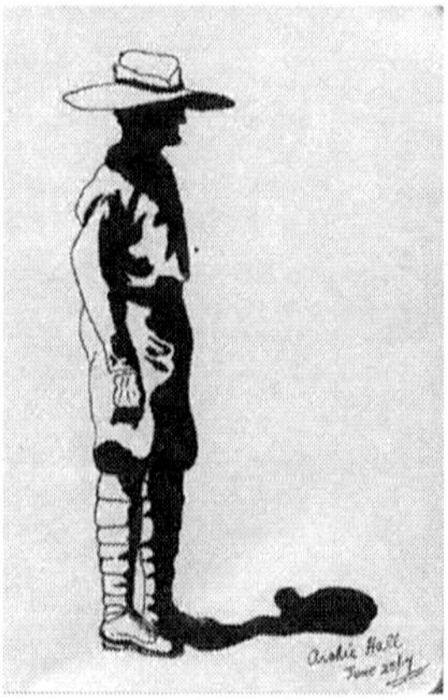

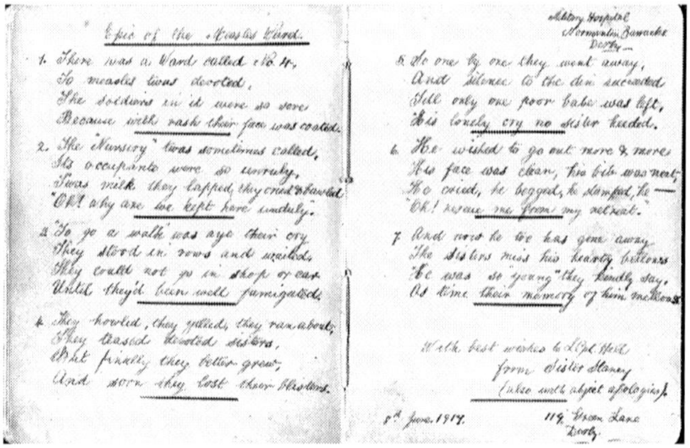

Military Hospital
Normanton Barracks
Derby

Epic of the Measles Ward.

1. There was a Ward called No 4,
To measles twas devoted,
The soldiers in it were so sore
Because with rash their face was coated.

2. The "Nursery" twas sometimes called,
Its occupants were so unruly,
Twas milk they lapped, they cried & bawled
"Oh! why are we kept here unduly."

3. "To go a walk" was aye their cry
They stood in rows and waited,
They could not go in shop or car
Until they'd been well fumigated.

4. They howled, they yelled, they ran about,
They teased devoted sisters,
But finally they better grew,
And soon they lost their blisters.

5. So one by one they went away,
And silence to the din succeeded
Till only one poor babe was left,
His lonely cry no sister heeded.

6. He wished to go out more & more
His face was clean, his bib was neat,
He cried, he begged, he stamped, he —
"Oh! rescue me from my retreat."

7. And now he too has gone away
The sisters miss his hearty bellows
"He was so young" they kindly say,
As time their memory of him mellows.

With best wishes to L/Cpl Hall
from Sister Slaney
(also with abject apologies).

8th June. 1917.
119 Green Lane
Derby

Whilst stationed in Ireland he sent postcards home to his family.

The bulldog postcard was sent to his son Frank.

The Knockdrin Castle and Waterford postcards were sent to his sister in law Mary

HALLAM, Lance Corporal – Walter

Regiment unknown

Walter was born in 1894, the son of Arthur and Sarah Elizabeth Hallam. Before the war he was a pupil-teacher. No record of his time in the forces has been uncovered

HARRIS BROTHERS

Charles and Samuel lived at Crich Carr, and their parents were William and Hannah Harris.

HARRIS, Sapper – Charles William ✝

North Staffordshire Regiment
East Lancashire Regiment
Royal Defence Corps
Royal Engineers

Charles was born in 1879. Before joining the army he worked as a stone dresser. He died on 14th June 1918 while serving with the Inland Water Transport unit of the Royal Engineers, and is buried at Newport (St Woolos) Cemetery.

HARRIS, Private – Samuel

Regiment unknown

Samuel was born in about 1885, and like his brother Charles worked as a stone dresser. He played cricket for the Alderwasley Cricket Club (see the photograph on page 239).

HARRISON BROTHERS

Arthur, Ernest, Herbert, Sydney and William were the sons of William and Catherine Harrison. The family lived on Roes Lane in Crich.

Derbyshire Advertiser 20th February 1915

FOUR SONS WITH THE COLOURS

> Crich figures amongst the list of Rural Parishes that has sent four sons from one family to serve with the colours. This proud distinction is claimed by Mr and Mrs Harrison of Roes Lane Crich who will have four sons in his Majesty's forces. Gunner Herbert Harrison is with the 4th Coy. Royal Field Artillery, at Swanage, Pte William Harrison another brother having been at the front since Sept. serving with the 2nd Battalion Sherwood Foresters, the third son Gunner Ernest Harrison is stationed at Sheerness, being attached to the 22nd Coy Ravelin Battery, Royal Garrison Artillery, whilst the youngest son Pte. Arthur Harrison is serving with the 5th Bttn. Sherwood Foresters, at present stationed at Hoddesdon, Herts.

The four sons mentioned became five when Sydney joined the Army at a later date. All five of them survived the war.

HARRISON, Private – Arthur

Sherwood Foresters (Nottinghamshire and Derbyshire Regiment)

Arthur Harrison was born in 1899. The newspaper article and his Medal Roll Index Card show him serving with the Sherwood Foresters in 1915, entering France on 28th June 1915, when he was only sixteen years old. He survived the war to be discharged on 17th February 1919. His brothers Ernest, Herbert, Sydney and William are also on the Roll of Honour.

HARRISON, Lance Corporal – Arthur Walker ◊

Army Service Corps
Royal Army Service Corps

Arthur Walker Harrison was born at Crich in 1889. He was the youngest of the children of Lewis Walker Harrison and Caroline Froggatt.

Prior to the war Arthur had worked for the Midland Railway as a goods porter, initially at Whatstandwell from 1904 and later at the stations at Matlock Bath, Cromford and Rowsley. Immediately prior to enlistment he was working as an insurance agent. Though Arthur's service records have not survived, his army pension records confirm that he enlisted in the army at Bakewell on 18th November 1915, joining the Army Service Corps, initially with the rank of Driver. Arthur served in France from 18th November 1916 as part of the British Expeditionary Force. During active service Arthur suffered with appendicitis and underwent an appendectomy operation in France in June 1917, subsequently being transferred to Dorset County Hospital in Dorchester. He saw out the remainder of his military service in England. During February 1919 he was treated for inflammation of the stomach and was transferred to the Norfolk War Hospital near Norwich where his condition was confirmed as gastritis. He was honourably discharged on 24th February 1919 on account of gastritis. By the time he was discharged from the army he had attained the rank of Acting Lance Corporal. Arthur was awarded the standard Victory Medal and British War Medal, and also the Silver War Badge, which was awarded to all military personnel who had served at home or overseas since 4th August 1914 and who had been discharged because of wounds or illness.

After he was honourably discharged from the army Arthur lived in the Derby area, latterly residing at Alvaston. Arthur's pension records show that he suffered with ill health in the years immediately after his discharge from the army and he appears to have been awarded a war pension. In his later years Arthur was employed as a works policeman at a local artificial silk works, probably at British Celanese Ltd at nearby Spondon. He married Doris Smith in 1940. They had no children.

Arthur Walker Harrison passed away at Alvaston on 15th July 1944, aged fifty-four years, of causes linked to gastritis. He was laid to rest in the churchyard of Christ Church at Alsager, Cheshire.

Arthur's nephews Norman Henson and George Henry Henson are also listed on the Roll of Honour, as is Arthur's cousin Henry Rawson.

HARRISON, Private – Ernest

Royal Garrison Artillery

Ernest was born in 1886 and worked for the Butterley Company before the war.

Ernest's brothers Arthur, Herbert, Sydney and William are also on the Roll of Honour.

HARRISON, Gunner – Herbert ◊

Royal Field Artillery

Born in 1883, like brother Ernest he worked for the Butterley Company. In 1900 he married Maria Violet Taylor from Wirksworth. He attested on 3rd January 1915 at Derby, a collier aged thirty-two living at Market Place, Crich. Before being posted to France he was stationed at Corfe Castle.

He went to France in July 1915 where he was gassed (for which he received a 20% disability pension). In January 1918 he overstayed his leave by four days and was reprimanded, and in the following May he was admitted into Abbeville General Hospital seriously ill. In December 1918 he was discharged, aged thirty-six, to the Army Reserve to work at South Wingfield Colliery. There is a note in his record which states that he was admitted to St George's Hospital Hyde Park Corner, but there were no details or dates.

Herbert's brothers Ernest, Arthur, Sydney and William are also on the Roll of Honour.

HARRISON, Gunner – Robert Bertram

Regiment unknown

Robert was born at Tibshelf in about 1888, the son of Robert and Martha Harrison. His widowed mother was innkeeper at the King's Arms, Crich before he went into the army.

HARRISON, Private – Sydney

Regiment unknown

Sydney was born in Crich about 1899 and worked as an apprentice grocer.

Sydney's brothers Ernest, Herbert, Arthur and William are also on the Roll of Honour.

HARRISON, Lance Corporal – William

Sherwood Foresters (Nottinghamshire and Derbyshire Regiment)

William was born in 1887. At one time he worked as a miner but in 1911 he was unemployed.

William's brothers Ernest, Herbert, Sydney and Arthur are also on the Roll of Honour.

HARTLE BROTHERS –

Charles, Elias William and Thomas were the sons of Elias and Lavinia Hartle who lived at Laburnum Cottage, Crich.

HARTLE, Private – Charles ✝

Lancashire Fusiliers

Charles was born at Crich in 1882. Before the war he was living at Healey in Yorkshire working for the Leeds Waterworks. He was killed, aged thirty-seven, on 27 March 1918 and is buried at the Abbeville Communal Cemetery Extension in France. He is also remembered in the Wesleyan Chapel at Chapel Lane, Crich (see page 228).

Photos Rosemary Hall

Charles's brothers Elias and Thomas are also on the Roll of Honour.

HARTLE, Lieutenant – Elias William

Corps of Military Mounted Police

Sherwood Foresters (Nottinghamshire and Derbyshire Regiment)

Elias, known as Bill or Will, was born in 4th March 1889 at Crich. After working as a farmer he joined the police force and was a constable in the West Riding at the time of his enlistment in June 1915. He served with the Military Mounted Police as a Lance Corporal then a Corporal. Will entered France in June 1916 returning in January before joining No. 7 Officer Cadet Battalion. He was promoted to Second Lieutenant and joined the Sherwood Foresters. Re-entering France on 21st March 1918 he was almost immediately wounded in the left leg by gun shot and then repatriated back to England on 24 March 1918.

He was ordered to report to his Regiment on 29th April 1918 but had a few problems finding his kit. He wrote explaining his difficulty.

> *Sir*
>
> *My leave expires on the 29th April 1918 when I have to report to the O.C. 7th Res, Bn. Sherwoods at Louth, Lincs. I am however, still awaiting the arrival of my kit from France. Could you possibly grant me an extension please for a few days as I am practically without kit? I was advised from France that it had been sent on.*
>
> *I have the honour to be Sir, Your obedient servant*
>
> *E.W. Hartle 2/Lieut*
>
> *1/8 Battn Sherwood Foresters*

In May 1919 he sailed to Canada aboard SS *Olympic* and he relinquished his commission having the rank of Lieutenant. He retired to Abernethy, Saskatchewan.

Photos Rosemary Hall

Will Hartle, back row extreme left, with fellow officers

Elias's brothers Charles and Thomas are also on the Roll of Honour.

HARTLE, Lance Corporal – Harry Sylvester ✝
King's Own Yorkshire Light Infantry

Harry was born in 1894 at Crich to Charles Jackson and Mary Ellen Hartle. He worked as a coal miner. Enlisted into the King's Own Yorkshire Light Infantry, he entered France in September 1915 and died on 29th June 1916. He was buried at the Faubourg D'Amiens Cemetery, Arras.

HARTLE, Corporal – Thomas ✝
Royal Garrison Artillery

Photo Rosemary Hall

Thomas was born in about 1880 in Crich. He worked as a quarryman in Teeside before joining the army around 1901. In 1911 he was a Bombardier at Farnham Barracks. He entered the Asian theatre of conflict in January 1915, and like his brother William was a member of the Military Mounted Police. He died of beri beri on 19 March 1916 when he was thirty-seven years old. He was buried at Kut War Cemetery, which is in modern day Iraq. His brothers Elias and Charles are also on the Roll of Honour.

Photos Rosemary Hall

Derbyshire Times 8 April 1916

DEATH OF A CRICH MAN

The sad news was received on Saturday morning last by Mr and Mrs Elias Hartle of the Tors Crich, that their son, Thomas Hartle, of the Military Mounted Police R.G.A. who, as previously stated in these columns, has been lying seriously ill in hospital in Mesopotamia, has died. He was amongst the first to join the Expeditionary Force, and was beleaguered at Kut-el-Amara under General Townsend. He had been 15 years in the Army, ten of which he spent in India. He was the eldest son of Mr and Mrs Hartle, was 36 years of age and single, and of his two brothers, William has been in the trenches for some considerable time and Charles is training in England.

Courier (date unknown)

CRICH N.C.O.'S DEATH

Mr and Mrs E.W. Hartle of Laburnum Cottage, Crich, received news on Saturday that their son Cpl Thomas Hartle, had passed away in hospital on 19 March at the Persian Gulf. The intimation was forwarded from the Dover Record Office. As stated in last weeks "Courier" Cpl Hartle was in hospital suffering from beri beri and his condition was reported as dangerous. He enlisted fifteen years ago and of this period he has spent about ten years in India. About six years ago he was at home on furlough and after a short stay in the south of England he again was sent to India and was stationed there at the outbreak of war. With his brigade, which formed part of the Indian Expeditionary Force, he was dispatched to Mesopotamia and he took part in a lot of the fighting there. Cpl Hartle, who was 36 years of age and single, was held in high esteem in Crich. His two remaining brothers are in the army. Prior to joining the Army Cpl Hartle was a mason and quarryman, and for a considerable time he worked on the Langsett waterworks along with other Crich artisans.

Brothers Charles and Thomas are both remembered on the Wesleyan Chapel Memorial in Crich; see page 228. Their mother, Lavinia, had a double-sided locket showing her sons.

Photo Rosemary Hall

HARTSHORNE BROTHERS

Isaac, Joseph, Wilfred and William were the sons of limestone quarryman Joseph Hartshorne and his wife Clara who lived in the church area of Crich.

John Isaac, Thomas and William were sons of limestone quarryman Thomas Hartshorne and his wife Elizabeth who lived at Park Head in Crich. The family followed son John to Canada 28 March 1913 aboard the *SS Victorian*, leaving Liverpool bound for Halifax, Canada.

HARTSHORNE, Private – Isaac

Sherwood Foresters (Nottinghamshire and Derbyshire Regiment)

Born in about 1894 Isaac worked as a pony driver in the pit. He entered France in September 1915. His brothers Joseph, Wilfred, and William are also on the Roll of Honour.

HARTSHORNE, Gunner – John Isaac

Canadian Expeditionary Force

Photo Carol Beadle

John Isaac, known as Jack, was born in March 1884. He worked as a limestone quarryman before emigrating to Canada from Liverpool on 15th March 1912 aboard SS *Victorian*. War was declared soon after he arrived in Canada so Jack enlisted at Toronto on 27th November 1914 aged thirty, an unmarried stoker. His papers stated the next of kin as his father Thomas Hartshorne of Georgetown, Ontario. He married Edith Parnham on 26th May 1917; she was the sister of George William Parnham who is also on the Crich Roll of Honour.

After the war Jack Hartshorne did not return to Canada but remained in Nottinghamshire where he worked at Glover's Factory making elastic stockings. He died in 1946 aged sixty-three. He and Edith had no family.

John Isaac's brothers Thomas and William are also on the Roll of Honour.

HARTSHORNE, Corporal – Joseph

Royal Garrison Artillery

Born in about 1890, Joseph was a grocer's assistant who was over six feet tall. He attested at Matlock in December 1915, under Lord Derby's scheme, aged twenty-four. In October 1917 he married Beatrice Annie Price at St Mary's Church, Crich. The Reverend W. Bunting (who was to die of influenza on Armistice Day 1918) officiated. He embarked from Folkestone on August 1916, but was given leave home in October 1917, which is when he married.

> *Bowns Hill Crich 12/11/17,*
>
> *Bombardier J Hartshorne 72906*
>
> *To Regimental Paymaster, Dover*
>
> *Dear Sir, Please note that I was married on 31/10/17 to the above named, who is serving with the 135 (S) Bty, he is making an allotment on my behalf of 6d a day from 31/10/17 date of marriage, marriage certificate herewith enclosed trusting you will return the same. Payee Mrs Beatrice A Hartshorne*

Joseph's brothers Isaac, Wilfred, and William are also on the Roll of Honour.

HARTSHORNE, Sergeant – Thomas

Canadian Expeditionary Force

Thomas was born in 1895 and enlisted in the Canadian Expeditionary Force during September 1915. He was an unmarried miner.

Derbyshire Times 16 March 1918

CRICH SOLDIER WOUNDED

> News has been received at Crich that Mr Thomas Hartshorne Junior, who went to Canada four years ago, and who enlisted in the Canadian Forces when war broke out, has been in France over a year is now in hospital at Shrewsbury suffering from the effects of a serious wound on the shoulders. He is single about 25 years of age and previous to going to Canada was employed at the Oakerthorpe Colliery.

Thomas's brothers John Isaac and William are also on the Roll of Honour.

HARTSHORNE, Private – Wilfred

Sherwood Foresters (Nottinghamshire and Derbyshire Regiment)

Born in about 1899, Wilfred must have been a later entrant into the forces. His brothers Joseph, Isaac, and William are also on the Roll of Honour.

HARTSHORNE, Bugler – William

Regiment unknown

William was born in about 1897 and worked as a pony driver in the pit. His brothers Joseph, Wilfred, and Isaac are also on the Roll of Honour.

HARTSHORNE, Private – William

Regiment unknown

It appears that William, born in about 1899, did not go to Canada with the rest of the family. His brothers John Isaac and Thomas are also on the Roll of Honour.

HASLAM BROTHERS

George, John and Wilfred were all born in Crich, the sons of Frederick and Sarah Haslam. Frederick was a stone mason who died in 1907.

George and James were the sons of Alfred and Emma Haslam. Their father was a farmer.

Harold and Roy were the sons of Arthur and Mary Elizabeth Haslam. Their father was a stonemason who died in 1900, leaving his wife, Mary Elizabeth, with three young sons, Samuel Maurice, Harold Arthur and Roy Edgar.

HASLAM, Lance Corporal – Arthur ◊

Army Service Corps

Arthur, born in Crich in about 1887, was the son of Thomas and Elizabeth Haslam. In 1911 he was a twenty-seven-year-old unmarried mechanic working in Salford.

He attested at Derby on 24th February 1905 aged eighteen, a fitter's labourer and Wesleyan. He was serving with the 3rd Notts and Derby militia. He was with the Expeditionary Force from August 1914 until March 1915, when he returned to the UK before being posted to Salonika. In May 1916 he was invalided home aboard HS *Formosa* after suffering from concussion of the brain; he was awarded the Silver War Badge as well as the Clasp and Roses (which was given to those who qualified for the 1914 Star and who served "under fire"). There was correspondence in his army record relating to confirmation of his rank.

> *Base Horse Transport Depot, Salonica*
> *T/22861 Driver Haslam A*
> *With reference to the reversion of the above named from a/Corpl. on 1/4/16 on admission to hospital, the Colonel i/c A.S.C. Records Woolwich informs me that he has no record of his appointment a/Corpl.*
> *Will you please furnish number and date of Part II orders in which the appointment was published. 11/7/1916*

To Officer i/c A.S.C. Section, A.G.'s Office at the Base, G.H.Q, E.E.F
This N.C.O. was a lance Coprl in the 2nd Divn. Trains who were in France at the commencement of the war, and was appointed Corporal at a time when a number of N.C.O.'s were given a higher rank and sent back to England in March 1915
I am unable to give further information as this N.C.O. was invalided to England on 29-3-16
This N.C.O. was posted to this Unit, upon the formation of No. 2 Reserve H.T. Depot, Blackheath
J. Cuthbertson (Lieut & Adjt. No 3 Base Horse Transport Dept) Salonica 19-7-16

After the war Arthur was living in Coventry and wished to join the Old Contemptibles.

Spring Rd, Coventry, Warks, 19-5-38
Dear Sirs
Please find enclosed my old army discharge papers I want to join the Coventry Branch of the Old Contemptables and I have not yet got a clasp for my Mons Star Medal. Will you kindly look into the same for me
Yours faithfully, Arthur Haslam

25/5/1938 T/22861 Dvr Haslam, A residing at Yew Tree Farm, Wheatcroft is eligible for the British War, Victory and 1914 star Roll No. 5. Also confirmation of eligibility for the Clasp and Roses.

By registered post 8 July 1938
Sir,
With reference to your letter of 19th May, I am directed to inform you, for the purposes of an application to the old Contemptibles Association, that according to the records of the Department No T.22861, driver Arthur Haslam, Royal Army Service Corps, was awarded the 1914 Star and Clasp and the British War and Victory Medals in respect of his services during the Great War.
It has been ascertained from the General Secretary that this letter will meet the requirements of the Association.
The enclosure to your letter (Army form B2067) is returned here with
I am, Sir,

HASLAM, Sergeant – George

South Wales Borderers

Photo Barbara Haslam

George was born in about 1895. He and best friend Jim Holmes were in Crich Brass Band before the start of the war. They were both in the regimental band of the South Wales Borderers and were demobbed as sergeants. Jim Holmes is also on Crich Roll of Honour. Before the war George worked as a blacksmith.

George's brothers Jack and Wilfred are also on the Roll of Honour.

Photos Barbara Haslam

Corporal George Haslam, third left

George seated first left with Jim Holmes standing seventh from the left on the back row

George Haslam standing sixth from the left with Jim Holmes next to him, seventh left

HASLAM, Lance Corporal – George ✝

Sherwood Foresters (Nottinghamshire and Derbyshire Regiment)

Born at Crich in about 1896, George was a farm worker. He entered France in June 1915 and was killed in action, aged twenty-two, on 31st December 1917. He is remembered on the Tyne Cot Memorial. His brother James is also on the Roll of Honour.

HASLAM, Private – Harold Arthur

Sherwood Foresters (Nottinghamshire and Derbyshire Regiment)
Labour Corps

Harold was born about 1896 and worked at Lea Mills before being conscripted in October 1915. He received parcels from Lea Mills and acknowledged their receipt. After the war he returned to work in the Mill.

At some time while in France he was hospitalised.

10 March 1917
No. 1 Camp c/o A.P.O. Base Details, B.E.F. France
Dear Sir
I now take the pleasure of writing these few lines, thanking you very much for your parcel which I have received quite safe. I am pleased to say I am out of Hospital and getting on well. I have seen several of your workmen, who wish to be remembered to you: namely Sergt. Walton, Pte Ellis and L/Cpl Oxspring who are still doing their bit towards victory. Wishing you and the Firm every success and a speedy return to England, again thanking you for your gracious gift.
I remain Yours Sincerely
Dr. H Haslam

8th Sept. 1917

Dear Sir

I received your parcel and its contents quite safe, thanking you and all my colleagues for the same. Trusting that you are all in good health, as it leaves me the same. I am looking forward to coming home shortly when I shall be able to thank you personally for your kindness to me whilst in France.

I remain Yours Sincerely

HA Haslam

Harold's brother Roy is also on the Roll of Honour.

HASLAM, Writer – James

Royal Naval Volunteer Reserve

Photo Ruth Haslam

James was born in Matlock in 1884, and started working as a clerk on the railway before becoming a schoolmaster. He engaged in the RNVR in September 1916, serving on HMS *Vivid I, Defiance, Thunderer* and *Orion*. He was with the grand fleet at Scapa Flow.

In the Christmas of 1918 he received a postal order for four shillings and a postcard from the Crich Knitting Guild. James's brother George is also on the Roll of Honour.

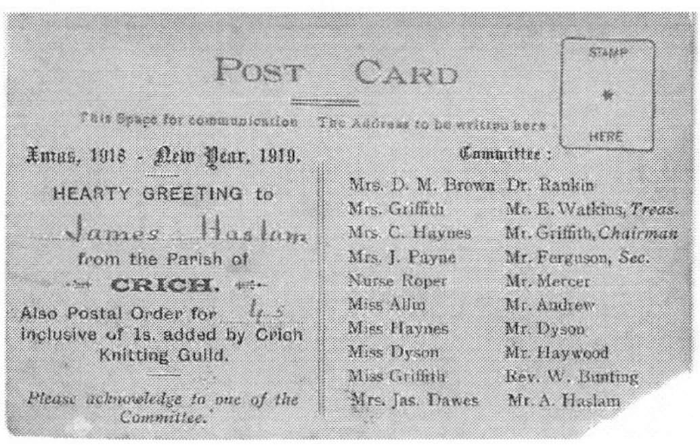

POST CARD

This Space for communication / The Address to be written here

STAMP HERE

Xmas, 1918 - New Year, 1919.

HEARTY GREETING to

James Haslam

from the Parish of

CRICH.

Also Postal Order for 4/-

inclusive of 1s. added by Crich Knitting Guild.

Please acknowledge to one of the Committee.

Committee:

Mrs. D. M. Brown	Dr. Rankin
Mrs. Griffith	Mr. E. Watkins, *Treas.*
Mrs. C. Haynes	Mr. Griffith, *Chairman*
Mrs. J. Payne	Mr. Ferguson, *Sec.*
Nurse Roper	Mr. Mercer
Miss Allin	Mr. Andrew
Miss Haynes	Mr. Dyson
Miss Dyson	Mr. Haywood
Miss Griffith	Rev. W. Bunting
Mrs. Jas. Dawes	Mr. A. Haslam

HASLAM, Corporal – John (Jack)

Machine Gun Corps

Photo Barbara Haslam

John was born in about 1892 and worked at Lea Mills. He was conscripted in June 1916 aged twenty-seven and sailed for France in December 1916. He wrote letters expressing his gratitude for the parcels sent to him by J.B. Marsden-Smedley, the Managing Director of Lea Mills.

Friday, Jan 5 1916
Pte J Haslam, No. 58413, 192 Company, M G C, B E F
Dear Sir
Many thanks for the parcel containing the pair of under shirts which I have received from you today. I must say it is very good of you to send me what I have received from you this Xmas and New Year and the shirts are just what I want as it is very cold here at night especially when we cannot get a fire in our billet. We have not had much snow here yet but I heard that you was having wintery weather in England. Dear I wish we was allowed to put more in our letters as I should be able to send you a very interesting letter but I hope it will soon be over and then I shall be able to tell all I have seen. Excuse this short letter, so I will now close.
Wishing you every success in the New Year I remain yours truly
J Haslam

December 29 1916
Pte J Haslam, No. 58413, 192 Company, M G C, B E F
Dear Sir
Many thanks for splendid parcel which I received from you on the 27th Dec. It was quite a pleasant surprise when I had the parcel handed to me. Of course these are the sort of surprises which we make a fuss of. You could hardly credit how the Boys anxiously await the mail from Dear old England. It does one good to leave home if it is only to appreciate what we have left behind. Dear Sir you must excuse this letter as I am writing under difficult conditions I am in a pig stye. So you will have an idea of the surroundings but we have to make the best of things in War time. We are having wet weather out here at present hope it is better in England. I must draw my letter to a close. Hoping to soon be back working for the Old Firm again. I will now close wishing you and your family a happy New Year.
I remain yours Truly
J Haslam

Thursday, Aug 30 1917
Dear Sirs
Many thanks for the parcel which I received yesterday, it was quite a pleasant surprise. I can assure you I little thought when I came in off duty what was waiting for me. Dear Sir I have

just come back into the trenches again as our Company has been out on rest for a month you must excuse this writing as I am down in a dugout. And they are not very ideal places for letter writing. Well I must now close hoping this short letter finds you all in the best of health. Hoping it will not be long before I am back with the old firm again. So I will now close.
I remain yours truly, Pte J Haslam
192 Company, M G C, B E F, France

Dec 25 1917
Dear Sirs
Many thanks for the shirts which I received a few days ago. I shall find them very usefull this winter. We are having as good a time as we can today under the circumstances. Hoping you have a merry xmas and a bright and happy new year.
I remain Yours Truly
Pte J Haslam

Either illness or injury put Jack into the VAD Hospital at Chudleigh.

Tuesday, Sep 24, 1918
Dear Sirs
Many thanks for the parcel which I received from you a few days ago. Well Sir everything was in perfect order and not in the least damaged but it had not got so far to go this time with me being in Hospital in Devonshire. But I can assure it was very welcome I will now close my letter again thanking you.
I remain Your Truly, Cpl John Haslam
58413, 6th M G C, V A Hospital, Chudleigh Devon

Soon after the Armistice Jack returned to work at Lea Mills. Jack's brothers George and Wilfred are also on the Roll of Honour.

HASLAM, Private – Roy
Sherwood Foresters (Nottinghamshire and Derbyshire Regiment)
Essex Regiment

Roy, born in about 1898, worked as a coal hewer before enlisting at Derby in April 1918 aged twenty. In August 1918 he was late returning from his final leave and was fined four days' pay. Shortly afterwards he was in France and transferred from the Sherwood Foresters into the Essex Regiment. His demob date was in December 1918.

Roy's brother Harold is also on the Roll of Honour.

HASLAM, Sapper – Wilfred

Royal Engineers

Photo Barbara Haslam

Born in about 1888 at Crich, he became a police constable stationed in Ilkeston. He joined the Army in January 1918 aged twenty-nine and was six foot tall. He was demobbed in January 1919.

Wilfred's brothers Jack and George are also on the Roll of Honour.

HAY, Driver – Alfred

Regiment unsure

In the records there is an Alfred Hay serving with the Royal Field Artillery, but it is unclear whether the record relates to this Alfred Hay. An Alfred Hay married Ethel Whitmore in 1912; she was living at Whatstandwell with her mother and sisters. The Derby Daily Telegraph dated 21st February 1936 recorded the award of a Belper special constable's long service medal to Alfred Hay of Whatstandwell.

HAYNES, Lance Corporal – John Roger ◊

Labour Corps

John Roger Haynes was born at Crich in about 1900, the son of John Roger and Emily Haynes. His father was a well-known Crich builder and his maternal grandfather was Vaughan Taylor, Crich butcher and farmer, who lived at the Mount on Bowns Hill. He had a short military career. In January 1918, he enlisted in the Army, aged seventeen, before contracting scarlet fever, and in May 1918 he was admitted to Cannock Chase Hospital. June 1919 found him in Bagthorpe Military Hospital with Disordered Action of the Heart (D.A.H.) before being transferred to the Cardiac Centre at Leeds General Infirmary. He was invalided out of the Army in August 1919.

Photo George Smith Collection

John R Haynes, Builders, at the bottom of Bowns Hill

HEAPPEY BROTHERS

Andrew, Ernest, Jesse and Lot were the sons of John and Sarah Heappey. The family lived at Town End, Crich.

HEAPPEY, Private – Andrew Frank

North Staffordshire Regiment

Andrew was born at Crich in about 1887. He married Sarah Elizabeth Greensmith in 1908 and worked in the limestone quarry. During the war he was wounded and lost an eye. He died in 1949 aged sixty-two.

The photograph shows Andrew with family members (date unknown).

Photo "elfiej7"

HEAPPEY, Private – Ernest

Regiment unknown

Ernest was born in about 1881 and worked in the limestone quarry. He died in 1926 aged forty-five.

HEAPPEY, Sapper – Jesse

Royal Engineers
Northumberland Fusiliers

Jesse was born in about 1883 and worked in the limestone quarry. He enlisted at Derby in September 1916 aged thirty-two.

HEAPPEY, Private – Lot

Regiment unknown

Lot was born in about 1890 and worked in the limestone quarry. He died in 1922 aged thirty-three.

HEATHCOTE BROTHERS

John William and Samuel Joseph were the sons of Edmund and Mary Heathcote. For a time they lived in the Hat Factory at Crich.

HEATHCOTE, Private – John William

Regiment unknown

Born in about 1883 at the Hat Factory in Crich, John married Florence May Brown in 1903 and they lived on Roes Lane. He worked as a shunter at the South Wingfield colliery.

HEATHCOTE, Sergeant – Samuel Joseph

Royal Field Artillery

Born in about 1887 at Crich Samuel worked as a railway locomotive fireman and married Helena Bate in 1909 before joining the Army and entering France in December 1915.

HENSON BROTHERS

George and Norman were two of the six sons of Lewis and Elizabeth Ann Henson. They were the nephews of Arthur Walker Harrison and cousins of George Cowlishaw, both of whom are also on the Crich Roll of Honour.

HENSON, Private – Frank

Regiment unknown

It has not been possible to identify Private Frank Henson. During the twentieth century, only one family named Henson appears to have resided within the Crich parish. Extensive family history research has been undertaken into this family, yielding no reference at all to a Frank Henson. This raises the possibility that the Frank Henson on the Roll of Honour was in fact an individual who, at the time of the First World War, had briefly moved to live in the Crich parish from elsewhere, and was therefore listed on the Roll of Honour. There is also the possibility that this individual had merely assumed the surname of Henson, making it difficult to identify him in available records.

Only two definite references have been found relating to this Frank Henson. Two entries from the court registers of the Wirksworth Petty Sessions dated 30 June 1914 refer to a defendant named Frank Henson of Crich. Henson and another Crich man named Walter Rogers were charged with having been on licensed premises during prohibited hours, and for having attempted to obtain liquor by falsely representing themselves to be travellers. Both men received fines for their offences.

It has been suggested that Frank Henson could in fact be an individual named Frank Ward (1874–1941), who was a close friend of the Henson family at Crich. Frank Ward was a native of the Chesterfield area who had lodged at the home of Caroline Harrison on the Common for many years. He worked as an engine driver on the mineral railway running between Cliff Quarry at Crich and the lime works at Ambergate. He became a close friend and work colleague of Caroline Harrison's grandson George Henry Henson, who is also listed on the Roll of Honour. However, no documentary evidence or family recollections exist to suggest that Frank Ward ever used the surname of Henson. Likewise, George Henson's daughter – who knew Frank Ward well – has no recollection of being told that he served in the armed forces during the First World War. It should also be noted that Frank Ward would not have been eligible for conscription until the final months of the war. The Military Service Act of January 1916, which introduced conscription, stated that men who reached the age of forty-one years prior to 15 August 1915 were not eligible for conscription. He reached his forty-first birthday only a few months before this date. This upper age limit was raised to fifty-one years in 1918, during the last few months of the war, which would have latterly made him eligible for conscription.

HENSON, Private – George Henry
King's Own Yorkshire Light Infantry

Photo Neta Stone

George Henry Henson was born at Crich on 14th October 1898. He was the second of the six children of Lewis Henson and Elizabeth Ann Harrison, all of whom were boys. George was a lifelong resident of Crich.

Prior to the war George was employed on the Clay Cross Company's mineral railway running between Cliff Quarry at Crich and the company's lime kilns at Ambergate. Initially George worked as an engine driver, but spent the majority of his working life maintaining the engines as a skilled engineer.

During the war George served as a Private with the King's Own Yorkshire Light Infantry and saw active service in France. He was wounded in action, being shot through the leg, and spent a period in convalescence. George was awarded the Victory Medal and British War Medal.

Like many of the Crich men he received a postcard and postal order from the Parish of Crich and the Crich Women's Knitting Guild.

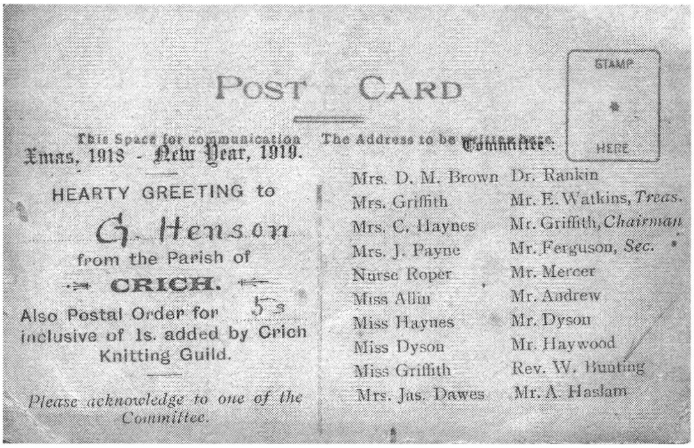
POST CARD

This Space for communication — The Address to be written here.

Xmas, 1918 - New Year, 1919.

HEARTY GREETING to

G. Henson

from the Parish of

CRICH.

Also Postal Order for 5s inclusive of 1s. added by Crich Knitting Guild.

Please acknowledge to one of the Committee.

Committee:

Mrs. D. M. Brown	Dr. Rankin
Mrs. Griffith	Mr. E. Watkins, *Treas.*
Mrs. C. Haynes	Mr. Griffith, *Chairman*
Mrs. J. Payne	Mr. Ferguson, *Sec.*
Nurse Roper	Mr. Mercer
Miss Allin	Mr. Andrew
Miss Haynes	Mr. Dyson
Miss Dyson	Mr. Haywood
Miss Griffith	Rev. W. Bunting
Mrs. Jas. Dawes	Mr. A. Haslam

STAMP HERE

After he was honourably discharged from the army, George returned to his occupation as an engineer on the mineral railway and married Eva Dorothy Roberts in 1926. They had three children together, a girl and two boys. After Cliff Quarry closed in 1957 and the mineral railway ceased to operate, George worked for Stevenson's Dye Works at Ambergate, retiring at seventy-two years of age. George Henry Henson passed away at Crich on 26th December 1978, aged eighty years.

George's older brother Norman Henson is also listed on the Roll of Honour, as is his uncle Arthur Walker Harrison and his cousin George Cowlishaw.

HENSON, 1st Stoker – Norman

Royal Navy

Photo Sheila Lockie and Maureen Austick

Norman Henson was born at Crich on 29th August 1896. He was the oldest of the six children of Lewis Henson and Elizabeth Ann Harrison, all of whom were boys.

His naval service records state that at the time of enlistment in 1916 he was employed as an engine driver. This was probably on the Clay Cross Company's mineral railway running between Cliff Quarry at Crich and the company's lime kilns at Ambergate. Norman's younger brother George is known to have been employed on the same railway at this time.

During the war Norman served as a stoker with the Royal Navy. His period of engagement dates from 14th June 1916, initially with the rank of Stoker 2nd Class. He was promoted to the rank of Stoker 1st Class on board HMS *Euryalus* on 14th June 1917. The majority of his naval service was spent aboard HMS *Euryalus* and

HMS *Venus*. Latterly he was stationed at HMS *Victory II*, which was the name given to a training depot which at the time of the First World War, was based at Crystal Palace in London. Norman received an honourable discharge on 19th December 1918 owing to organic heart disease and was awarded the British War Medal and the Victory Medal.

After he was honourably discharged from the Royal Navy, Norman married Beatrice May Dexter in 1920. They had two daughters. Almost all of their married life was spent living in the Derby area, where they lived at Allenton for many years. For much of his working life Norman was employed as a boiler stoker for various employers in the Derby area, most notably at Queen Street Baths when it opened in 1932. Shortly after his wife's death in 1983 he moved to live at Holbrook, near Belper.

Norman Henson passed away at Holbrook on 6th October 1990, aged ninety-four years. He was laid to rest in the churchyard of the Parish Church of St Michael and All Angels at Alvaston.

Norman's younger brother George Henry Henson is also listed on the Roll of Honour, as is his uncle Arthur Walker Harrison, and his cousin George Cowlishaw.

Norman Henson's Discharge Certificate

HINDS, Gunner – George Henry

Royal Field Artillery

George was born in Fritchley in about 1893, the son of George and Elizabeth Hinds. He joined the Army at Derby in July 1915 aged twenty-two, and entered France in January 1916. In July 1916 he was hospitalised with scabies and in January 1917 he was in hospital again in the Canadian General Hospital, this time with a foot injury. In May and July 1918 he was again in hospital with a urinary infection and then influenza. Demobbed in December 1918, he left France aboard the *SS Princess Victoria.*

HITCHCOCK: Corporal – Samuel ◊

North Staffordshire Regiment

Samuel was born in Holloway in about 1885, the son of Samuel and Phyllis Hitchcock. The family lived at Wheatcroft and Samuel junior worked at Lea Mills as a framework knitter. He joined the Army in November 1915 aged thirty and was discharged, having been wounded in August 1919 and being awarded the Silver War Badge. He spent time in a VAD hospital in Devon.

HODGKINS, Private – Matthew

Sherwood Foresters (Nottinghamshire and Derbyshire Regiment)

Matthew was the son of William and Matilda Hodgkins, born at Buckland Hollow in about 1885. He worked as a limestone quarryman.

HOLLINGSWORTH, Gunner – Samuel

Sherwood Foresters (Nottinghamshire and Derbyshire Regiment)

Royal Garrison Artillery

Photo Hilda Turner

Samuel was born at Crich in 1881, the son of Henry and Ellen Hollingsworth. He worked at Lea Mills before enlisting at Crich in December 1915 aged thirty-four, suffering from rheumatism. He had married Martha Ann Allen in July 1904. He was with the Foresters on enlistment and transferred to the Royal Garrison Artillery as a signaller and gunner. Although he had enlisted in 1915 it was not until January 1918 that he was mobilised as a gunner entering France in June 1918, before being demobbed to Mount Pleasant, Crich, in April 1919.

He was a gifted tenor horn player, playing for both Lea Mills Band and Crich Brass. Before the war he used to play for the famous "Besses o' th Barn Band", from

Lancashire, when they were at their best, touring America, Canada, Australia and New Zealand with them and winning many solo contests.

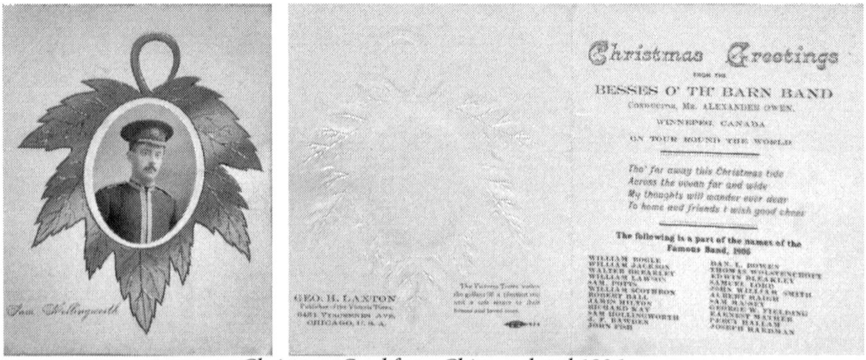

Christmas Card from Chicago dated 1906

Sam Hollingsworth on tour

Samuel conducted Crich Brass from 1952 to 1953; he died in 1959.

HOLMES, Private – Charles ✝

South Staffordshire Regiment

Essex Regiment

Charles was the son of James and Harriet Holmes; he was born in about 1890 at Crich and worked as a colliery hewer. He originally enlisted at Alfreton in the South Staffordshire Regiment and was killed on 21st September 1918, aged twenty-eight, and is buried at the Unicorn Cemetery, Vendhuile. He is also remembered on the Crich War memorials inside and outside St Mary's Church (see page 224).

HOLMES, Private – Charles Francis ✝

King's Own Yorkshire Light Infantry

Charles was born at Crich in 1898, the son of William and Eliza Holmes. He enlisted while working at Lea Mills, joining the King's Own Yorkshire Light Infantry in February 1917. His record states that he died on 7th February 1918 and is buried at Tincourt New British Cemetery. He is also remembered on the Lea Mills Memorial and on the Crich War memorials inside and outside St Mary's Church (see pages 230 and 224).

HOLMES: Sergeant – James Edgar

Sherwood Foresters (Nottinghamshire and Derbyshire Regiment)

South Wales Borderers

James (Jim) Edgar Holmes was born in 1892 at the Old Vicarage, Crich to Samuel and Elizabeth Holmes. He joined the Army in January 1916, originally with the Sherwood Foresters before transferring to the South Wales Borderers along with his best friend George Haslam, who is also on the Crich Roll of Honour. He worked at Lea Mills and received various parcels from the Managing Director, J. B. Marsden-Smedley, to which he replied.

Photo Margaret Charboneau

Battalion Grenade Section, 6th Sherwood Foresters, B E F c/o Y.P.O.L.
October 5th
Sir
I am just writing these few lines to you, I hope you wont think it too much, but I am asking you if you can kindly get us a football, there is myself and a lot more Matlock Boys, we have got a good team and have played a lot of games when out of the trenches, but at present we are without a ball, we have a bit of time when we are out of the trenches and we like a game to keep us fit. I must say that all the Matlock boys read in the paper of the death of your brave son, and we all join in sending our deepest sympathy, I will close now hoping you will oblige your Obedient Servant,
Pte J. Holmes 2050

L/Cpl J. Holmes, 58 T.R. 4/4370 A Coy., No. 9 Camp, Kinmel Park, Nr Rhyl. N.W.
Mr. Smedley
Dear Sir
Many thanks for your kind Xmas gift. I'm sure it is very good of you to think about us while we are at War and I hope before long we shall return to Lea Mills and settle down in peace and Comfort. Once more wishing you a Merry Xmas and a Happy New Year when it comes.
Yours Truly, J. Holmes

Sgt J C. Holmes, 51st. S.W.B., Sgt's Mess Alderburgh, Suffolk
Dear Sir
Thanks very much for parcel received quite safely. It is very kind of you to think of the boys who went from Lea Mills some of them now killed.
It hardly seems true. I don't know what to think of the war, Sir there isn't any sign of it being over. Once more thanking you very much for parcel.
Wishing you a Prosperous New Year.
Yours Very Truly, J.E. Holmes

51st S. W. B., Stowlangtoft Camp, Nr. Bury St. Ed., Suffolk
Sir
I wish to thank you for the splendid Parcel you have sent me — I can assure you it was very acceptable. Just coming off a Physical Drill & Bayonet Fighting Course.
Yours Faithfully, Sgt JE Holmes

Photos Barbara Haslam

George Haslam seated first left with Jim Holmes standing seventh from the left on the back row

Music was Jim Holmes' life-long interest. While he served with the 12th Welsh Regiment he became bandmaster, and after the war, during the days of silent films, he played for a number of years in the orchestra of Ripley Hippodrome. A keen sportsman, he played football with several local clubs. His father Samuel was a semi-professional footballer for Derby County, playing between 1889 and 1891. James was a member of Crich United Prize Brass Band for fifty-six years, several years as conductor. He married and moved to Heanor to work in the hosiery trade before moving back to Crich in later years.

George Haslam standing sixth from the left with Jim Holmes next to him, seventh left

HOLMES, Private – John Henry ◊

Durham Light Infantry

John was born at Crich in about 1894, the son of George and Mary Holmes. He enlisted at Matlock in December 1915 aged twenty-two, a miner working for the Butterley Company. John married Mary Hayne in May 1919 after being discharged from the Durham Light Infantry suffering from hammer toes in March 1919. He was awarded the Silver War Badge.

HOMER, Stoker Petty Officer – Harry

Royal Navy

Harry was born at Belper in August 1886, the son of Thomas and Harriet Homer. He worked as a bricklayer before joining the Royal Navy in May 1906 for a twelve-year period. He married Fritchley-born Harriett Elizabeth Curzon in 1916. Harry served throughout the war period, extending his twelve-year period to thirty-two years, finally demobbing in October 1938.

HOPKINSON BROTHERS

Thomas Humphrey and George Job were the sons of Job and Elizabeth Hopkinson who lived at Park Head, Crich.

HOPKINSON, Private – George Job
Sherwood Foresters (Nottinghamshire and Derbyshire Regiment)
Leicestershire Regiment

Photo David and Liz Houlden

George was born in about 1899. His collar insignia on the photograph show him as a Pioneer when he was serving with the Leicestershire Regiment. His family remember him suffering from trench foot and being wounded by shrapnel. As a result he was in hospital during the latter part of the war and came home during 1919. He died aged eighty in 1979.

Photo David and Liz Houlden

A souvenir sent home in 1918

HOPKINSON, Private – Thomas Humphrey
Regiment unknown

Thomas was born in about 1896 and worked as a grocer's errand boy. In 1922 he married Adelaide M. Stewardson. He died in 1976 aged eighty. His brother-in-law, Robert Stewardson, is also in the Roll of Honour.

HOUSLEY BROTHERS

George Samuel and William were the sons of George and Eve Housley of Crich.

HOUSLEY, Private – George Samuel

Royal Army Medical Corps

George was born at Crich in about 1886 and worked as an insurance agent before the war. He was five foot six inches tall and weighed one hundred and thirty-four pounds. His medical record noted an old fracture to his left patella. During 1918 he suffered from malaria and his record stated that he had 30% disability

HOUSLEY, Private – William

Sherwood Foresters (Nottinghamshire and Derbyshire Regiment)

Photo Michael Dawes

William, born in about 1894, worked for a time at Lea Mills but must have left before the start of the war as he does not feature in their records for this time. In 1921 he married Nora Mason.

His memorabilia includes matchbox cases showing photographs of himself and his wife Nora, and various items of his kit and uniform.

William and Nora on matchbox tins

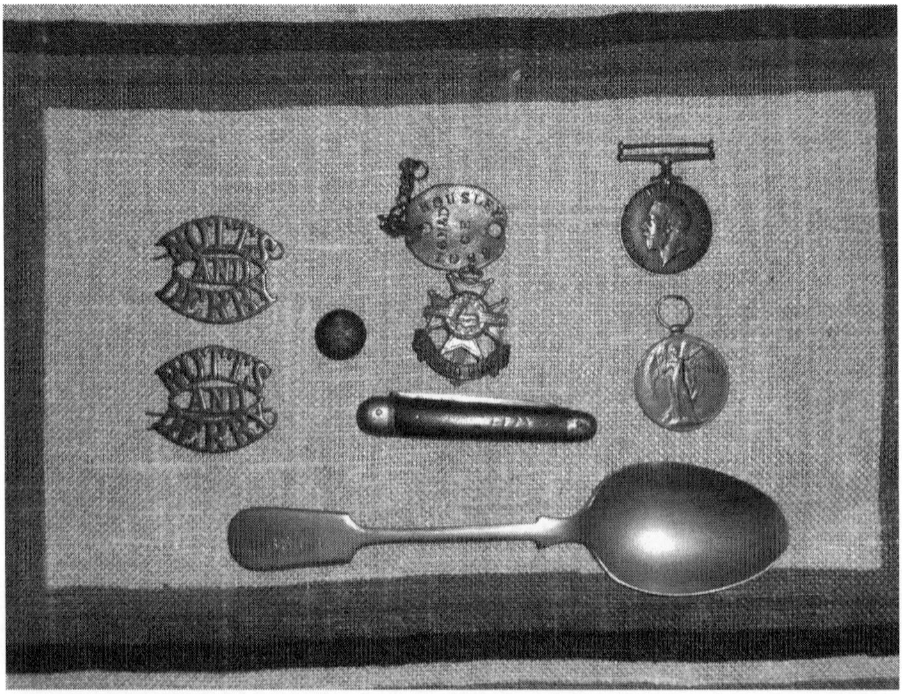

Shoulder flashes, button, dog tags, penknife, spoon, British War and Victory medals

HOWITT, Sapper – George Henry

Royal Engineers

George Henry was born in about 1883 and lived in Crich with his uncle and aunt, John and Margaret Taylor, until he married Lillian Fletcher in 1908 when he moved to Crich Carr. The records show him as Henry Howitt working as a stone mason.

HUGHES BROTHERS

George Andrew and James were sons of Joseph Hughes and Caroline Barton Pearson. Their father was born at Tansley and worked as a wheelwright. Around 1900 the family moved from Holloway to Crich.

HUGHES, Private – George Andrew

Sherwood Foresters (Nottinghamshire and Derbyshire Regiment)

Army Service Corps

George Andrew Hughes was born at Holloway on 30 December 1895. He was raised at Crich, though the family later moved to live at nearby Whatstandwell. Prior to the war, George had worked as a wood machinist at Yelverton Dawbarn Brothers at Whatstandwell.

At the time of enlistment George was living at Barrow-in-Furness in Cumbria, where he enlisted in the army on 6th December 1915. He initially served as a Private with the 3rd Battalion of The Sherwood Foresters, though was later transferred to the Army Service Corps, and was employed as a lorry driver. George was wounded in action in August 1918, having received a gunshot wound to the left forearm, and was transferred to a hospital in England.

After he was honourably discharged from the army, George married Ada Taylor at Derby in 1920. They emigrated to the US shortly afterwards and had a son and a daughter. For many years the family lived at Somerville in Middlesex County, Massachusetts. Throughout most of his working life George worked as a machinist and had worked for the Massachusetts Bay Transport Authority.

George Andrew Hughes passed away at Lowell, Middlesex County, Massachusetts, on 26 November 1968, aged seventy-two years. He was laid to rest in the Puritan Lawn Cemetery at Peabody in Essex County, Massachusetts.

He was not listed on the original Roll of Honour inside Crich Parish Church. This might be due to him being based at Barrow-in-Furness in Cumbria at the time of enlistment in 1915. His brother, James Hughes, was listed on the original Roll of Honour.

HUGHES, Telegraphist – James

Royal Naval Volunteer Reserve

Photo Gina Hewitt

James Hughes – known as Jim – was born at Matlock on 11th March 1894. He was raised at Crich, though his family later moved to live at nearby Whatstandwell. At this time Jim worked locally as a railway porter. In 1914 he moved to live at Hyde in Cheshire where he found employment as a railway booking clerk. He remained a resident of the Hyde area for the rest of his life.

During the war Jim served in the Royal Naval Volunteer Reserve (RNVR). His period of engagement dates from 22 August 1916, initially with the rank of Ordinary Seaman. He undertook training at the naval training establishment HMS *Victory VI* at Crystal Palace in London. After completing his training he progressed to the rank of Ordinary Telegraphist, then later Telegraphist. During the early days of wireless telegraphy, telegraphists became indispensable at sea, where they used Morse code in order to communicate via radio waves. On 10 April 1917, he was posted to HMS *Dalhousie*, which had been among the first ships to be involved in the Mesopotamian campaign. By the time Jim was posted to HMS *Dalhousie,* it was moored at Basra as the depot ship for a number of gunboats further up river. Crews came in and out of the region and swapped boats due to promotions and injuries via HMS *Dalhousie*. Jim served on the Euphrates and Tigris rivers on board the gunboat HMS *Gadfly*, though the majority of his service was aboard HMS *Gnat*. Jim reported in a 1980 newspaper article that he had travelled to Mesopotamia, China and India during his naval service. He recalled combatting pirates in the Far East, and helping to sink a submarine in 1917. He was shore demobilised on 11 December 1919.

After he was honourably discharged from the Royal Navy, Jim returned to his occupation as a clerk at Hyde railway station and married Edith Marshall in 1924. They had one daughter. After his wife's death in 1927, Jim married Alice Wilson in 1930. In total, Jim spent forty-eight years as an employee of British Railways (and predecessors), retiring from Marple railway station. After Jim's daughter and her husband emigrated to Canada in 1951, Jim and his wife spent some time in Canada visiting them. James Hughes passed away in Tameside on 8 February 1983, aged eighty-eight years.

His brother-in-law George Job Hopkinson is also listed on the Roll of Honour. Jim's younger brother George Andrew Hughes (1895-1968) served during the war as a Private in the Sherwood Foresters, and later in the Army Service Corps, but was not listed on the original Roll of Honour at Crich as he was living at Barrow-in-Furness in Cumbria at the time of enlistment.

JARVIS, Second Lieutenant – John Allan William

Royal Flying Corps
Royal Air Force

John, more commonly known as Jack, was born in Alfreton on 8th November 1889, the son of Leonard Arthur and Annie Jarvis. His maternal grandfather, the aptly named Charles Brewer, was one-time landlord of the Four Horseshoes in Alfreton and Jack's father Leonard Jarvis was a landlord at the Jovial Dutchman in Crich.

Jack was educated at the Herbert Strutt Secondary School in Belper before going on to become a bank clerk in Alfreton. He enlisted on 30th October 1917 stating that he wished to join the Royal Flying Corps or the Royal Engineers. At the time he was living in Crich at the Jovial Dutchman. He was commissioned into the RFC as Pilot or Observer. It was noted that he could ride a motor cycle, cycle and horse.

Jack transferred into the RAF as Second Lieutenant Observer Officer when it was formed in 1918 .

The photograph shows the Jovial Dutchman, by Crich Cross, where Jack lived from about 1912 (taken about 1915). Leonard A Jarvis's name is on the wall.

KEY, Private – James

Regiment unknown

The only James Key found with Crich connections was the son of Martha Key, born in about 1876 in the Heage area. He married Mary Alice Litchfield of Crich in 1900. Mary was the daughter of William Litchfield and the family lived at the Hat Factory in Crich.

KNEEBONE, Trooper – Gerald

Derbyshire Yeomanry

Sherwood Foresters (Nottinghamshire and Derbyshire Regiment)

Gerald Needham Albarn, born in 1890 at Crich, became the adopted son of John and Emily Kneebone and was then known as Gerald Kneebone. He attested at Derby in November 1915, a twenty-five year old grocer living at Tor View, Crich. In December 1916 he was transferred from the Derbyshire Yeomanry into the Sherwood Foresters, entering France a few days later. In November 1917 he was awarded a good conduct badge and was demobbed to Lodge Hall Farm, Wingfield Park in February 1919. Gerald married Ellen Shelton at Pentrich in December 1916.

KNEEBONE, Private – John (Jack) Thomas ✝
Sherwood Foresters (Nottinghamshire and Derbyshire Regiment)

Jack was born at Crich in about 1896; his parents were Thomas and Elizabeth Kneebone of East View, Crich. Before joining the Army he worked at Manor Colliery, South Wingfield. Jack was one of the first to enlist, doing so in August 1914 – see the photograph of the Crich volunteers on page 237. He died 20th September 1917 aged twenty-one, and is remembered on the Tyne Cot Memorial near Ypres. The Derbyshire Times reported him as missing (presumed dead) but they appear to have his regiment incorrectly stated as the Royal Field Artillery rather than the Sherwood Foresters.

Derbyshire Times 10 November 1917

CRICH SOLDIER MISSING

Mr and Mrs Thomas Kneebone, of Crich Common, have received news from the military authorities at Lichfield that their eldest son, Pte. John Thos. Kneebone who is a gunner in the R.F.A has been missing for about eight weeks. He enlisted in August 1914 and previous to joining the Army was employed at the Manor Colliery, South Wingfield. He is single and 23 years of age.

KNOWLES, Private – Charles Herbert
Royal Marines

Charles was the son of William and Sarah Knowles, born in about 1880 in Ripley. In 1901 he was with the Royal Marines in Plymouth aged twenty-two, but in 1911 he was at Bullbridge, Crich with his wife Clare (née Bond) and their three children, working as a train examiner. When the war started he must have re-engaged with the Royal Marines.

LAWRENCE, Private – Bryant Henry
Middlesex Regiment

Bryant was born in about 1879 at Goldalming; his parents were Reuben and Alice Lawrence. He attested at Bakewell in August 1915, a navvy, aged nearly forty, living at The Common Crich. He had married Annie Shaw in 1908. In January 1916 he was discharged from the Army on grounds of ill health although his request for a pension was denied. His army pension record wrongly named him as Henry Lawrence Bryant.

LEAFE BROTHERS

Arthur and James were the Crich-born sons of Edwin and Mary Ann Leafe. The family were Baptists.

James and Thomas were the sons of Edwin and Sarah Leafe living at Fritchley.

LEAFE, Private – Arthur

Sherwood Foresters (Nottinghamshire and Derbyshire Regiment)

Arthur, born at Crich in about 1882, attested at Clay Cross in October 1914 aged thirty-two, an unmarried labourer. However, shortly afterwards in December 1914 he was declared medically unfit to serve and was discharged. His brother James is also on the Roll of Honour.

LEAFE, Cyclist – Edwin ◊

East Yorkshire Regiment

Edwin was born in Crich Carr in about 1898 to John and Thirza Leafe. His father worked at Lea Mills and Edwin joined him there when he left school. He enlisted in February 1916 and was discharged in December 1917 having been awarded the Silver War Badge. He returned to live at Fern Leigh in Holloway and to work at Lea Mills.

LEAFE, Private – James ◊

Sherwood Foresters (Nottinghamshire and Derbyshire Regiment)

Born in about 1876 in Crich, James left as a young man to work as a labourer in the ironworks, living at Ilkeston. He attested in December 1915, a forty-year-old foundry worker, quoting Alfred Leafe of Roes Lane, Crich as his next of kin. He was discharged, of good character, in October 1917 aged forty-one, having been awarded the Silver War Badge. He did not serve overseas. His brother Arthur is also on the Roll of Honour.

LEAFE, Private – James

North Staffordshire Regiment
King's Shropshire Light Infantry

Born in 1893 at Fritchley, James, like his father, worked at Lea Mills. He joined the forces in June 1916 aged twenty-two, initially into the 3rd North Staffordshire Regiment but the Lea Mills Company and his medal index card identify him as being in the King's Shropshire Light Infantry. The Sherwood Foresters cap badge in the photograph does not match either of these two regiments.

He received parcels from Lea Mills and responded to them.

Feb. 7th 1917
Dear Sirs
Pleased to say that I received the parcel of underwear on the 5th Feb. in good condition. I thank you very much indeed for it. We are in the first line trenches, and having some very wet & cold weather. So you are sure the goods will be very useful. Sorry to hear that they are still calling your workmen away, But hope we shall soon all return home again. Wishing you & the firm the best of luck. Thanking you again for the parcel.
I Remain, Yours Sincerely
James Leafe

18/12/17
Dear Sirs
Very pleased to say that I have received your welcome parcel with the two vests in. I thank you very much indeed for them. We are out of the trenches at present, Have had some awfully cold weather, but it is a good deal warmer again now. The vests you sent me last year are in good condition even now. It will be a welcome time when we can come & make them again from the good old Firm. It is very hilly on this front, with a few fine lakes on the lower ground.
This last summer we got plenty of grapes & figs out of the old vineyards. The guns are firing at a Bulgar plane overhead as I am writing this. He has also tried a few raids on the front lately, But pleased to say he has had to retire in a hurry. I am in the best of health, hoping this will find you the same. Wishing you the Best of Luck & a Happy New Year.
I remain, Yours Sincerely
James Leafe (countersigned by J A Swindell)

After the war he returned to work at Lea Mills. James's brother Thomas is also on the Roll of Honour.

LEAFE, Private– Thomas Edwin ✝
West Yorkshire Regiment (Prince of Wales's Own)

Thomas was born in 1899 and after joining the army he was killed on 12th April 1918, aged nineteen. He was buried at Le Grand Beaumart British Cemetery, Steenwerck, near Armentières. His brother James is also on the Roll of Honour.

LEE BROTHERS

George Eric and Thomas Sanders were the Wirksworth-born sons of William and Mary Lee who lived near the Crich Parish Boundary at Longway Bank and Wigwell Mill. Some of the family were born at Crich.

LEE, Corporal – Arthur ◊

Sherwood Foresters (Nottinghamshire and Derbyshire Regiment)

Arthur was born in about 1893 at Alderwasley, son of Benjamin and Sarah Ann Lee. He played cricket with the Alderwasley Cricket Club (see the photograph on page 239). He worked at Lea Mills as a clerk and was one of the men who volunteered at the meeting in the factory on 17th August, 1914. He joined the forces on 25th August, 1914. He enlisted as a Private and initially served in the Balkans but by the time he went to France he was a Corporal. When the Company sent a parcel of groceries to him in France during October 1916, it was returned as he was in hospital.

A parcel containing vests reached him in December 1916, finding him in Cavendish Bridge VAD Hospital, Shardlow, Derby. He was discharged as the result of his wounds in October 1917 aged twenty-four, having been awarded the Silver War Badge. On his discharge record his given address was Meerbrook, Whatstandwell. He was transferred to Class P Army Reserve as Lance Corporal, no longer fit for War Service and not to be compulsorily posted for service under the Military Act 1917.

The original Crich Roll of Honour recorded him as receiving the Military Medal but this has not as yet been verified in any record.

After enlistment in the Sherwood Foresters he was in the local newspaper along with James Toplis, another Lea Mills worker.

High Peak News, 7 November 1914

MATLOCK LOCAL PATRIOTS

Above is photograph, by Barnett, Middlesborough, of some of our local patriots now at ––, ready for the front:–

Standing (at extreme left) Private J. Toplis; 4th from left, Private B. Checkley; next on right, Private Lee (Whatstandwell), and Private Travis, on the extreme right. Left, (sitting) Private J. Margerrison; on the extreme right-hand, Private George Stacey

Mr J. B. Marsden-Smedley, Managing Director of Lea Mills, wrote personally to Arthur.

Lea Green, Near Matlock

23rd Oct. 1916

Dear Lee,

I have sent you a parcel of eatables from Austin, Grocer, Derby, which I hope you will safely receive, and I shall be pleased to have a letter from you telling me how you are and whether the contents of the parcel are what you like. I have taken some trouble in choosing these contents and should like to know whether what has been sent is liked, so that I can have some guide when I next want to send you a parcel.

I fear the war is not over yet and that you may be some time away, and I should like you to know you are not forgotten and from time to time should like to send you a parcel. If you want any hosiery or a waistcoat write and let me know and I will do my best to send what you want.

I believe all the Derbyshire men are to have a parcel at Christmas, sent by a Committee, of which the Duke of Devonshire is chairman. They have been asking for subscriptions and you will have to look out that you get your parcel.

I hope you are well and that you may have good luck and a safe return.

Yours very truly,

J. B. Marsden-Smedley

Cpl Arthur Lee 13271, C. Coy, 9th Batt. 11th Division, Sherwood Foresters, B. E. F. France

Cavendish Bridge, V.A.D. Hospital, Shardlow, Nr. Derby

18.12.16

To Messrs John Smedley Ltd

Dear Sirs

Many thanks for your kind gift which has reached me quite safely.

The Vests were most acceptable and I'm sure that the lads in France, if they have received the same gift will appreciate your kindness very much.

My wounds are nearly healed, although; I shall never be able to walk properly again, as the principal nerve in my left leg has been severed and it has rendered my foot practically useless.

Yours respectfully

Cpl Lee A. No 13271

LEE, Private – George Eric

Regiment unknown

George was born in about 1893. By 1911 he had left the area and was working in Durham as a domestic groom. After the war he returned to Crich where he worked at Wingfield Manor Colliery. A newspaper report in the Derby Daily Telegraph dated 16th October 1922 reported on a fatal accident at the colliery. John Beresford and George Eric Lee were "ripping" when a fall of bind[1] occurred injuring both men, but John Beresford died of his injuries. George's brother Thomas is also on the Roll of Honour.

[1] Bind is believed to be shale or clay.

LEE, Trooper – James Stanley

Regiment unknown

James was the son of James and Hannah Lee, born in about 1892 in Crich. By 1911 he had left home and was working as a grocer's assistant in Hereford.

LEE, Private – James William

Labour Corps

James William was born at Crich in about 1886 to Edward William and Clara Lee. Sometime between 1891 and 1901 the family moved to the Sheffield district where they settled. James worked as a gardener and married Annie Swift in 1906. He enlisted in January 1918 and was posted to the Labour Corps. However, a medical report of March 1918 reported that he had tuberculosis disease of the arm so he was discharged on the grounds of being medically unfit for war work. His report stated that he was of good character.

LEE, Private – John William ◊

Sherwood Foresters (Nottinghamshire and Derbyshire Regiment)
South Staffordshire Regiment
Army Service Corps (Royal Army Service Corps)

John was born in about 1898 at Crich Carr to John and Anne Lee. He enlisted in 1916 aged eighteen whilst working as a clerk. In April 1918 he suffered a gun shot wound to his right thigh and was discharged in February 1919 having been award the Silver War Badge.

LEE, Private – Thomas Sanders

Regiment unknown

Thomas was born in about 1899. His brother George is also on the Roll of Honour.

LIMB, Private – William

Regiment unknown

William, born in about 1880 at Wheatcroft, was the son of James and Jane Limb. He worked as a farm labourer before joining the forces.

LISTER, Lance Corporal – John

Regiment unknown

Although John has not been found in Crich records up to 1911 he does make an appearance after the war as president of the Crich Branch of the British Legion.

Derby Daily Telegraph; 13 November 1933

EX-SERVICEMEN ON PARADE

CRICH PROCESSION

> Members of the Crich British Legion, Old Comrades, Parish Council, School Managers, Rural Council, Boy Scouts, Cubs, Brownies, Girl Guides, Friendly Societies, Welfare Committee and other organisations, headed by Crich Silver Band, paraded to Crich Parish Church yesterday for a Remembrance Service conducted by the Rev H.E. Jones (Vicar), who was assisted by Captain Graham. "O Valiant Hearts" was sung, Mr A. Pearson being the organist. The "Last Post" and "Reveille" was sounded by Bandsman J. Holmes.
>
> Mr John Lister (chairman of the British Legion) was in command of the parade. British Legion officers assisting were Mr E Burtt (secretary) and Mr A Day (Treasurer). Mr N. Smith was in charge of the Comrades, and Commissioner Flora MacDonald assisted by officers of the other organisations, also assisted. Councillor F.J. Lynam (chairman of the Parish Council) was present.

The bandsman J. Holmes mentioned in the report was James Holmes who is also on the Roll of Honour.

Other newspaper reports mention John Lister of Derwent Villas, Whatstandwell.

LITCHFIELD BROTHERS

Abraham and John were two of the sons of William and Mary Litchfield. In 1891 the family were living at the Hat Factory at Crich where William was a widower working as a framework knitter.

LITCHFIELD, Private – Abraham

Sherwood Foresters (Nottinghamshire and Derbyshire Regiment)

Born in about 1883, Abraham worked as a coal miner before joining the Sherwood Foresters very early in the war. He disembarked with the 2nd Battalion in September 1914.

LITCHFIELD, Lance Corporal - John

Regiment unknown

Born in about 1874, John worked on the railway and married Frances Burton in 1909.

LOCKEY, Lieutenant - Ernest **MM**

Kings Own Royal Lancaster Regiment

Ernest was born in 1892 at Gomersal in Yorkshire, the son of George and Emma Lockey. By 1911 his parents had moved to Thurlow Booth Farm at Whatstandwell while Ernest was working as a schoolmaster at Barrow in Furness. He was posted abroad in July 1917 and was subsequently awarded the Military Medal.

> 1st/4th King's Own, for Ypres 20 to 24 Sep 1917.
>
> To O/C 1/4 RLR
>
> No 201104 Corporal Lockey, Ernest.
>
> During the attack on Strong Point D13 d12 58 this Corporal organised a system of defence in adjacent shell holes while under MG fire and sniper fire from Gallipoli.
>
> He also assisted in bringing in wounded during this period although under heavy fire and later took charge of our line of defence on the right flank while we reorganised and advanced some 100 yards.
>
> He personally visited posts on a 150 ft front and distributed rations though sniping was prevalent.
>
> 27 September 1917 MM
>
> 2nd Lieutenant Paterson, D Company, 1/ RLR

This award was reported in the London Gazette 30715, published on 31st May 1918.

He was commissioned on 29th May 1918 and then transferred to the Reserve Battalion. After being demobbed in January 1919 he had an address of *The Royal Albert Orphanage, Worcester,* and he went on to marry Edith Lawton in 1923. He died in 1958 aged sixty-six.

LOWE, Private – John

Derbyshire Yeomanry

John was born in Whatstandwell in about 1885, the son of Robert and Maria Lowe. Before the war in 1910 he married Susan Margaret Cupit and lived at Somercotes where he worked for miller and baker J.A. Taylor. He joined the Army, at Somercotes, in February 1914, aged twenty-eight. He was discharged in July 1916 under the Military Services Act 1916. This could possibly be through ill health or "*as a member of the regular or reserve forces or of the Territorial Force who are liable for foreign service or who are, in the opinion of the Army Council, not suitable for foreign service*".

LUDLAM BROTHERS

Charles and Ernest were the sons of John and Sarah Ann Ludlam who lived at Mill Green, Crich.

LUDLAM, Private – Charles

Regiment unknown

Charles, born in about 1898, worked at Ambergate wire works before the war. After the war he had a lorry working as a haulage contractor with Clarence Wainwright.

LUDLAM, Lance Corporal – Ernest

Regiment unknown

Ernest, born in about 1896, worked as a butcher before joining the Army.

A view of Fritchley, familiar to the Ludlam family and other local residents.

LUDLAM, Rifleman – John (Jack) Charles
Leicestershire Regiment

Jack was born at Crich in 1898, the son of Henry and Eliza Ludlam. His maternal grandfather John White farmed at Cliffside, Crich and Jack worked as a farm hand before enlistment.

Photos Sue Worboys

LYNAM, Lance Corporal – John (Jack) Thomas ✝
Seaforth Highlanders

Jack was born in 1887, the son of James and Elizabeth Mary Lynam, who kept the Post Office in Fritchley. He worked as a clerk on the railway and enlisted in 1915, joining the Seaforth Highlanders. He died, the result of illness, on 10 December 1916 and is buried at Contay British Cemetery, near Amiens. His death was reported in the Derbyshire Times on 23 December 1916. He left a will leaving his estate to his brother Joseph Henry Lynam.

The will of John Thomas Lynam of The Cottage Fritchley dated 8/6/1911.
Appointed Hugh Spence, Railway Clerk of Little Eaton, and Charles Fredrick Pemberton of 13 Nether Close St Derby as executors.
The whole of my money and possessions to my brother Joseph Henry Lynam of The Cottage, Fritchley.
Probate granted 22/8/1917
Effects £181-12s-3d

Derbyshire Times 23 December 1916

CRICH SEAFORTH'S DEATH

Information was received last weekend that Lance Corporal J. T. Lynam of the Seaforth Highlanders, son of Mr and Mrs Lynam of the Post Office Fritchley, had died at the Front in France. The Matron of the 49th Casualty Clearing Section wrote saying that Lance Corporal Lynam died on the 10th last from pneumonia and that the funeral took place at the British Military Cemetery, Contay. The sad news caused widespread sorrow and regret in the Fritchley and Crich district, where the deceased soldier was well-known and respected. He enlisted about fifteen months ago and saw much hard fighting at the

Western Front. In the terrible battle of the Somme he had many narrow escapes and it is the bitter irony of fate that he should come through all this and then die from illness. One incident which occurred is worth recording. During one engagement some elaborate German dug-outs were captured and Lance Corporal Lynam was in charge of the party which took possession. On entering one of the dug-outs he found a German inside and ordered the latter to come out. The "Boche" however, beckoned to Lance Corporal Lynam to come further inside and then whilst parlaying the treacherous German fired point blank at the Britisher, but fortunately missed. What happened to the Hun is not recorded! The late Mr Lynam was about 30 years of age and single. He was a member of the Fritchley Congregational Church, the members of which will keenly feel his loss. He formerly took an interest in local football and was at different times goalkeeper for the Fritchley Congregational and Alderwasley football clubs. He also had association with Cromford at which place he spent several summers camping out. Before he joined the Army he was employed at the Chief Goods Manager's Office, Midland Railway, Derby. The utmost sympathy is felt for the bereaved family.

LYNAM, Driver – Samuel

Royal Field Artillery

Samuel was born at Fritchley in 1896, the son of Frederick and Elizabeth Ellen Lynam who had a butcher's shop on the Green at Fritchley and also kept the village pub, the Red Lion. After the war in 1922 he married Myrtle Allen and ran the Fritchley butchery. Sam died at Fairfield Farm, Fritchley in 1954 aged fifty-seven.

Red Lion in Fritchley, one-time home of Samuel Lynam

Sam was a "village character" and in the Lynam family archives there is "A Little Tale of Samuel Lynam" written as Sam would have spoken:

Samuel Lynam, the butcher of Fritchley, was passing the time of day with the doctor (John Stewarts) chatting that witch-craftery was at least as effective as some of the drugs prescribed and made his patients feel so much better – with no side effects!

John Stewarts mentioned the forthcoming wedding of a well-known Fritchley character when Sam then said "Ar suppose thay'll bay cummin ter borra me payjarmers". Dr John looked puzzled so Sam explained "Durst say I nivvawore owt i' bed – nubbdi in Fritchley could afford few – an when ar got wed t'missus made me buy a pair. Ar've nivva worn 'em sin – but ar lend'em aert fer honeymoons wenn ar'm arsked!"

Pony and trap outside Sam Lynam's butcher's shop

MACDONALD, Lieutenant – Ian Petrie

Royal Army Medical Corps

(attached to Sherwood Foresters (Nottinghamshire and Derbyshire Regiment))

Ian was born at Crich in 1892, the son of village doctor George Macdonald. There were two doctors in partnership at this time – Doctors Macdonald and Rankin. He was one the first to enlist (see the two group photographs taken at his family home, Roskeen in 1914 on pages 237 and 238). In December 1915, whilst a Lieutenant in the RAMC, he joined the 11th Battalion Sherwood Foresters as Medical Officer. During June 1916 he was wounded near Bouzincourt.

Doctors Macdonald and Rankin outside Roskeen on Surgery Lane, Crich

MAES, Frank

The Maes family arrived in Crich during November 1914 as Belgian refugees. Two of the children, Madeleine and Jules (also known as Saul) were enrolled at Crich School. In 1916 Jules left school to work and in 1919 Madeleine returned to Belgium.

It is assumed that Frank Maes is related to this family. On the Medal Roll index cards there is Rev. Francois E. Maes, Belgian Agent, who was awarded the British War Medal. Belgian Agents were Belgian civilians in British service, but not with a regiment.

In April of 1915 the High Peak News reported that two Belgian refugees from Crich, Mlle Anna De Ridder and M. Joseph Maes, were married by father Le Roy at St Joseph's Catholic Church in Matlock. Most of the twenty-minute ceremony was in Flemish, but the bride and bridegroom had learned sufficient English to be able to respond to the wedding questions in that language.

See the photograph on page 247 of the Maes and De Ridder families.

MARSDEN, Private – Joseph

Canadian Expeditionary Force

Joseph was born on 9 February 1895 at Crich; his parents were Robert and Annie Marsden. On 1 April 1897, when he was aged two, the family left Liverpool aboard *SS Mongolian* bound for Halifax, Canada. The family were Robert, Annie, Henry, Millicent, Joseph and Minnie, who was an infant. He attested on 22nd May 1918 aged twenty-three, an unmarried Methodist, working as a farmer. He was living at Excel, Alta.

MARTIN BROTHERS

Alfred and John were the sons of Alfred and Catherine Martin. The family variously lived at Matlock, Crich and Somercotes.

MARTIN, Private – Alfred Bertram

Sherwood Foresters (Nottinghamshire and Derbyshire Regiment)
South Staffordshire Regiment

Alfred was born in 1892 at Matlock and worked as a labourer in the coal mines. He joined the Army in September 1914 at Derby aged twenty-one and entered France in July 1915. In September 1915 he suffered a gunshot wound at Etaples and was returned to the UK for treatment before returning to his unit.

Derbyshire Times 16 October 1915

FORMER CRICH MAN WOUNDED

> Mr Alfred Martin, late of Crich, now residing at Somercotes, has received the following tribute from the Commanding Officer to his son, Pvte. A.B. Martin, No 14116, D Co. 10th Battalion, Notts and Derby. Private Martin was struck by a bullet which passed right through the muscle of his arm, causing paralysis for the time. He was conveyed to Etaples Hospital, but is now at Nether Court V.A.D. Hospital, Ramsgate where he is progressing favourably. "Had it not been for the spade he was using he would have been killed; he was a credit to his platoon, and was very calm under fire. He was a man with very high ideals, and always tried to live up to them. Such men do their comrades good, and I was very sorry to lose him." Mr Martin also has another son Pvte. John Martin in the Notts and Derbys.

He was transferred to the South Staffordshire Regiment in January 1917 before moving out to India where, in October 1918, he contracted malaria and was treated at Colaba War Hospital (Northern India) and Bombay Hospital. Leaving India aboard the hospital ship HS *Castalia* he was demobbed, with a 20% disability allowance, in March 1919. His brother John is also on the Roll of Honour.

MARTIN, Private – Charles Walter

Regiment unknown

Born in 1887, Charles was the son of Crich barber William Martin and his wife Mary Ann. In 1910 he married Alice Briddon and moved to Pinxton where he worked as a pit banksman.

MARTIN, Corporal – Herbert Wilfred **MM**

Army Service Corps
North Staffordshire Regiment

Photo Keith Fretwell

Wilfred was born in Crich in January 1894, the son of Frederick Martin and Mary Ann Taylor. He was a member of the Boys Brigade and Crich Church Choir in his youth. Wilfred worked as a miner at Wingfield Manor Colliery for most of his working life. He married Alice Clarke at St Mary's Church, Crich in January 1915 and lived in the village all his life, dying there in November 1965 aged seventy-one.

He enlisted in the Army Service Corps in September 1914 and was later transferred to the North Staffordshire Regiment. During August 1918, whilst serving with the 8th Battalion in France, he was awarded the Military Medal. This was published in the London Gazette on 26 August 1918.

Derbyshire Times 17th August 1918

MILITARY MEDALS

CORPL. W. H. MARTIN CRICH

Corpl. Wilfred H. Martin, son of Mr Fred Martin, North View Crich, writes to his parents and wife that he has been awarded the Military Medal. He enlisted in the ASC in September 1914 and was afterwards transferred to the North Staffs Regiment and drafted into France. He is 22 years of age and was a member of Crich Parish Church Choir and Boys Brigade.

Derbyshire Times 15th February 1919

MILITARY MEDALS

Corpl. Herbert Wilfred Martin, 8th North Staffs Regt, of Crich, was presented with the Military Medal by Major Hurt, of Alderwasley, at the Parochial School, Crich, on Saturday. After pinning the medal on his breast, the Major warmly shook hands and heartily congratulated him on his bravery. He also paid a high tribute to the Crich boys for their splendid response to the call, many of whom have laid down their lives for their King and Country. Dr Harry Rankin likewise referred to the great effort made by Crich in the war. The act of bravery which won for Corpl. Martin the medal occurred on Palm Sunday 1918 at Beugny, near Bapaume. The ribbon was presented to him by General Birdwood in front of the Division. Corpl. Martin enlisted in October 1914 and was wounded in action.

MARTIN, Private – John Henry

Sherwood Foresters (Nottinghamshire and Derbyshire Regiment)

John was born in 1897 and worked as a ganger in the coal mines. His brother Alfred is also on the Roll of Honour.

MASON BROTHERS

Arthur, Charles, James and William were four of the six sons of James and Eliza Mason. Their father was a Liverpool-born stonemason. Before the war the family were living at Whatstandwell.

MASON, Driver – Arthur

Royal Field Artillery

Photo Simon Johnson

During Arthur's youth, his family moved from Crich to Whatstandwell and were notable for being a musical family. As a young man Arthur was involved with Whatstandwell Brass Band and later became involved with Crich United Silver Prize Brass Band, which he regularly conducted. He also played the organ at the Baptist Chapel at Crich. Prior to his military service during the war, Arthur was employed as a wire drawer at the wireworks at Ambergate. He married Annie Cowlishaw in 1916, either prior to his military service, or whilst back home on a short furlough. They had four children, two boys and two girls. After the war Arthur returned to Whatstandwell and spent periods working at the wireworks at Ambergate, and at the joinery works of Yelverton Dawbarn Brothers at Whatstandwell. In later years Arthur and his wife moved to live at Crich. Several years after the death of his wife, Arthur Mason passed away at Derby in 1980, aged eighty-six years.

Arthur, centre, with the Whatstandwell Brass Band in about 1920

Arthur's older brothers William Mason, Charles Richard Mason and James William Mason are also listed on the Roll of Honour, as is his brother-in-law George Cowlishaw.

MASON, Sergeant – Charles Richard

Sherwood Foresters (Nottinghamshire and Derbyshire Regiment)

Charles was born at Crich in 1882, and like his father he worked as a stonemason. In 1903 he married Eunice Hawksley.

In 1932 he represented the Sherwood Foresters Old Comrades Association at a memorial service at the Thiepval Memorial in France.

Derby Evening Telegraph Tuesday August 2 1932

Veteran Foresters in France

SOMME MEMORIAL TO BRITISH DEAD

Among the 73,000 names inscribed on the panels of the Somme memorial to the British armies at Thiepval are those of 1,483 Sherwood Foresters

The memorial was unveiled by the Prince of Wales yesterday as president of the Imperial War Graves Commission. Beside him stood the president of the French Republic. The names of 73,367 British dead who have no known grave are commemorated by this memorial.

The general committee of the Sherwood Foresters Old Comrades Association decided that the association should be represented at the unveiling ceremony, and the following representatives of the Association were selected: –

COUNTY REPRESENTATIVES

Mr H. Allsop, of Ripley who enlisted in 1886 served with the 1st Battalion in the South African war, re-enlisted for active service in 1914, and served for seven months on the Somme with different service battalions of the regiment.

Mr F. Flowers of Whitwell, near Mansfield, who served with the 1st Battalion Sherwood Foresters in India before the war, went to France with the 2nd Battalion in 1914, and after being wounded fought with the 2nd and 10th Battalions on the Somme; and

Mr C. R. Mason, of Crich who, as a Territorial soldier served with the 5th, 11th, and 12th Battalions of the regiment on the Somme.

It was also intended that the 1st and 2nd Battalions of the regiment should be represented by a senior serving officer, and Major R. L. Sherbrooke, D.S.O., was selected, but at the last moment was prevented from attending the ceremony.

MASON, Private – James William †

South Staffordshire Regiment

Born in 1883, James was a quarryman. He married Emma Limb at St Mary's, Crich in 1909. He enlisted in 1917 and was killed in action on 21st August 1918 – he was buried at Fouquieres Churchyard Extension, near Béthune.

Derbyshire Times 31 August 1918

CRICH SOLDIER KILLED

> Mrs Mason, of Crich Common, received the news on Monday that her husband Pte. James Wm. Mason, South Staffs, was killed in action in France on the 20th inst and was buried on the 22nd. He was 34 years of age and leaves a wife but no family. He enlisted just over a year ago and went to France last November, and had been wounded and gassed. Prior to joining up he was superintendent of the Wesleyan Sunday School, organist and a vocalist of some repute.

James is remembered on the memorial tablet in the Wesleyan Chapel, Crich; see page 228.

MASON, Private – William

Regiment unknown

William was born in 1880 and worked as a machine minder in a factory.

MASSEY, Lance Corporal – Hugh

Regiment unknown

This is possibly the Hugh Massey born in 1891 at Oakerthorpe. During 1915 Hugh J. Massey married Ada M. Bowler in the Belper district.

MCLARTY, Lance Corporal – Hector †

King's Own Yorkshire Light Infantry

Hector was born in 1893, the son of police inspector John McLarty, a Scotsman, and his wife Ellen. Hector was born in Willington near Derby but in 1911 the family were living at Plaistow Green, Crich. Hector was killed on 20th September 1918 aged twenty-five and is buried at Five Points Cemetery, Lechelle, near Arras.

Photos Joyce Denton

Hector is on the back row, fifth from the left

In Joyce Denton's family album are several photographs of Hector's Battalion band. Was he a member?

Hector Mclarty received postcards and postal orders from Crich Ladies' Knitting Guild.

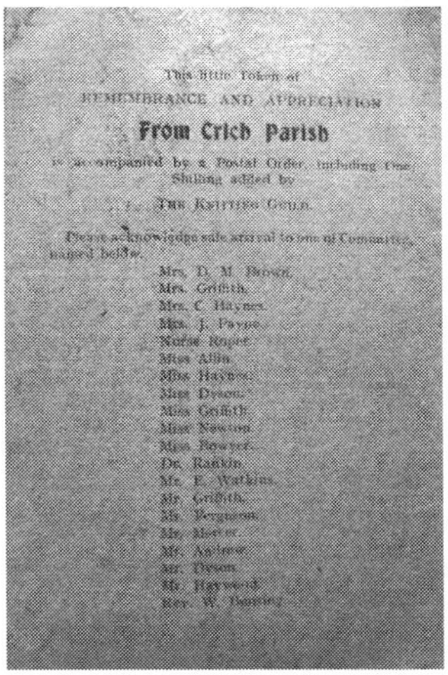

This little Token of

REMEMBRANCE AND APPRECIATION

From Crich Parish

is accompanied by a Postal Order, including One Shilling added by

THE KNITTING GUILD.

Please acknowledge safe arrival to one of Committee named below.

Mrs. D. M. Brown.
Mrs. Griffith.
Mrs. C. Haynes.
Mrs. J. Payne.
Nurse Roper.
Miss Allin.
Miss Haynes.
Miss Dyson.
Miss Griffith.
Miss Newton.
Miss Bowyer.
Dr. Rankin.
Mr. E. Watkins.
Mr. Griffith.
Mr. Ferguson.
Mr. Mercer.
Mr. Andrew.
Mr. Dyson.
Mr. Hayward.
Rev. W. Dunning.

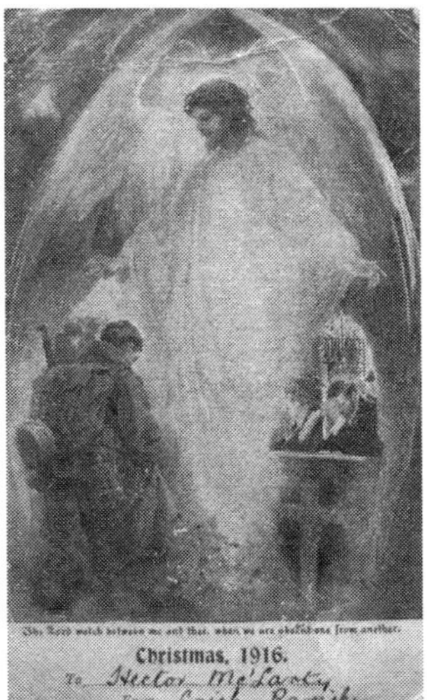

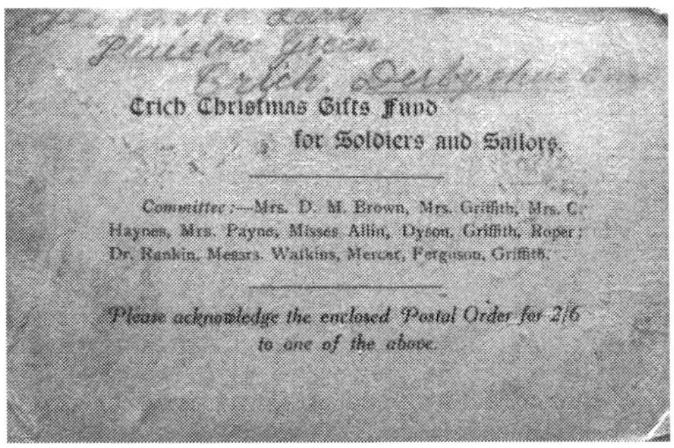

Plaistow Green
Crich. Derbyshire

Crich Christmas Gifts Fund for Soldiers and Sailors.

Committee:—Mrs. D. M. Brown, Mrs. Griffith, Mrs. C. Haynes, Mrs. Payne, Misses Allin, Dyson, Griffith, Roper; Dr. Rankin, Messrs. Watkins, Mercer, Ferguson, Griffith.

Please acknowledge the enclosed Postal Order for 2/6 to one of the above.

He also sent home postcards to his sisters and mother.

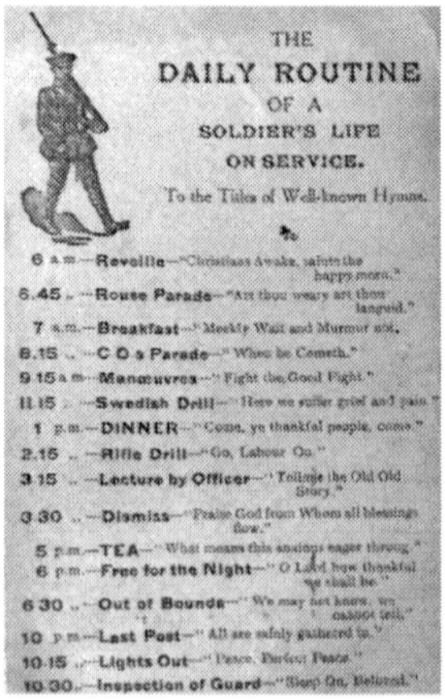

Many of the soldiers had access to embroidered cards, often very sentimentally written, and Hector was no exception. He sent several home to his sisters and mother.

Hector's family received the scroll sent to families of those who died.

MEE BROTHERS

Clement and Maurice's parents were William and Lydia Mee – the family lived at Crich Carr.

MEE, Private – Clement

Regiment unknown

Clement was born at Crich Carr in 1881. He married Edith Simpson in 1902 and worked as a joiner and cabinet maker. He died in Cheshire during 1966 aged eighty-six.

MEE, Driver – Maurice

Army Service Corps
Royal Army Service Corps

Maurice was born in 1889. He married Elizabeth Amatt in December 1914, at Holloway, and worked at Ambergate wireworks. When he enlisted in December 1916, aged twenty-seven, he was living at Lower Hartshay, Ripley. In February 1917 he was in hospital with scabies, and then embarked from Southampton for Le Havre in May 1917. His record shows that in October 1919 he was in Cologne. When demobbed in November 1919 he was described as being sober, reliable and intelligent.

The Army Service Corps became the Royal Army Service Corps in 1918.

MELLORS BROTHERS

John and Walter were the sons of James and Maria Mellors.

MELLORS, Sapper – George ✞

Royal Engineers

George was the son of George (senior) and Sarah Mellors. He was baptised at St Mary's Crich in July 1888 aged ten, and joined the regular army in about 1900. He died of pneumonia in a Norfolk sanatorium on 6th April 1915 aged thirty-six. He is buried in the north west of the churchyard at Cley-next-the-Sea (St Margaret), near Cromer. Sometimes his name was recorded as Mellows.

He is probably the George Mellows (sic) who is named on the Wesleyan Chapel Memorial Tablet; see page 228.

Ripley & Heanor News 16 April 1915

DEATH OF A CRICH SAPPER

News was received last week by Mr and Mrs George Mellors, of the Common, Crich, of the death of their eldest son Sapper George Mellors of the Royal Engineers, in a sanatorium in Norfolk. Mellors, who was 36 years of age, had seen 16 years service in the Army and was a reservist. He took part in the fighting at Mons and the Marne and Aisne, and apart from a very slight shrapnel wound escaped injury. He, however, contracted a severe chill, and pleurisy and pneumonia set in, and he was invalided back to England.

MELLORS (MELLOWS), Private – John ✝
King's Own Yorkshire Light Infantry

John was born at Crich in 1892 but did not live with his parents, but with his uncle and aunt Thomas and Mary Ann Marshall. The records show that his name was recorded as Mellows. He married Hannah Beardsley in 1913 while living in Nottinghamshire and enlisted in 1914 at Doncaster. Entering France in May 1915 he was wounded in 1916 and then killed in action on 3rd May 1917 aged twenty-five. He was buried at Arras.

Derbyshire Times 2 June 1917

CRICH CASUALTIES

Mr and Mrs James Mellors of Crich have received news of the death of their second son, Pte John Mellors, of the King's Yorkshire Light Infantry, who was killed in action on the 3rd of May. He was wounded 13 months ago in France, and had seen much fighting. He had enlisted at the beginning of the War, while at Doncaster. He was 25 years of age and married. The deceased's brother Cprl. Walter Mellors, of The Sherwoods, who enlisted at the same time is now a prisoner of war in Germany.

John's brother Walter is also on the Crich Roll of Honour.

MELLORS, Lance Corporal – Walter (Wammy)
Sherwood Foresters (Nottinghamshire and Derbyshire Regiment)

Walter was born in 1896 and worked in the stone quarries. He was one of the first to enlist (see photographs of recruits at Roskeen, Crich on page 237) and he entered France in June 1915.

By June 1917 he was a prisoner of war – see the newspaper article above. He was demobbed in May 1919.

After the war Wammy Mellors was a member of the Crich United Silver Prize Brass Band.

Wammy Mellors with the big drum

Walter's brother John is also on the Crich Roll of Honour.

MERCER, Corporal – Herbert

Royal Fusiliers
Royal Engineers

Herbert was born in 1896 at Rochdale, the son of Alfred and Elizabeth Alice Mercer. His father was the pharmacist in Crich and his mother was very active in the parish church. He enrolled at Derby in June 1915, aged nineteen, an unmarried chemist's assistant; his address was Hill Crest, Crich. Originally he was with the Royal Fusiliers, then in September 1915 he was transferred as depot chemist to the Royal Engineers and promoted to Corporal. His clothing statement recorded him as having: two boots, one cap, two drawers, two jackets, one puttees, two trousers, one waistcoat/cardigan, one great coat, one kit of necessities. He had an aggregate musketry score, Part I and II, of 92 (possible 260). When demobbed in February 1919 he was recorded as being of good character.

MINKLEY, Corporal – Horace James

Sherwood Foresters (Nottinghamshire and Derbyshire Regiment)
Royal Engineers

Born in 1884 at Swinderby Horace was living with his grandparents Thomas and Jane Minkley in 1891. He moved to Derbyshire and married Lily Nash in 1908. They lived in Fritchley and Horace worked on the railway.

MOUNTNEY, Second Lieutenant – James Oscroft

Royal Air Force

James was born in 1899 at Whatstandwell where his parents, Herbert and Elizabeth, were publicans at the Derwent Hotel. He joined the RAF in May 1918 as a cadet and left the service in January 1919 as a second lieutenant.

He was a supporter of the Whatstandwell Football Club (see photograph on page 243).

MURPHY, Private – James Crowder ✝

Sherwood Foresters (Nottinghamshire and Derbyshire Regiment)

James was born in 1886 at Crich, the son of John and Eliza Murphy. Like his father James worked at Ambergate wireworks.

On the 9th October 1916 he was killed in action, aged thirty-one, during the attack on the Schwaben Redoubt, Somme, and is remembered on the Thiepval Memorial.

NEEDHAM, Private – Jim

Sherwood Foresters (Nottinghamshire and Derbyshire Regiment)
North Staffordshire Regiment

Jim was born at Bullbridge in 1894, the son of James and Lucy Needham. Before the war he worked as a horse driver.

NEWTON, Private – Norman

Sherwood Foresters (Nottinghamshire and Derbyshire Regiment)
Queen's (Royal West Surrey) Regiment
Labour Corps

Norman was born at Lea in 1880; his parents were Adam and Matilda Newton. In 1911 he was living at Crich and working as a banksman in the colliery. When he enlisted in February 1916, at Matlock, he was aged thirty-six, an unmarried cowman living at Carr Farm, Wheatcroft. In January 1917 he was transferred from the Foresters into the Queen's (Royal West Surrey) Regiment, then in May 1917 he was transferred into the Labour Corps. He must have served in France as he embarked from Dunkirk back to the UK in February 1919 to be demobbed.

NOWELL, Sapper – Ernest Albert

Royal Engineers

Ernest was born in 1890 at Gorton, Manchester, the son of Arthur and Emma Nowell. His father was an inspector of waterworks and Ernest worked as a skilled walling mason before becoming an inspector of public works. He married Essie England at Derby in December 1912 before attesting to join the Army in December 1915 at Mold, aged twenty-five. His record shows that he had previously served with the 5th Battalion Sherwood Foresters. In April 1917 he was sent to Mesopotamia. Two years later, in April 1919, he was in a military hospital with dysentery, dermatitis and boils; he was demobbed five months later with a 20% disability allowance.

Newspaper cutting (date and publication unknown)

> Mrs E. Nowell of Church View, Crich, received news from her husband, Sapper Ernest Nowell, last weekend, stating that he is ill in hospital, having had an attack of "sandfly" fever. Soon after landing in Mesopotamia he had an attack and, after recovery, rejoined his company. A couple of days later the fever again attacked him, and he had to return to hospital. Sapper Nowell has been in the Engineers since joining up in October last year. He went to the Eastern front last Easter. Before joining up he was water-works inspector at Mold, Wales.

PARKIN BROTHERS

Frank, George and Harold were the sons of John James and Annie Elizabeth Parkin, a Fritchley family. Their father worked at the lime works.

PARKIN, Corporal – Frank Ashton

Royal Field Artillery

Born in 1887 at Fritchley, Frank was a clerk who attested at Derby in January 1915 aged twenty-seven, unmarried and employed at the Midland Railway. He was promoted to Corporal in June 1915 but in May 1917 he was suffering with defective teeth, had discharge from his ear, had Valvular Disease of the Heart (VDH) and deafness. He was posted to the Army Reserve to work on munitions with the Midland Railway Coy at Derby before being demobbed in December 1918.

PARKIN, Sapper – George Norman

Royal Engineers

George was born in 1885, and like his two brothers he worked as a railway clerk. He married Mary Radford in 1910.

PARKIN, Sergeant – Harold John

Regiment unknown

Born in 1886, Harold worked as a railway clerk.

PARNHAM, Private – George William ◊

Sherwood Foresters (Nottinghamshire and Derbyshire Regiment)

Photo Carol Beadle

George William Parnham was born in January 1890 at Alfreton. His father was Benjamin Parnham, a plate-layer for the railway, and his mother was Ellen Rebecca (née Poundall). In the early 1900s the family took over the tenancy of Hill Top Farm, Crich. His father became a farmer and as a young child George helped. He kept a few pigeons in the barn and it was while trying to catch one of these that he fell from the barn roof and broke his leg. The family were staunch Methodists so George went to Bible class with his sister Edith, and also he belonged to the Boy's Brigade. When he was fifteen his father died leaving his mother to run the farm and make ends meet. She took in washing. George would go and collect the washing in a pony and trap. Eventually the farm had to be given up and the family moved to a small house in Crich village, but six months later Ellen Rebecca died. George had missed a lot of schooling because he had to help on the farm, so he was not considered bright. A family story tells that when the school inspectors visited the school, he would be sent to fill up the ink wells so that he was not questioned. Upon becoming an orphan George went to lodge with the Ludlow family; he was then a miner at Tibshelf pit. When the War broke out he joined the army in 1914, leaving his few belongings with the Ludlow family. During fighting in September 1916 at Ypres he was shot, the bullet lodging itself in a main artery. George was shipped back to England and then taken by train to a hospital in Sheffield, but by this time gangrene had set into his leg and he had to have the limb removed just above his knee. George was discharged from the army in January 1917 as 100% disabled. On 17th April 1917 he married Florence Martha Love at Skegby Church. In 1951 he died aged sixty-one.

PATILLA, Sapper – Frederick

Royal Engineers

Frederick, born in 1873, was one of the thirteen children of William Patilla and Mary (née Fletcher), a Brackenfield family. In April 1911 he married Sarah Saunders of Lindway Lane; the Saunders family were also a well-known Brackenfield family. He worked as a farm labourer before enlisting, aged forty-three, in January 1917. Initially he was with the Railway Corps of the Royal Engineers, but while serving in France and Belgium between February 1917 and January 1919 he was a labourer on the roads. During December 1918 he was in hospital with influenza and on demob in March 1919, was in Middlesex War Hospital with rheumatism. His first cousin, George Patilla, is also on the Roll of Honour.

PATILLA, Sapper – George

Royal Engineers
South Wales Borderers
Army Service Corps

George was born in 1881, the son of George Patilla and Maria (née Brown). At the time of the war he was living with his parents at Wheatcroft, Crich, working as a stonemason for A. Sims stone yard at Whatstandwell. While he was serving in France he was severely wounded in the leg and admitted to Rouen General Hospital before being transferred to the Auxiliary Military Hospital at Ashton under Lyne. His married sister, Frances Radford, received notification of his injuries.

After the war, in 1920, he married Ethel May Keeton and they continued to live in Wheatcroft. Ethel was very active with the Methodist Chapel in Wheatcroft, especially with the Rechabite movement. George died in 1942 aged sixty.

Newpaper cutting (date and publication unknown)

> Mrs Philip Radford, of Plaistow Green Crich, received news last week that her brother, Private George Patilla, South Wales Borderers, had been wounded in action. Further details came to hand on Wednesday, the official intimation from the Shrewsbury Record office stating that Private Patilla had been admitted to the 6th General Hospital, Rouen on 14 November suffering from severe gunshot

wounds in the left thigh. He was wounded on 10 November. A letter was also received from Private Patilla on Wednesday, stating that he was at the Auxiliary Military Hospital, Ashton under Lyne, and that he was making satisfactory progress. Private Patilla, who was a stone mason at Messrs. A. Sims' stone yard, Whatstandwell was in the RE as a sapper, but on being drafted to France last December he was transferred to the South Wales Borderers.

PAYNE, Gunner – Joseph

Royal Garrison Artillery

Joseph, born in about 1878 at Heage, was the son of Joseph and Leah Payne. He married Florence Elizabeth Smith in 1905 at Crich and the couple lived on the Dimple, Crich. He enlisted in June 1916 and was called up in March 1917, at Derby, aged thirty-nine, a married building contractor. Serving with the 431 Siege Battery in France from September 1917, he was demobbed in February 1919.

PEACH, Private – Francis William Bryan

Middlesex Regiment

Born in 1889 at Bents Hill, Crich, Francis was the son of farmers John and Elizabeth Peach. In some records the family surname is given as Bryan. Before the war he worked on the farm.

PERRY BROTHERS

Arthur, Charles Henry, George Geoffrey and Maurice lived at the Market Place in Crich and were sons of Charles and Eliza Perry.

PERRY, Gunner – Arthur

Royal Field Artillery

Arthur was born in 1896 and worked as an underground colliery pony driver. He joined the Army in 1914. A newspaper report dated 20th January 1917 stated that Arthur's brother Maurice had been wounded; it also stated that Arthur and Charles Henry had been wounded.

Arthur's brothers Charles, Geoffrey and Maurice are also on the Roll of Honour.

PERRY, Lance Corporal – Charles Henry

Sherwood Foresters (Nottinghamshire and Derbyshire Regiment)
Gloucestershire Regiment
Suffolk Regiment
London Regiment
Labour Corps

Charles Henry had an interesting military career. Born in September 1890, he attested at Matlock in August 1914, an unmarried miner at Wingfield Colliery who was living at Crich. He was one of the first volunteers once war had been declared. Serving with the Foresters, he entered France in June 1915 and then, in the September, was admitted to the Canadian General Hospital at Etaples suffering with otitis. After treatment he returned to his battalion, but a few weeks later in November he was diagnosed as having defective vision and was returned to the base depot at Rouen before being transferred to England and the Provisional Battalion of the Sherwood Foresters, where he remained until February 1917. He was then sent as a reserve to work at Wingfield Manor Colliery, but in April 1917 he wrote to the Army stating that he was unable to work underground and asking what he should do.

> *"I was sent home from France (on or about the 18th of January 1916) owing to the vision of the right eye failing, suffering from rheumatism and bad discharge from the left ear. Eyesight was alright when I enlisted but cannot say what was the cause of failure, I never suffered from rheumatism prior to enlistment, but suffered from ear trouble about 12 years"*

In May 1917 he was discharged from the Foresters on grounds of his disability, when his address was Church View House, Crich.

The Army wrote to Wingfield Manor Colliery querying whether he was still working there and received the following response –

> *"In reply to your enquiry this man started work underground but was unable to do it and we were not in a position to find him work on the surface so that at present he is not employed by us. Yours truly for the company, William Curzon."*

In August 1917 the Crich policeman, Sergeant Wyles, reported back to the Army what had happened to Charles (the copy in his record is very feint and parts are unreadable) –

> *"I have seen the above mentioned man today the 6th inst. He states he only worked one day in the pit after being transferred to Army Reserve but he could not stand it. He wrote to Lichfield asking what he was to do but got no reply. He appeared before ... board at Derby ... told to remain in ... He is now working at the Wire Works at Ambergate where he has been since last March. Wyles, Sergt 70"*

The Officer Commanding the TF Depot at Derby then received the following communiqué –

"Please note that instructions have been issued to No 331238 Pte C.H.Perry to report to the Depot under your command for clothing &c. on 6/9/17. He should be posted forthwith to the 21st Notts & Derby Regt Frinton-on-Sea. This man is rejoining from Class W (T) T.F. Reserve"

At the same time Charles received his orders –

"To Pte. C.H.Perry (331238; 21st Notts & Derby Regt), Market Place, Crich – I again forward A.F. D463b for the purpose of joining the T.F. Depot Drill Hall, Derby on 6/9/17, I have been informed that the return of your protection certificate has been applied. The consequences if you do not present yourself on the date stated are fully given on the attached Form."

In September 1917 he was at Frinton-on-Sea with the Sherwood Foresters; in November 1917 he transferred to the London Regiment; in March 1918 he transferred to the Suffolk Regiment Cycling Battalion, when he was promoted to unpaid acting Corporal; in July 1918 he transferred to the Gloucester Regiment when he was made paid Lance Corporal; in August 1918 he transferred to the Labour Corps before being demobbed in March 1919.

Charles's brothers Arthur, Geoffrey and Maurice are also on the Roll of Honour.

PERRY, Private – George ✝
Sherwood Foresters (Nottinghamshire and Derbyshire Regiment)

Photo Alan Perry

George was born in 1893, the son of Joel and Alice Perry. His father was an old soldier who had served in the 95th Foot during 1879, serving in Ireland, Egypt and India.

George was one of the first to enlist and is on the photograph of the 1914 Crich recruits on page 237. He was killed, aged twenty-four, on 29th October 1917 and is remembered on the Tyne Cot Memorial. His death was reported in the Derbyshire Times.

Derbyshire Times 17 November 1917

CRICH SOLDIER KILLED IN DUG-OUT

Mr Joel Perry, of the Market Place, Crich, received the sad news last week that his youngest son Pte George Perry, of the Sherwoods, was killed in action on the 29th ult., as the following letter from Lance-Corpl. Summers indicates: – "It is with my deepest sympathy I have to announce the death of your son, George Perry, attached to the Sherwoods. It was on Monday afternoon the 29th Oct. that the enemy opened a terrible bombardment on our strong-point, and about 4.30 a shell struck the main dug-out, and the captain and sergeant major and your son and several other fine fellows bravely gave their lives, and I can only thank God that I am here to write these sad lines to you. I and all our men send our deepest sympathy to you, as he was one of the finest men in the Company. If you wish to know further details I am willing to help you." Pte. George Perry was employed at the Butterley Co's Quarries, Crich, previous to enlisting in August 1914. He was 24 years of age last January, single, and lived with his father. His father is also an old soldier having served the 95th Foot in 1879 and served in Ireland and fought at the Chitral, the Egyptian War, and the Indian Frontier. In fact the deceased belongs to a fighting family, as he had six nephews in the present war, and his grandfather, Mr John Perry, fought in the Crimean War.

It is assumed that George's father Joel received a missing in action telegram. He sent a photo (which includes another soldier) with an enquiry regarding George to the War Office and received the following reply.

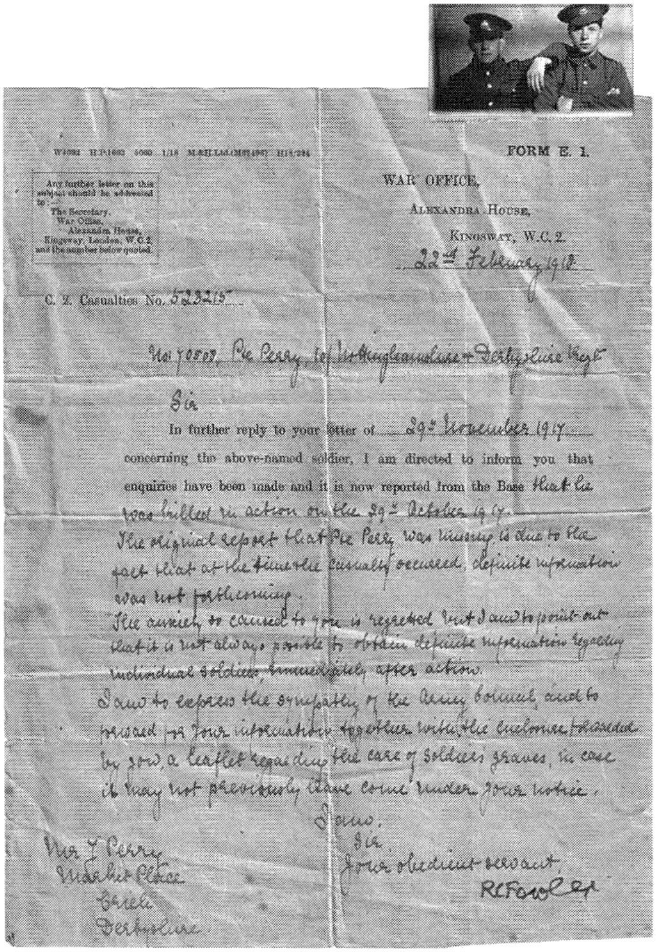
W4094 H.P.1003 4000 1/18 M.&H.Ltd.(M8496) H13/234

FORM E. 1.

Any further letter on this subject should be addressed to:— The Secretary, War Office, Alexandra House, Kingsway, London, W.C.2. and the number below quoted.

WAR OFFICE,
ALEXANDRA HOUSE,
KINGSWAY, W.C. 2.
22nd February 1918

C. 2. Casualties No. 533215

No 70509, Pte Perry, 1st Nottinghamshire & Derbyshire Regt

Sir

In further reply to your letter of 29th November 1917 concerning the above-named soldier, I am directed to inform you that enquiries have been made and it is now reported from the Base that he was killed in action on the 29th October 1917.

The original report that Pte Perry was missing is due to the fact that at the time the casualty occurred, definite information was not forthcoming.

The anxiety so caused to you is regretted but I am to point out that it is not always possible to obtain definite information regarding individual soldiers immediately after action.

I am to express the sympathy of the Army Council, and to forward for your information together with the enclosure forwarded by you, a leaflet regarding the care of soldiers' graves, in case it may not previously have come under your notice.

I am,
Sir,
Your obedient servant,
R C Fowler

Mr J Perry
Market Place
Crich
Derbyshire

Sir, In further reply to your letter of 29th November 1917 concerning the above named soldier, I am directed to inform you that enquiries have been made and it is now reported from the Base that he was killed in action on the 29th October 1917. The original report that Pte. Perry was missing is due to the fact that at the time the casualty occurred definite information was not forthcoming.
The anxiety so caused to you is regretted but I am to point out that it is not always possible to obtain definite information regarding individual soldiers immediately after action.
I am to express the sympathy of the Army Council and to forward for your information together with the enclosure forwarded by you a leaflet regarding the case of soldiers' graves in case it may not previously have come under your notice.
I am sir, your obedient servant, R. C. Fowler
Mr J. Perry, Market Place, Crich, Derbyshire

PERRY, Signaller – George Geoffrey
Royal Garrison Artillery

Born in 1901 George enlisted when only sixteen during March 1917, to be called up a year later in March 1918 when his stated aged was given as nineteen (he was seventeen). He was posted to the Royal Garrison Artillery where he qualified as a first class signaller. November 1918 found him in Kinghorn Auxiliary Hospital with influenza, and he was discharged a month later on grounds of ill health. His brothers Arthur, Charles and Maurice are also on the Roll of Honour.

PERRY, Private – John Henry ✞
Sherwood Foresters (Nottinghamshire and Derbyshire Regiment)
Border Regiment

John Henry, born at Crich in 1882, was the son of Fountain and Hannah Perry. Before the war he worked in the Belper area as a cowman. He was killed on 23rd April 1917 with the 5th Border Regiment and is remembered on the Arras Memorial.

PERRY, Lance Corporal – Maurice
Duke of Cornwall's Light Infantry

Maurice was born in 1897. He entered France in July 1915 and was wounded in January 1917. This was reported in the Derbyshire Times –

Derbyshire Times 20 January 1917

CRICH MAN WOUNDED

Mr and Mrs Charles Perry, Market Place Crich, have received a field service postcard from their son Lance Corporal Maurice Perry (Duke of Cornwall's Light Infantry) stating that he had been wounded and was in hospital. He has been in France for the last two years and has been in almost all the big battles. He has two other

> brothers in the Army, vis. Gunner Arthur Perry (R.F.A.) and Private Henry Perry (Sherwoods). The two latter have also been wounded. The three brothers joined immediately the war broke out.

Maurice's brothers Arthur, Geoffrey and Charles are also on the Roll of Honour.

PETTS BROTHERS

George and Hubert's parents were estate bailiff George Petts and his wife Mary Ellen. Both were born in Alderwasley and in 1911 the family were living in Whatstandwell.

PETTS, Sergeant – George William

Sherwood Foresters (Nottinghamshire and Derbyshire Regiment)

Royal Defence Corps

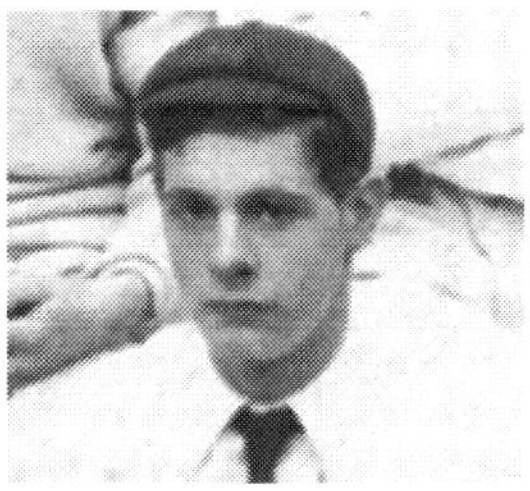

George was born in 1892 and worked as a joiner before joining the Army. He entered France on 2nd March 1915 and his promotion to Sergeant was reported in the Derbyshire Times.

Derbyshire Times 21 August 1915

DCM FOR ALDERWASLEY MEN

> Alderwasley people have been very pleased to hear during the past week of the achievements of two of their soldiers, viz., George Petts, jnr, of the 5th Sherwood Foresters, who has been promoted to full sergeant while in the fighting line somewhere in France, and George Repton, son of Mrs Repton, who has gained the DCM in the Dardanelles where he is working with the Field Services Telegraph Department. Two more young fellows from Alderwasley have joined the forces, viz,. Frank A Alsop and Dennis Griffin, who were both employed at Bury Hill Farm, Alderwasley.

The newspaper title should be "DCM for Alderwasley Man" as it was only George Repton who was awarded the medal.

George's brother Bert Petts is also on the Roll of Honour.

PETTS, Lance Corporal – Hubert (Bert) ✝
Sherwood Foresters (Nottinghamshire and Derbyshire Regiment)

Bert was born in 1896, worked at Lea Mills, and enlisted into the Foresters in September 1914. Entering France in July 1915 he was promoted to Lance Corporal and then killed in action at St. Eloi on 3rd March 1916. His death is commemorated at the Ypres (Menin Gate) Memorial, on the Lea Mills Memorial (see page 230) and on the Alderwasley Memorial (see page 235).

Bert's brother George William is also on the Roll of Honour.

PIERPOINT, Private – Robert
Regiment unknown

Robert was born in 1898, the son of George and Agnes Pierpoint who farmed at Culland Farm, Crich.

PLATTS, Private – Harold Allison ◊
Durham Light Infantry

Harold was born in 1898 at South Wingfield, the son of Thomas and Mary Jane Platts. In 1911 the family were living at Plaistow House Farm, Park Head, Crich. He enlisted in May 1918 aged twenty, an unmarried spar miner, but was discharged in May 1919, being of good character, suffering from Graves Disease, or goitre. He was awarded a 20% disability allowance and the Silver War Badge. He did not serve abroad.

PORTER, Corporal – John (Jack) William ◊
Sherwood Foresters (Nottinghamshire and Derbyshire Regiment)

Photo Michael Porter

Jack was born in July 1891; his parents were John Alfred and Ann Porter. He was a limestone quarryman who was one of the first to enlist in the Foresters in 1914 (see photographs on page 237). He joined the 17th Battalion Sherwood Foresters in October 1915 and entered France in March 1916. Although wounded in his left hand he was back in the trenches two weeks later. In October 1916 he was again wounded by shrapnel through the neck, narrowly missing his jugular vein, and was returned to England for hospital treatment before being discharged as unfit for further service in February 1919. He was awarded the Silver War Badge.

Like many of the servicemen he sent postcards back to his fiancée and family.

Photos Michael Porter

Jack Porter seated

Jack Porter centre

He married Rose Allen in 1918 and during the Second World War he served in the Home Guard for which he received a medal.

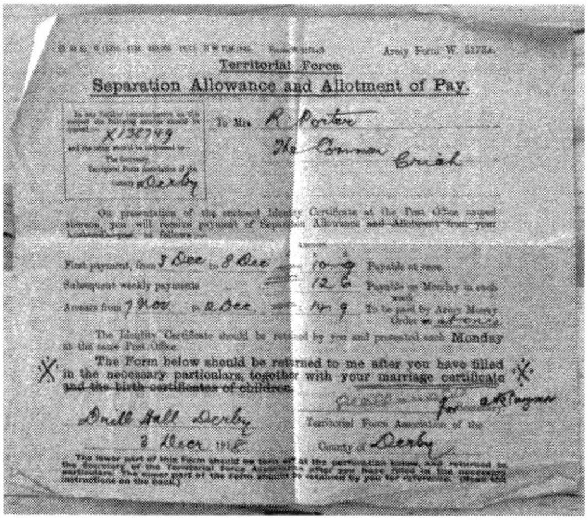

Army Form W. 5173a.
Territorial Force.
Separation Allowance and Allotment of Pay.

X136749

To Mrs R Porter
The Common Crich

County of Derby

First payment, from 3 Dec to 8 Dec 10 9 Payable at once.
Subsequent weekly payments 12 6 Payable on Monday in each week.
Arrears from 7 Nov to 2 Dec 14 9 To be paid by Army Money Order

The Identity Certificate should be retained by you and presented each Monday at the same Post Office.

The Form below should be returned to me after you have filled in the necessary particulars, together with your marriage certificate ~~and the birth certificates of children.~~

Drill Hall Derby
3 Dec 1918

Territorial Force Association of the County of Derby

Jack's allotment of pay to his wife, Rose

Photo Michael Porter

Jack in the Home Guard

Jack's WWI memorabilia

Jack's wife Rose died in 1967 and he died eight years later in 1975.

POYSER BROTHERS

Gilbert and Ralph were the sons of blacksmith Ralph Poyser and his wife Margaret.

POYSER, Rifleman – Gilbert N. ◊

Kings Royal Rifles Corps

Gilbert was born in 1891 and took up his late father's occupation of blacksmith before enlisting in the Kings Royal Rifle Corps in August 1915. He was discharged through sickness in May 1918, aged twenty-seven, and was awarded the Silver War Badge.

POYSER, Private – Ralph William

Sherwood Foresters (Nottinghamshire and Derbyshire Regiment)

Ralph was born in 1883 and worked as a colliery labourer before joining the Foresters.

PRICE, Rifleman – George

Regiment unknown

We cannot find any George Price with Crich connections. There is a Gunner George Price from Holloway who worked at Lea Mills, but he has no apparent link to Crich Parish. In 1922 George H. Price married Florence E. Lee in the Belper registration district. She is believed to be the daughter of Benjamin and Sarah Ann Lee, who was born at Alderwasley.

RADFORD BROTHERS

Arthur, Fred and George were the sons of John Widdowson Radford and his wife Martha Ann. In 1911 the family were living at The Canal Inn, Bullbridge.

Austen and Thomas were the sons of William and Matilda Radford. Their father was a Wessington-born coal miner.

RADFORD, Ordinary Seaman – Arthur

Royal Navy

Born in March 1896 Arthur joined the Royal Navy in November 1915. He was described as a Congregationalist, non-swimmer, planer (he was a wood machinist). He was not in the Navy very long as he was discharged as being medically unfit for service in January 1916. His brothers Fred and George are also on the Roll of Honour.

RADFORD, Private – Austen Ellis

Lincolnshire Regiment

Born in 1890 at South Wingfield, Austen worked as a cowman on a farm at Wakebridge before joining the Lincolnshire Regiment. His brother Thomas is also on the Roll of Honour.

RADFORD, 3rd Air Mechanic – Fred

Royal Air Force

Born in 1901, Fred must have joined the RAF right at the end of the war. His brothers Arthur and George are also on the Roll of Honour.

RADFORD, Sergeant – George

Regiment unknown

George was born in 1893 and, like his father and brother Arthur, worked in the timber yards. He was a timber clerk. His brothers Fred and Arthur are also on the Roll of Honour.

RADFORD, Farrier – Horace Joseph

Army Service Corps
Royal Field Artillery
Labour Corps

Born in 1877 at Fritchley, Horace was the son of Thomas and Phoebe Radford. Married in 1900 to Sophia Marsh, he worked as a blacksmith at Tupton, near Chesterfield. He enlisted at Chesterfield in March 1915, aged thirty-eight, with a Fritchley address. Horace entered France in July 1915 and was invalided out in December 1919 suffering from rheumatism and with a head injury giving him a 20% disability allowance.

RADFORD, Private – John George

Sherwood Foresters (Nottinghamshire and Derbyshire Regiment)

John was born in 1888 at Crich to John and Annie Radford, and he worked with his father on Hollins Farm at Crich.

RADFORD, Private – Thomas **MM**

Sherwood Foresters (Nottinghamshire and Derbyshire Regiment)

Thomas was born in 1886 at Crich, and worked as a farm labourer before joining the Foresters. In 1918 he was awarded the Military Medal.

Derby Daily Telegraph Wednesday 18 September 1918

MILITARY MEDALISTS

The latest official list of awards of military medals includes the names of Corpl. F. Mosely (Derby) and 28702 Pte. T. Radford (Crich) both of the Notts and Derby Regiment.

Thomas's brother Austen is also on the Roll of Honour.

RAWSON, Private – Henry (Harry)

Regiment unknown

Henry Rawson – better known as Harry – was born at Fritchley in 1885, the son of Robert Rawson and Mary Ann Harrison. Of the children who survived beyond infancy, Harry was the fifth of seven, with two sisters and four brothers. Harry married Alice Calladine in 1906. They appear to have had no children.

Harry's service records have not survived, so it hasn't been possible to identify his regiment. His grand-niece, Rosemary Tomlinson, recalls her grandmother (Harry's younger sister Lily) telling her that she can remember Harry joining up, and also remembers him coming home in his uniform, which had a red jacket.

After the war Harry spent periods living at Crich and Swanwick and worked for a number of years as a coal miner. His later life was spent living on Chapel Lane at Crich. After his wife's death in 1960 he married Sarah Ann Redfern in 1961 and inherited an adult stepdaughter.

Harry passed away at Belper on 6 November 1964, aged seventy-nine years. His cousin, Arthur Walker Harrison, is also listed on the Roll of Honour.

REDFERN: Lance Corporal – J. Herbert

Regiment unknown

We cannot find J. Hbt. Redfern as listed on the original Crich Roll of Honour. However, there was a Job Henry Redfern, the son of Herbert and Eliza Redfern who were living at Whatstandwell during the war (they are recorded on the 1918 Electoral Register). Job had a younger brother called George Herbert Redfern. It is possible that this is another name error on the original Roll.

RODGERS BROTHERS

The Fritchley-born Rodgers brothers, Amos, George, James plus Frederick Wragg, were the sons of William and Harriet Rodgers. Frederick Wragg was born to their mother, Harriett Wragg, in 1886 before she married William Rodgers in 1889. William and Harriett were to lose three of their sons.

Amos, James and Frederick Rodgers are remembered on the Sawmills Memorial see page 231.

RODGERS, Driver – Amos ✝
Royal Field Artillery

Born in 1889, Amos worked as an engine driver before joining the Royal Field Artillery. He entered France in September 1915 and was transferred to Salonika where he died on 20th October 1918. He was buried at Struma Military Cemetery.

The Salonika Campaign was part of the Greek/Bulgarian Campaign and for every man killed in battle three died of malaria or flu. In the Battle of Doiran, or Vardar or Strumica Valley, British troops were massacred charging through their own gas, unprotected, up a sheer hillside. This is a forgotten battle which is barely reported. There were about four thousand dead.

RODGERS: Private – George William
West Yorkshire Regiment

Born in 1898, George served in the West Yorkshire Regiment.

Photo Allan Rodgers

RODGERS, Stoker – Harry
Royal Navy

Harry was born about 1877 at Belper, the son of William and Ann Rodgers. He married Ellen Hannah Bowler during 1901 and they went to live at Bullbridge, where he worked on the Midland Railway as a goods checker.

RODGERS, Able Seaman – James ✝
Royal Naval Volunteer Reserve

James was born in 1892 and worked as a miner before joining the Royal Naval Volunteer Reserve. He was killed at the Battle of Jutland on 31st May 1916, aged twenty-four, aboard HMS *Black Prince* along with the whole ship's company. The ship exploded, killing thirty-seven officers, eight hundred and fifteen men and five civilians. As well as being on the Crich memorials he is remembered on the Sawmills Memorial (see page 231) and the Plymouth Naval Memorial.

RODGERS (WRAGG), Private – Frederick ✝
Grenadier Guards

See the record for Frederick Wragg.

ROE BROTHERS

John Thomas and William were the sons of John and Martha Roe who lived on Sun Lane, Crich.

ROE, Private – John Thomas ✞

Sherwood Foresters (Nottinghamshire and Derbyshire Regiment)

Born in 1896, John entered the war as an early volunteer, entering the Balkans in December 1915. He died of his wounds in October 1917, aged twenty-one. He is buried at Dozinghem Military Cemetery.

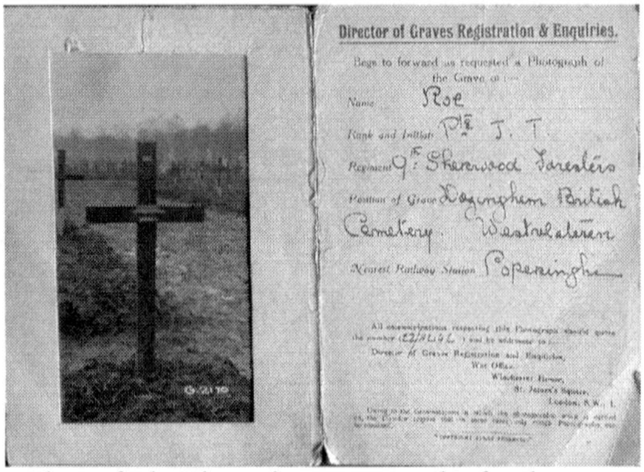

Director of Graves Registration & Enquiries.

Begs to forward as requested a Photograph of the Grave of :—

Name Roe

Rank and Initials Pte J. T.

Regiment 9th Sherwood Foresters

Position of Grave Dozinghem British Cemetery. Westvleteren

Nearest Railway Station Poperinghe

Photo of John Thomas's grave sent to his family.

A permanent headstone replaced the original wooden cross

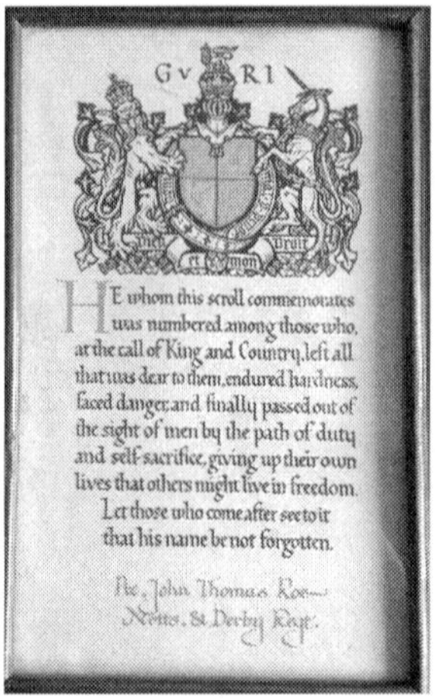

GvRI

HE whom this scroll commemorates was numbered among those who, at the call of King and Country, left all that was dear to them, endured hardness, faced danger, and finally passed out of the sight of men by the path of duty and self-sacrifice, giving up their own lives that others might live in freedom.

Let those who come after see to it that his name be not forgotten.

Pte. John Thomas Roe
Notts. & Derby Regt.

Memorial Certificate

"Death Penny" for John Thomas Roe

ROE, Stoker – William

Royal Navy

Born in October 1893, William enlisted in the Royal Navy in January 1916. He served in Malta on HMS *Egmont* as well as on HMS *Victory II* and *Penstemon.*

William, front row extreme right.

ROLLINSON, Lance Corporal – John (Jack) William

Regiment unknown

We can only find one local Jack Rollinson in the records. If this is the correct Jack Rollinson he would have entered the war at its end and must have been promoted rapidly. He was born in 1900, at Crich, the son of Albert and Ada Rollinson.

ROSS, Private – Alexander ✝

Sherwood Foresters (Nottinghamshire and Derbyshire Regiment)

Alexander Ross, born in Manchester in 1880, was the son of William and Ellen Ross (née Curzon). He married Sarah Colledge in 1907. He was killed in action, aged thirty-seven on 15th April 1917 in the trenches on the Brown Line, near Arras. He is remembered on the Arras Memorial, on the Wesleyan Chapel memorial tablet (see page 228) as well as the Crich Church memorials.

ROWE BROTHERS

Archie, Thomas and William were the sons of Tom Anthony and Henrietta Rowe, publicans of Fritchley. After their father died Henrietta married Caleb Minard, but upon his death she reverted to the name Rowe. On the original Crich Roll of Honour the brothers are recorded as Roe instead of Rowe.

ROWE, Private – Archibald

Army Service Corps
Royal Irish Rifles

Born in 1881, Archibald worked as a wood turner for Joseph Glossop before joining the Army at Ripley in December 1915 aged thirty-four. He entered France on *SS Archangel* in October 1916 and worked in the field butchery. In September 1917 he was compulsorily transferred to the Royal Irish Rifles as rifleman "*in the interests of the Service*". He had several hospital admissions for boils and skin problems. In May 1918 he was transferred to the Army Service Corps.

ROWE, Private – Thomas Joseph

Regiment unknown

Thomas was born in 1883, worked as a sawyer in the local woodyard and married Martha Ann Coleman in 1908.

ROWE, Private – William

Regiment unknown

Born in 1885, William married Ellen Ann Barber in 1907 and worked in the woodyard before becoming a collier. After the war William is remembered as having a wooden leg, the result of a wound. There is insufficient information known about him to discover if he was awarded the Silver War Badge.

ROWLEY, Flight Commander – Herbert Victor
Royal Naval Air Service
Royal Air Force

Photo Scott Hamilton

Herbert Victor Rowley was born in Crich on 20 October 1897, the son of Arthur and Agnes Rowley. His father was a Church of England clergyman serving in Crich Parish at the time of his birth. By 1901 the family had moved into Nottinghamshire from where Herbert joined the Royal Naval Air Service in April 1916.

He had a distinguished record becoming one of the few Flying Aces of the Great War. His service record described him as a good Scout Pilot with experience of air fighting tactics, a hardworking officer and a brilliant fighter. He was forced to land during one aerial fight and during another he was shot down. There were nine aerial victories to his name. He transferred into the RAF when the RNAS and RFC were amalgamated in April 1918 and continued his service with them after the war. He retired as Air Commodore in 1944.

Date	Time	Unit	Aircraft	Opponent	Location	Location
29/04/17	1150	1N	Sopwith Triplane (N5425)	Albatros D.III	Villers les Cagnicourt	Victory shared with another; Rowley forced to land
13/07/17	1025	1N	Sopwith Triplane (N6308)	German reconnaissance plane	E of Warneton	Victory shared with two others; Rowley shot down
17/07/17	1805	1N	Sopwith Triplane (N5373)	Albatros D.V	4 mi E of Messines	Victory shared with seven others
26/08/17	0750	1N	Sopwith Triplane (N6301)	DFW reconnaissance plane	E of Deulemont	Victory shared with another
13/11/17	1210	1N	Sopwith Triplane (N5472)	German reconnaissance plane	SE of Nieuport	
12/03/18	1315	1N	Sopwith Camel (B6429)	Observation Balloon	Ypres	Victory shared with another
16/03/18	1145	1N	Sopwith Camel (B6429)	Albatros D.V	Dixmude	
21/03/18	1550	1N	Sopwith Camel (B6429)	Albatros D.V	Nieuport	
01/04/18	1300	201	Sopwith Camel (B6429)	Albatros D.V	Nieuport	

From the collection of the Royal Aero Club.

RUSSELL, Lance Corporal – Charles Henry **MM**

Machine Gun Corps

Charles Henry was a gardener at Alderwasley Hall, home to the Hurt family. In 1915 he married Crich-born Lucy Alice Wragg. His parents-in-law were Edward and Rebecca Wragg of Thurlow Booth, Whatstandwell and his brothers-in-law George and John Edward Wragg are also on the Roll of Honour. In 1917 he was awarded the Military Medal.

Derbyshire Times 11 August 1917

> Mr and Mrs Edward Wragg, of The Tors Crich, have received official information that their son-in-law, Private C. H. Russsell has been awarded the Military Medal for bravery on the Western Front. The official record of Private Russell's gallantry reads as follows: – "69th Company, Machine Gun Corps, No 8906, Private Charles Henry Russell, Conspicuous energy, ability and devotion to duty while employed as a runner during the assault of the 69th Brigade on the Hill 60 Sector on June 7th 1917. Private Russell, who had already made several journeys as a runner, was sent to find and guide to their positions two gun teams which had been misdirected. This accomplished with success and subsequently guided up a party carrying ammunition to these guns. Private Russell worked indefatigably and cheerfully without any rest for a very long period under trying conditions. Military Medal. (Signed) E. F. Falkner, Lieut. Colonel A.A.and Q.M.G. 23rd Division." Private Russell was formerly a gardener at Alderwasley Hall.

SADLER, Private – Arthur

Regiment unknown

The only local person found who corresponds to this entry on the original Roll of Honour is Arthur Ernest Sadler, born in 1893 at Wessington, the son of John and Mary Sadler. Before the war he worked as a colliery banksman and lived with his married brother Samuel at Amber Row. At one time Wessington was part of Crich Parish and people living at Amber Row often appear in the Crich Parish Records.

SANDERS, Company Sergeant Major – William

Canadian Expeditionary Force

William was born on 7th August 1888, at Crich, to Francis and Rose Sanders. Some time between 1901 and 1911 the family suffered some form of upheaval as Francis and Rose were living apart in 1911. The indications are that, in July 1901 William was sent to Canada aboard *SS Numidian* when he was only thirteen. The passenger list shows all the passengers to be children.

In April 1913 he married Harriett Annie Pearle Allen at Brandon, Manitoba. The

1916 census shows him aged twenty-seven living with Hattie in Saskatchewan. He was a farmer and both were Methodists.

William attested on 19th April 1916 at Winnipeg when he was working as a lumber merchant; his address was Eugenie Street, Norwood, Winnipeg. Previously he had served three years with the 13th Battery of the Canadian Field Artillery and was in the militia serving with the 79th Cameron Highlanders of Canada. He was 5 foot 8 inches tall with grey eyes and fair hair. In September 1919 he was declared medically unfit.

The 1921 census recorded him with his wife, Hattie, and three children, working as a farmer with Canadian nationality after emigrating to Canada in 1902.

SARGENT, Second Lieutenant – Henry (Harry) Westbury ✝

Royal Fusiliers (City of London Regiment)

Sherwood Foresters (Nottinghamshire and Derbyshire Regiment)

Henry was born on 31st March 1895 at Walton-on-Thames to chartered accountant Henry Crunden Sargent and his first wife Amy Sophia (née Westbury). Before the war the family moved to live in Brook Cottage, Fritchley where Henry worked as a clerk to railway engineers.

He enlisted at Derby on 18th December 1914 aged nineteen as a Private into the Royal Fusiliers. In May 1915 he was commissioned into the Special Reserve of Officers (Infantry) Sherwood Foresters and he entered France in May 1916. He was killed two months later in July 1916 when he was twenty-one. He is buried at the Albert Communal Cemetery Extension.

There was some confusion over the date and circumstances of his death as correspondence in his service record showed. Initially he was recorded as being killed in action on 5th July 1916 but elsewhere he was recorded as dying of wounds on the 6th July. He did die of his wounds – in No. 57 Field Ambulance, France on the 6th July 1916.

Telegram: 19 July 1916
To Sargent , Brook Cottage, Fritchley, Derbyshire
Deeply regret to inform you 2/Lt HW Sargent Sherwood Foresters was killed in action July 5th. The Army Council expresses their sympathy, this information could not be communicated before as your address had not been registered and all efforts to trace have failed

5 August 1916
The Military Secretary presents his compliments to Mr H. G. Sargent, and begs to inform him that a report has just been received which states that 2nd Lieut. H.W. Sargent 1st Sherwood Foresters died of wounds on July 8th (sic), and was not actually killed in action.

19 August 1916

The Military Secretary presents his compliments to Mr H. G. Sargent, and begs to inform him that a report has just been received from Army Headquarters in the Field which states that the late 2nd Lieutenant H. W. Sargent, 1st Battalion Sherwood Foresters, died in No. 57 Field Ambulance, France and was buried at Albert Cemetery.

The Military Secretary ventures to send this information now, as Mr Sargent may not have previously received it.

The effects sent to Henry's father comprised: identity disk, wrist watch, nickel mirror, whistle and lanyard, cigarette lighter, cigarette case, key chain, bottle of morphine tabloids (sic), leather wallet, book of 1d stamps, Officer's Advance Book, AB 153 book, letter and photos, broken ruler

[Officers did not carry a pay book, they had an Advance Book which was like a cheque book. The AB 153 was the standard field message book]

Derby Daily Telegraph Tuesday 8 August 1916

OLD DERBEAN KILLED

Second-lieut. Henry Westbury Sargent , of the Sherwood Foresters, who is reported killed, was born in 1895 at Walton-on-Thames. He was the only son of Mr Henry Crunden Sargent, now of Fritchley, Derbyshire, and the late Mrs Sargent. He was educated at Berkhamsted and Derby Schools.

SAYLES, Nurse – Elsie Marina

Red Cross

Photo Fred Sayles

Elsie was born at Fritchley in 1889, the daughter of William and Alice Sayles. In 1911 she was a nurse at Smedley's Hydro at Matlock. In 1917 she joined the Red Cross for war work. August 1917 found her working at Salonika in the Military Hospital, where she served until February 1919 before being transferred to Netley Military Hospital, Southampton. While in Salonika she met her nephew Percy Sayles who was with the Derbyshire Yeomanry. Percy is also on the Roll of Honour.

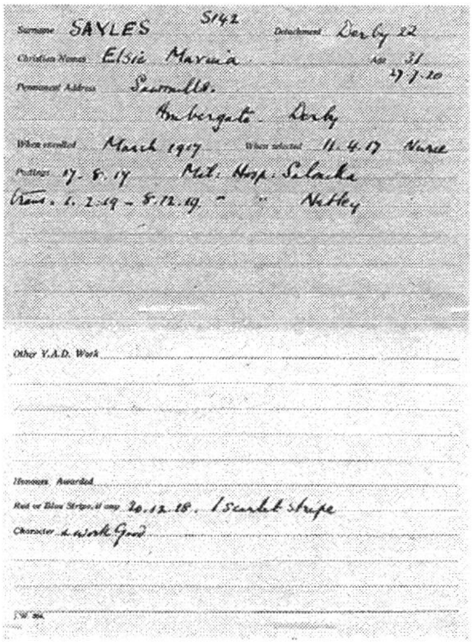

Surname SAYLES S/42 Detachment Derby 22
Christian Names Elsie Maria Age 31
27.7.20
Permanent Address [illegible]
Ambergate Derby
When enrolled March 1917 When selected 11.4.17 Nurse
Postings 17.8.17 Mil. Hosp. Salonika
[illegible] 1.2.19 – 8.12.19 " " Netley

Other V.A.D. Work

Honours Awarded
Red or Blue Stripe, if any 20.12.18. 1 Scarlet stripe
Character & work Good

Elsie's record card, courtesy British Red Cross

SAYLES, Trooper – Percy

Derbyshire Yeomanry

Percy was born at Crich in 1896, the son of Joseph and Emma Sayles. Before the war he was a grocer's assistant and spent some time in Ridgeway Isolation Hospital with his sister Ethel. He served in Salonika where he had his horse shot from under him and where he met his aunt, Elsie Sayles, who was working as a nurse at the Military Hospital there.

Photo Percy Sayles

SEALS BROTHERS

Alfred, Curtis and Victor were born in Dethick at Manor Farm, the sons of John and Annie Seals.

SEALS, Gunner – Alfred

Royal Garrison Artillery

Alfred was born at Parwich in 1895 and worked as a shepherd, horseman and waggoner before the war. Along with his two brothers he enlisted at Matlock in February 1916 aged twenty-one, when his address was Common Farm, Crich. He entered France in September 1916, serving with the 112 Heavy Battery of the Royal Garrison Artillery, and he was demobbed in May 1919.

SEALS, Bombardier – Curtis William

Royal Field Artillery

Curtis was sometimes recorded as Charles. He was born in 1897 at Parwich and worked as 'a cowboy on a farm'. Along with his two brothers he enlisted at Matlock in February 1916 aged nineteen, when his address was Dethick Farm. His record shows that he had flat feet, a chronic cough but had good teeth. He entered France in May 1917 and suffered a gunshot wound to his left arm. He was demobbed in October 1919.

Photo Carole Rayner

SEALS, Gunner – Victor James

Royal Garrison Artillery

Victor was born in 1892 at Parwich and worked as a cowman. Along with his two brothers he enlisted at Matlock in February 1916 aged twenty-three. He had a slight deformity of the right hand small finger and left hand index finger. The address noted was Common Farm, Crich which was the same as that for his brother Alfred. In March 1916 he was posted to the Royal Garrison Artillery as Gunner; he gained a third-class certificate of education in April 1917 and was posted to Siege Artillery Reserve Battalion (S.A.R.B.) in June 1918 before being demobbed in January 1919. His army record stated that he was very good, intelligent, honest, sober, hardworking and willing; he would make a good NCO.

SELF BROTHERS

Charles, Joseph and Stephen were all born at Crich Carr, the sons of Stephen and Sarah Self.

SELF, Private – Charles

Regiment unknown

Charles, born in 1881, worked as a gardener, as did his father. He married Tamar Ann Taylor in 1908 and died in 1963 aged eighty-two. It is possible that he was with the Sherwood Foresters but this has not yet been proved.

SELF, Driver – Joseph

Army Service Corps (Horse Transport)

Joseph was born in 1889 and, like his father, worked as a gardener. He attested at Buxton in March 1915 aged twenty-four while living at Whatstandwell. He entered France in May 1915. During May 1917 he was confined to camp as punishment for not being shaven on General Officer Commanding Parade. This seemed a bit harsh, as a short time later he was hospitalised with scabies. July 1918 saw him driving with the Field Ambulance at Abbeville. He was demobbed in July 1919.

SELF, Lance Corporal – Stephen ◊

Sherwood Foresters (Nottinghamshire and Derbyshire Regiment)

Stephen was born in 1892. Before the war he worked at Lea Mills, and then as a miner. He enlisted in January 1915 and entered France in October 1915, and then two years later, he was wounded and hospitalised. He was discharged with the Silver War Badge in May 1918.

Derbyshire Times 19 May 1917

> Mr and Mrs Stephen Self of Whatstandwell have received the news that their youngest son Lance Corporal S. Self of the Sherwoods, was wounded on the 25th ult by the bursting of a shell from which he received a compound fracture of the right arm and a wound on the left side to the neck. He is now in hospital at Chatham. Previous to enlisting he worked as a miner at Staveley where he enlisted in January 1915 and has seen nearly two year's service at the front. He is single 34 years of age, and a native of Whatstandwell.

SELLORS, Driver – George David

Regiment unknown

George David Sellors was known by his middle name. He was born David Eaton at Cromford in 1875, the son of Hannah Eaton who married James Sellors in 1877; David then took the surname Sellors. After James Sellors' death Hannah married John Harrison.

David Sellors worked as a quarryman and married Mary Alice M. Taylor in 1899. After the war the family lived at Ladygrove, Whatstandwell where he died in July 1934 aged fifty-nine.

SHELDON BROTHERS

Joseph and William were the sons of George and Mary Sheldon. .

SHELDON, Gunner – Joseph Henry ◊

Royal Field Artillery

Born at Crich in 1885, Joseph was the son of George and Mary Sheldon. Before the war he worked as a stone mason. He enlisted in January 1915, entered France in November 1915 and the following November was wounded; this was very briefly reported in the Derbyshire Times on 4 November 1916. He was discharged with the Silver War Badge on 5 September 1917.

SHELDON, Driver – William ◊

Army Service Corps

Photo courtesy Louis Sheldon

William Sheldon was born at Sutton-in-Ashfield, Nottinghamshire, in 1870. He was the oldest child of George Sheldon and Mary Ward. His parents had twelve children, of whom ten were still living in 1911. William was raised at Sutton-in-Ashfield, but by 1881 the family had moved to live at Crich.

During the 1880s, William worked as a factory hand in the Crich area. As a young man he was part of a volunteer battalion of the Sherwood Foresters. At eighteen years of age he left Crich to become a regular soldier, enlisting as a Private in the King's Royal Rifle Corps at Winchester. He served with his regiment in India, Burma and South Africa.

William married Sarah Ann Eastwood at Skipton in the West Riding of Yorkshire, in 1898. They had eight children, six boys and two girls. In November 1899, only a few months after his marriage, William was recalled to active service as a result of a Special Army Order and served with the King's Royal Rifle Corps during the Second Boer War in South Africa.

By the time William returned from South Africa the family were living at Westmorland Street in Skipton and he soon found employment as a railway porter. The family remained in Skipton for a number of years, where William is known to have worked as a lamplighter for the Urban District Council, and later as a chauffeur for a local jeweller. The family later moved close to Bradford at the village of Saltaire, near the town of Shipley, where he worked at the mills of Sir Titus Salt.

During the early stages of the First World War, as an experienced former solider, the call to arms found William ready to respond. He was attested as a Private with the Army Service Corps at London on 25 March 1915, aged forty-five years. He served in Mechanical Transport as a driver, and most of his service was spent with the rank of Acting Corporal. From October 1915 he served in France as part of the British Expeditionary Force, but he was invalided home in November 1916 due to failing health, for which he was later awarded a pension and the Silver War Badge. He was discharged on 2nd October 1917.

As William's parents George and Mary were still residents of Crich until after the First World War, they had William's name listed on the Roll of Honour inside Crich Parish Church alongside that of his brother Joseph. It is notable that all of William's six sons also served in the armed forces.

After he was discharged from the army, William returned to his family at Saltaire, and remained in the Shipley area for the rest of his life. Only a month after the death of his wife, William Sheldon passed away at Shipley on 18th February 1952, aged eighty-two years. He was laid to rest in Nab Wood Cemetery at Saltaire.

SHIPSTON BROTHERS

George and Thomas were the sons of William and Sarah Shipston (Shipstone). William was a Crich grocer who died in March 1877, aged forty-three, when his children were still very young.

SHIPSTON, Private – George ✝

South Staffordshire Regiment
King's Own Scottish Borderers

Born in 1876, George worked as a wheelwright before enlisting into the South Staffordshire Regiment at Matlock. He was later transferred into the King's Own Scottish Borderers and died in Flanders, of wounds received, on 17th October 1918 aged forty-two. He was buried at Duhallow A.D.S. Cemetery at Ypres.

SHIPSTON, Private – Thomas

Regiment unknown

Thomas was born in 1878, and before the war he worked as a stonemason.

SIMS, Corporal – Herbert Charles

Sherwood Foresters (Nottinghamshire and Derbyshire Regiment)
Royal Engineers

Photo Sue Worboys

Born in 1883, Charles married Lily Winson in 1900 at Belper Baptist Chapel – he was a gritstone quarryman. Aged thirty-three, he attested at Derby in September 1914. His first posting was to the Sherwood Foresters. During 1915 he was late, or missed, one or two roll calls and on each occasion he was confined to barracks for a few days. He embarked to France on *SS Empress Queen* in August 1915. In May 1917 he was transferred to the Royal Engineers Quarrying Corps as a Sapper. He was injured on 24th November 1918 and an enquiry had to be made. The injury to his right hand was over the base of the thumb and the back of his hand. It was recorded as being "*less severe but troublesome to heal*". The result of the enquiry was:

> *This NCO was preparing a large hole in the macadam ready for firing when a piece of stone struck the knuckle of his right hand, date of accident 24 November 1918, no Court of Inquiry held, no one to blame.*

Herbert Sims second left on back row

SLACK, Driver – Walter

Royal Field Artillery

Walter was called up for service on 4 November 1916 aged forty-one an unmarried lime worker of Prospect Terrace, Crich. His height was 5ft 3¾ and his father was Joseph Slack of Scarthin, Cromford. In September 1917 Walter was transferred from hospital to Class W (Army Reserve) after a hernia and varicocele operation. His disability was aggravated by riding whilst in training at Doncaster. He was finally discharged under Paragraph 392 on 14 December 1918. The address on his correspondence was c/o Butterley Co. Ltd., Bull Bridge Lime Works, Ambergate.

SMITH BROTHERS

Arthur and Herbert were the sons of Raymond and Ann Smith; the family lived at Fritchley where their father worked as a lime burner.

Henry and Norman were the sons of Joseph Roe Smith and his wife Annie Elizabeth.

SMITH – FATHER and **SON**

Frederick John and his son Charles George were both in the Army. Frederick was the coachman at Chase Cliffe, Whatstandwell and was married to Sarah Ann.

SMITH, Sergeant – Arthur Δ

Northumberland Fusiliers

Arthur was born in 1896 and worked as a farm labourer before joining the army. A newspaper report in the Derbyshire Times dated 25th May 1918 stated that "*Sgt. A Smith of the Northumberland Fusiliers from Fritchley was a Prisoner of War.*"

SMITH, Private – Charles George

Regiment unknown

Charles was born at Blidworth in 1898.

Charles's father Frederick John is also on the Roll of Honour.

SMITH, Private – Fred

Machine Gun Corps

Fred was born in 1896, the son of Joseph and Sarah Ann Smith. Before the war he worked at the limestone quarry. He attested in December 1915 aged nineteen living at Folds Yard, Crich. He was a Primitive Methodist. Although he had enlisted in 1915 he was not mobilised until April 1918, only to be released eight months later to work in a coal mine. He was demobbed in January 1919.

SMITH, Trooper – Frederick John

Regiment unknown

Frederick was born at Ratby, Leicestershire, in 1873. His son Charles George is also in the Roll of Honour.

SMITH, Corporal – George Parkinson †

Sherwood Foresters (Nottinghamshire and Derbyshire Regiment)

Photo Stan Smith

George was born in 1888, the son of James and Jane Smith. His father was a navvy so they travelled around a little before settling in Fritchley. Before he joined the army George worked as a wood sawyer and married Elizabeth Reed of Fritchley in 1913. He was killed in action during an attack on Lens on 1 July 1917 when he was aged twenty-nine. He is remembered on the Arras Memorial.

Like many of the soldiers George sent back home beautifully embroidered cards and postcards. The cards were usually sentimental or amusing.

Sent to his wife Elizabeth in 1916

To his son George, sent June 1917. He was killed 24 days later.

SMITH, Sapper – Henry Victor

Royal Engineers

Photo Hilary Welby

Henry was born in 1898 and joined the Royal Engineers. His brother Norman is also on the Roll of Honour.

SMITH, Private – Herbert

Sherwood Foresters (Nottinghamshire and Derbyshire Regiment)

Photo Mick Smith

Born in 1893, Herbert worked at Ambergate wireworks. 1911 found him as a patient in Ridgeway Isolation Hospital. His brother Arthur is also on the Roll of Honour.

SMITH, Private – Herbert

Regiment unknown

The 1918 Electoral Register shows Robert and Mary Smith living in Crich Carr with an absent voter named as Herbert Smith. It is presumed that the family moved into the area between 1911 and 1918 as the family cannot be found locally on the 1901 nor 1911 censuses.

SMITH, Driver – James Alfred

South Staffordshire Regiment
Herefordshire Regiment

Born in Manchester during 1892, the son of James and Harriet Smith, he married Crich-born Florence Stocks in 1914. He worked as an underground coal-filler. While serving with the South Staffordshire Regiment he was wounded, and this was briefly reported in the Derby Daily Telegraph dated 12 June 1918.

SMITH, Gunner – John Henry

Regiment unknown

John was born in Crich during 1888, the son of George and Emma Smith. However, he was brought up by his grandparents George Ashbourne and Mary Smith. A newspaper cutting reported his wounding.

Derbyshire Times 2 June 1917

Crich Casualties

> Details of Gunner John H Smith's wounds have been received in a letter he sent to his uncle and aunt Mr and Mrs J Roe Smith of Ashbourne House, Roes Lane, Crich. He says that he was wounded by a shell, which caused severe injuries to his right side and arm. After being taken to a hospital in France, he underwent two operations, and later was drafted to England. He is now at Bellahouston Red Cross Hospital, Glasgow, where he is improving. His chum, who was hit by the same shell, died in the next bed to his shortly afterwards. Gunner Smith went across to France in May this year. Before joining up he was a butcher, and had a business on the marketplace, Crich.

There is not enough information to find out whether he was awarded the Silver War Badge.

SMITH, Private – John Thomas ◊
East Yorkshire Regiment

John was born in about 1884, the son of Crich butcher Arthur and Ann Smith. Before joining the army John Thomas worked as a joiner. In May 1917 he was seriously wounded during action on the Western Front. He was in the Kitchener Australian Hospital, Brighton and was awarded the Silver War Badge.

Derbyshire Times 2 June 1917

CRICH CASUALTIES

Private J. T. Smith, of the East Yorkshire Regiment, was seriously wounded in the thigh whilst in action on the Western Front on the 13th May. He is now lying at the Kitchener Australian Red Cross Hospital, Brighton, from which place he has written to his mother, Mrs Arthur Smith, of The Archway, Crich, as follows: – I should not have sent you the field card, but that I thought you would be wondering what had become of me. I had begun to think that I would not get out of here. You have no need to worry, as my leg is going on as well as it can. I was under the X-Rays, but nothing was found in. I thought I had a bad wound until I got to hospital, but then I saw many much worse. The week before I was hit we had bad luck: the place where I was billeted – a large warehouse with shells stacked outside – took fire. There were between two hundred and three hundred men in the place, and it was a rush to get out, many having neither coats nor boots on. Everything was burned. I received my wound when going to the front line whilst I was in the communication trench. 'Fritz' had started sending shells over and one burst just at the back of me, and a piece of the case must have hit me".

SMITH, Lance Bombardier – Lawrence Henry
Royal Garrison Artillery

Lawrence, born in about 1888, was the son of Samuel Smith and Annie. Samuel was publican at the Bull's Head on Cromford Road, Crich. Lawrence attested in February 1916 at Ripley, aged twenty-eight, an unmarried grocer's warehouseman. In April 1916 he was admitted into the Military Hospital, Great Yarmouth, suffering from influenza. He entered France in August 1916, was appointed Lance Bombardier in January 1919 and demobbed the following March.

You can see the Bulls Head pub sign on the left where Lawrence's father was publican.

SMITH, Sergeant – Norman Δ

Royal Fusiliers (City of London Regiment)

Photo Jennifer Teague

Norman Smith

Born in 1894, Norman worked as a joiner before the war. Enlisting in the Royal Fusiliers he entered France in November 1915. The Derbyshire Times dated 24th August 1918 reported him as a Prisoner of War, which he remained for nine months before repatriation.

After the war he became a well-known local businessman and involved himself fully in parish matters. He died in 1952 aged fifty-eight.

Derbyshire Times 1952

MR NORMAN SMITH

Death of Former Crich Councillor Mr. Norman Smith (58) died on Wednesday at his home, "Penfold," Crich. He had never fully recovered from a serious illness in November last year. He leaves a widow and one daughter. The third son of the late Mr. and Mrs. Roe Smith, of Crich, Mr. Smith was well known in Crich and district. Educated at Wirksworth Grammar School, he joined the Public Schools' Battalion of the Royal Fusiliers on the outbreak of the Great War and served on the Western Front. For nine months he was a prisoner-of-war in Germany. On demobilisation he and his eldest brother took over their father's old established business and formed the partnership of Smith Bros., builders and contractors.

For the last 25 years he has been prominent in the public life of Crich, positions he had held at various times including Foundation member, Chairman and Treasurer of Crich Comrades Club up to the time of his death, Chairman of Crich British Legion, People's Warden at Crich Parish Church, Manager of Crich CE. Schools, Chairman of Crich Conservative Association, member of Finance and General Purposes Committee of Belper Conservative Association, Crich Parish Council, Crich Old People's Welfare Committee and Matlock and

> District Building Trades Employers' Association.
>
> For the last three years he had represented the Crich Division on the Derbyshire County Council, but on medical, advice did not seek re-election at the recent elections.
>
> The funeral will be at Crich at 11a.m. tomorrow (Saturday).

Norman's brother Henry is also on the Roll of Honour.

SMITH, Private – Samuel ✝

Manchester Regiment
Labour Corps

Born in about 1886 at Crich Samuel moved to Seaton Carew. When he attested at West Hartlepool in November 1914 he was aged twenty-eight. It was recorded that he was married and that he had previously served with the Manchester Regiment for four years, being discharged in January 1907. He had married Florence Martha Mellors, of Sun Lane, Crich, in July 1911 at Belper. Florence was the sister of John and Walter Mellors who are also on the Crich Roll of Honour.

On enlistment in November 1914 he was posted to the Manchester Regiment and in September 1915 was appointed unpaid Lance Corporal. In January 1916 he arrived in Rouen, only to be returned to England twelve days later to work in munitions at the Central Zinc Company at Seaton Carew, West Hartlepool.

May 1918 saw him posted back to France at Etaples with the Manchester Regiment. In October 1918 he was sick and hospitalised for about a month. He was demobbed in March 1919.

After being demobbed he re-enrolled in May 1919 into the Labour Corps, aged thirty-six, and re-entered France in June of that year. During July 1919 he was admitted into hospital where, on 10 July 1919, he died of acute septic endocarditis at the Casualty Clearing Station, Ruitz, Germany. He was buried at Houchin British Cemetery. His wife, Florence, was living at Oak Cottage, Crich.

SMITH, Gunner – Samuel

Regiment unknown

He is on the original Crich Roll of Honour but no further information has been found.

SMITH, Private – Samuel Henry ✝
Sherwood Foresters (Nottinghamshire and Derbyshire Regiment)

We believe this to be the Samuel H. Smith on the Roll of Honour. His mother Ellen Smith (née Burton) came from Fritchley. He was born in 1887 at Borrowash, Derby to William and Ellen Smith. He died, aged thirty, on 10 June 1917 and is remembered at the Ypres (Menin Gate) memorial.

SMITH, Private – Thomas **MM** ✝
South Staffordshire Regiment

Thomas was born in about 1886. His father was George Smith, who in 1891, aged thirty-four, was a widower. Before he enlisted in the South Staffordshire Regiment Thomas worked as a limestone quarryman. He died of his wounds on 27th April 1918 and was buried at Haringhe (Bandaghem) Military Cemetery, near Ypres. He was awarded the Military Medal.

SNOW, Corporal – Oscar
Sherwood Foresters (Nottinghamshire and Derbyshire Regiment)
Cheshire Regiment

Photo Linda Hardy

Oscar Snow was born at Bonsall, Derbyshire, on 11th October 1894; the only child of Frederick Snow and Hannah Welch. He was raised at Alderwasley and Whatstandwell, where his father worked as a farmer. Oscar worked as a carpenter and joiner for the joinery firm of Yelverton Dawbarn Brothers at Whatstandwell.

He attested with the Sherwood Foresters at Derby on 1st February 1915 and shortly afterwards was posted to the 3rd Battalion. He was later transferred to the 3rd Battalion of the Cheshire Regiment and arrived in France on 14th July 1915 as part of the British Expeditionary Force where he served as a Lewis Gunner. From October 1915 Oscar served as part of the Mediterranean Expeditionary Force at Salonika. He was promoted to the rank of Corporal in May 1918. He was demobilised on 16th February 1919 and was awarded the British War Medal, Victory Medal, and the 1914–15 Star. He was also honoured with the Medalia Barbatie si Credinta (3rd Class) awarded by the King of Roumania. The medal which translates as 'Manhood and Faith', was awarded to non-commissioned officers for acts of bravery on the Eastern Front.

After he was discharged from the army, Oscar returned to his employment at the steam joinery works at Whatstandwell and married Mary Petts in 1919. They had a daughter and a son. Most of Oscar's married life was spent living at Longway Bank at Whatstandwell. During the Second World War, he served as a member of the local corps of the Home Guard. He was musically-inclined, and as a young boy he joined the choir at All Saints Church in Alderwasley and later became choirmaster and organist. He served as the secretary of the Church Council until he retired in 1968. There is a brass plaque placed in his memory by the side of the organ.

Oscar Snow passed away at Longway Bank, Whatstandwell, on 11 September 1970, aged seventy-five years. He was laid to rest in Alderwasley Cemetery.

STANLEY BROTHERS

John Robert and Percy were the sons of Malcolm and Eliza Stanley. The family lived at Fritchley.

STANLEY, Sapper – John Robert

Royal Engineers

Sherwood Foresters (Nottinghamshire and Derbyshire Regiment)

John was born in 1898 at Heage and worked as a pit-pony driver.

STANLEY, Private – Percy

Regiment unknown

Percy was born at Kirkby in Ashfield in 1899.

STEVENSON, Private – Robert ✝

Grenadier Guards

Photo Glynne Hickman

Robert, born in 1884, was the son of Joseph and Alice Stevenson of Fritchley. In 1903 he married Tamar Ann Payne and they lived at Wingfield Park. He died on 28th March 1918 and is buried at Bucquoy Road Cemetery, Ficheux, near Arras.

Robert's name is also inscribed on his mother's headstone in Crich Churchyard.

STEWARDSON, Gunner – Robert

Royal Marines Artillery

Robert was the son of mole-catcher Robert and Maria Stewardson. He was born in 1899 at Matlock. In 1911 the family were living at The Orchard, Whatstandwell. He enlisted, at Tansley, aged seventeen in June 1915. He was recorded as being "underage" from 3 June 1916 until 6 June 1916. He enlisted for twelve years and was of "very good character" throughout his record.

From June 1915 until January 1916 he appears to have been shore-based. From February 1916 until January 1920 he was posted to *Revenge* (he had chevrons awarded in June 1917). In July 1921 he had a Jutland Bounty paid to him of 5s 1d. He re- enrolled to complete twenty-seven years' service in October 1938. In January 1944, during WW2, he was a dispatch rider.

STOCKS BROTHERS

Albert and Fred were the sons of John and Sarah Ann Stocks.

STOCKS, Private – Albert

Regiment unknown

He was born in about 1899 at Crich.

STOCKS, Private – Fred

Regiment unknown

Fred was born in about 1882 and worked in the limestone quarry.

STORER, Pioneer – Charles

Royal Engineers

Charles was born in about 1878 in Fritchley. He married Ada Harriett Wesley in 1902 at Ambergate Parish Church. He attested in February 1916 aged thirty-eight, a married brick-setter living on Front Street, Fritchley. In July 1917 he left Southampton as part of the Mediterranean Expeditionary Force, arriving at Basra in August. After a spell in hospital he was posted to Nasiriyah Front Signal Coy. September 1918 saw him in hospital with influenza, and then in the October he was in Baghdad. He left for England aboard SS *Aduza* in March 1919 and was demobbed in the following May.

STORER, Trooper – Hiram

Derbyshire Yeomanry

Hiram Storer was the son of Hiram and Hannah Storer; he was born in Fritchley in 1896 and worked as a carter.

STORER, Trooper – Matthew

Derbyshire Yeomanry

There are two possible Matthew Storers in Crich Parish. He could be the brother of Hiram Storer, born in 1898. Hiram also served in the Derbyshire Yeomanry, so this is a likely match. However, there is Matthew Storer, brother of Charles Storer, born in 1880, who also is a possible.

STRAW, Private – Walter

Regiment unknown

Walter, born in about 1876, married Mary Ann Bradley during 1912 and was living in Fritchley at the time he would have enlisted.

STREET BROTHERS

Albert, Edwin and Frederick were the sons of Joshua and Agnes Street. Their father Joshua was variously a police constable, an inn keeper and a shop keeper. From 1901 they were living in Crich.

STREET, Private – Albert Percy

King's Own Yorkshire Light Infantry

Albert was born in about 1886 at Baslow, and in 1913 he married Margaret Daisy Ashforth at Fylde, Lancashire. He attested in December 1915 aged twenty-nine, a married slag loader living in Ripley. Previously he had served three years with the Sherwood Foresters. During June 1918 he was inattentive on parade and was confined to barracks for four days. His Army Record shows he served in India and present day Pakistan, including Sialkot and Bombay. He was finally demobbed in October 1919 aged thirty-three with a 30% disability pension (caused by malaria) of 12s 0d.

STREET, Private – Edwin Joshua

Army Service Corps

A slight note of caution over this record. The original Crich Roll of Honour lists J. Edward Street, but no such person has been found for the Crich area.

Edwin Joshua Street was born about 1878 at Borrowash and worked as a stonemason.

STREET, Lance Corporal – Frederick Vincent

Royal Field Artillery

Royal Engineers

He was born in about 1885 at Baslow but left the UK from Southampton on SS *Araguaya* for Buenos Aires on 27 May 1910. He was listed as a twenty-three-year-old fireman. Returning in 1914 he attested in January 1915 aged twenty-nine, an unmarried engine driver (superior) living at Derwent Terrace, Whatstandwell. He entered France in September 1915. In April 1916 he was attached to the Royal Engineers Railway Coy.

A note dated 1 May 1919 stated "*request for passage to Buenos Aires from 2nd Corporal Frederick Street who will be departing 01/07/19; free passage overseas granted*".

On his Repatriation Application he asked to be repatriated to Buenos Aires, Argentina with the comment under "*Grounds on which claim is based*" as: "*To return home where a situation awaits me. Came to England to join up voluntarily in 1914.*" He arrived at Liverpool aboard the SS *Amazon* from Buenos Aires, on the 29th November 1914, to join the war effort. The passenger list recorded him as an engine driver. He returned to Argentina in 1919.

SULLEY, Private – John William

Sherwood Foresters (Nottinghamshire and Derbyshire Regiment)

John was born at Ripley in 1884; his parents were Joseph and Hannah Sulley. Between 1891 and 1901 the family moved to live in Crich. Before joining the Foresters John was employed in the iron works.

SWANWICK, Driver – Arthur

Royal Field Artillery

Arthur has been difficult to track down in the records. He married Myra Hannah Hayes, of Crich, in 1913.

SWIFT, Private – John William

Sherwood Foresters (Nottinghamshire and Derbyshire Regiment)
Labour Corps

John was born in Cromford in about 1881, the son of Samuel and Mary Ann Swift. He attested at Derby in December 1915, aged thirty-five, an unmarried ganister miner living at Church Terrace in Fritchley. In October 1917 he was late back by a few hours from his embarkation leave and was punished by losing two days' pay. A few days later he entered France. In July 1918 he transferred to the Labour Corps and was posted to 153 POW Coy. He was eventually discharged in February 1919.

SWINDELL BROTHERS

Fred, Samuel and William were the sons of Samuel and Harriet Swindell.

SWINDELL, Driver – Fred

West Yorkshire Regiment
Labour Corps

Fred was born in about 1885 at Ripley. For a time he lived with his family on Cowper Lane, Crich and worked as a farm labourer. After the war he had an address at Moss Farm, Dore, Sheffield.

Fred's brothers Samuel and William are also on the Roll of Honour.

SWINDELL, Private – James

Regiment unknown

James was born in Crich Parish in about 1898.

SWINDELL, Private – Samuel

Royal Army Medical Corps

Samuel was born in about 1881 at Ripley. He attested in December 1916 at Derby, aged thirty-five, a married fruiterer living on the Common, Crich. He had married Elizabeth Eperson in December 1907 at Belper. He was discharged in November 1917 owing to osteo-arthritis (attributed to his service). He had a weekly pension of 27s 6d for four weeks and then 5s 6d per week thereafter. Samuel's brother-in-law, Edwin Eperson, is also on the Roll of Honour.

Samuel's brothers Fred and William are also on the Roll of Honour.

SWINDELL, Private – William

Sherwood Foresters (Nottinghamshire and Derbyshire Regiment)
Durham Light Infantry
Labour Corps

Photo Betty Nadin

Born in about 1878 at Crich, William worked as a gritstone quarryman. He attested in July 1916 at Derby, aged thirty-nine, a married stone cutter living at Thurlow Booth, Whatstandwell. He had married Lydia Eperson in September 1902 at Crich. His brother Samuel was to marry his wife's sister, Elizabeth, some five years later. He transferred from the Sherwood Foresters to the Durham Light Infantry in October 1916, and then was moved to the Labour Corps in April 1917. He was demobbed in March 1919.

William's brothers Samuel and Fred are also on the Roll of Honour.

TAYLOR BROTHERS

James Frederick and John Arthur were the sons of John Bown Taylor and his wife Mary Ann who lived at The Fields, Crich. Their father was a joiner, builder and contractor.

Herbert, Joseph Henry and John William were the sons of Herbert and Hannah Taylor. Although born at Darley Dale the family moved to the Whatstandwell area just before 1911. Their father was a railway porter.

TAYLOR, Corporal – George Bertram

Grenadier Guards

George Taylor was born at Crich Carr in about 1894, the son of Samuel and Ellen Taylor. Before the war he worked with his father at the Ambergate wireworks. He joined the Grenadier Guards on 3rd February 1915 and entered France with the British Expeditionary Forces on 5th October 1915. A few days later on 25th October he received a shotgun wound to his knee and after treatment at a Casualty Clearing Station and the Military Hospital at Rouen he was transferred back to the UK. While serving with 5th Reserve Battalion in the UK he was promoted to acting Sergeant. George returned to France having been posted to the 4th Battalion Grenadier Guards at Etaples. His gunshot wound must have been significant because he was examined at Cologne, Germany in February 1919 and had a disability certificate placed in his pension record. He was demobbed via Dunkirk in March 1919.

TAYLOR, Private – Gervaise Edward
Derbyshire Yeomanry
Devonshire Regiment

Gervaise was born on Spout Farm, Tansley in 1894, the son of Gervaise and Sarah Taylor. He married Elsie Thorpe during 1916 and served with the Derbyshire Yeomanry and Devonshire Regiments.

Photo Nigel Turner

Gervaise in the Derbyshire Yeomanry

Photo Keith Fretwell

Gervaise in the Devonshire Regiment

Photo Nigel Turner

Gervaise Taylor, Derbyshire Yeomanry, on the extreme right

After the war Gervaise lived in Crich and started the Crich bus service between the village, Ripley and Derby called "My Lady Coach".

Photo Nigel Turner

The first My Lady coach was a converted army lorry, seen here outside the butcher's in Crich Market Place

TAYLOR, Lance Corporal – Herbert

Royal Field Artillery
Corps of Military Foot Police

Herbert Taylor was born at Two Dales, near Darley Dale, on 24th July 1896. He was the second of seven children of Herbert Taylor and Hannah Barker. By 1911 he was living with his family at Longway Bank, Whatstandwell, which is on the outskirts of the parish of Crich. The family remained in the Whatstandwell area throughout the duration of the war, and for some time afterwards. Prior to his military service, Herbert worked as a delver at a local limestone quarry.

During the war, Herbert served as a gunner with the Royal Field Artillery and entered the Western Front on 13th December 1915. It is known that by September 1918 he had transferred to the Military Foot Police, with whom he served as a Lance Corporal. Whilst based at Dieppe in France, Herbert met his future wife Edith Mary Covell, who was serving in Dieppe with the Queen Mary's Army Auxiliary Corps (formerly the Women's Army Auxiliary Corps). They were married by a regimental chaplain at the Garrison Church in Dieppe on 26th September 1918.

Photo Christine Taylor

Herbert in WW2

After the war Herbert returned to the Crich area with his wife, and they lived for a time on Carr Lane and had nine children. He played football for Whatstandwell Football Club (see page 243). Herbert's wife was a native of Norfolk, and the family relocated to the Norfolk village of Worstead in 1929.

During the Second World War, Herbert served with the Corps of Military Police. Following the war he had a prominent role working on a project to repair the sea defences at the coastal town of Cromer which had been damaged by severe storms.

Herbert Taylor passed away at Norwich in 1968, aged seventy-two years. He was laid to rest in the churchyard of the Parish Church of St Catherine's in Ludham.

Both his brothers, John William and Joseph Henry, served in the army during the war, but were not listed on the original Roll of Honour at Crich as they were living just outside the boundary of the parish of Crich at the time of enlistment.

TAYLOR, Private – James

Regiment unknown

There are two possible matches for James Taylor in the Crich area:

James, born in about 1886 the son of James and Eliza Taylor of Crich; his father died at an early age and Eliza remarried to William Holmes.

James, born in about 1879, the son of Reuben and Elizabeth Taylor of Fritchley. Unfortunately we are unable to prove which one was on the original Roll of Honour.

TAYLOR, Private – James Frederick

Sherwood Foresters (Nottinghamshire and Derbyshire Regiment)

Although records show him as James Frederick, his preferred name was Frederick. He was born in 1891 and worked as a labourer in the spar works. During the war he was wounded in the left hand. After the war he worked as a greengrocer before dying in the Derbyshire Royal Infirmary, aged forty-one, in 1931. At the time of his death he was engaged to Freda Marsden.

DEATH OF MR F. TAYLOR,

CRICH

Mr Frederick Taylor, aged 41, of Rock House, Crich died on Wednesday week, at Derbyshire Royal Infirmary, where he had been a patient for about three weeks.

Mr Taylor, who conducted a green grocery business, was a native of Crich, being born at the White House Farm at Plaistow Green. He was the eldest son of Mr John and the late Mrs Taylor. During the war he served in the 2nd Battalion of Notts and Derbys and was wounded through the left hand. The news of his death caused a shock throughout the village, for he had only been ill a comparatively short time.

The funeral took place at Crich Parish Church on Sunday, the vicar (the Rev H.E.Jones, BSc) officiating.

James's brother John Arthur is also on the Roll of Honour.

TAYLOR, Private – John Arthur

Royal Army Veterinary Corps

John was born in about 1897 and he attested in January 1917 aged nineteen an unmarried farm labourer. February 1917 found him in Salonika where he served until 1919.

During his time in Salonika he failed to correspond with his parents. His Army Service Record contains letters written by his parents and the Army responses. Some of the letters were rather difficult to read.

{unclear text} *heard of the whereabouts of my son the above named, since September last, so I have become most anxious as to his whereabouts and trusting no ill has befallen him.*
I shall be most grateful to you if you would have enquiries made at your earliest convenience
Yours anticipation
{unclear text}

9 ? 1918
In reply to your enquiry No 3/8813/? with reference to the attached No 24525 Taylor J. A. RAVC is at present serving with the Veterinary Section, is quite well and has been requested to write to his father .
A. Brock Major 3rd Echelon, British Salonika Force

15 January 1919
Please pass attached letter to O.C. Unit in which the above mentioned soldier is serving in order that he may be interviewed with a view to communicating with his father, PA Bosher Capt, R.A.V.C Records

9 July 1919
Not having heard from my son Pte J.A. Taylor 24525 ? Veterinary section ? Division Salonica Forces Salonica for about eight weeks I am anxious as to his whereabouts. The last letter he stated that he was expecting coming home on leave as we have never seen him in kharki at all, and as he has been gone going on for three years we begin to think it due time we heard from him. So you may greatly oblige me by letting me know at your earliest convenience. I remain, Yours truly Mrs J. Taylor

12 July 1919
24524 J A Taylor RAVC
Attached letter passed to you for necessary action please
HW Badgett

22 July 1919
Madam, I beg to acknowledge receipt of your letter dated 9th July in reply have to inform you that according to information in this office No 24525 Pte J A Taylor is still serving in Salonica. A letter addressed as follows will be duly forwarded No 24525 Pte J. A. Taylor, c/o O i/c RAVC Base Records, Army of the Black Sea

In October 1919 John embarked for the UK via Taranto, Italy and was demobbed shortly afterwards. His brother James Frederick is also on the Roll of Honour

TAYLOR, Corporal – John Walter

Northumberland Fusiliers
Army Pay Corps

John, born in 1891 at Crich Market Place, was a son of Vaughan and Emily Taylor, butcher and farmer of The Mount, Crich. He enlisted in November 1916 aged twenty-six. He was also a butcher who had married Gertrude Bird in August 1915. His Army Record stated that in 1917 he suffered from D.A.H. (Disordered Action of the Heart) caused by some serious event connected to air raids while he was serving on the South Coast. This caused chest pains and palpitations. In January 1918 he was transferred from the Northumberland Fusiliers into the Army Pay Corps and then promoted to Corporal one year later. He elected to defer his demob until December 1919, then elected to defer this further until March 1920. When he was discharged his address was given as Derwent Villas, Whatstandwell.

TAYLOR, Corporal – John William

Royal Army Medical Corps
Royal Engineers

Photo Jenny Smith

John William Taylor was born at the Derbyshire hamlet of Two Dales, near Darley Dale, on 13th December 1894. He was the oldest of the seven children of Herbert Taylor and Hannah Barker. By 1911 the family had moved from Two Dales to live at Whatstandwell. Prior to his military service John was employed locally as a railway clerk.

He initially served as a Private with the Royal Army Medical Corps before being transferred to the Royal Engineers with whom he served as a Sapper before being promoted to the rank of Corporal. He entered the Western Front on 7th June 1915. In April 1916 during his furlough, John married Lilian Maud Viner at Wirksworth. Family recollections are that John was the first man from the local area to be married in military uniform. They would later have two daughters.

After the war, John and his family moved to the West Riding of Yorkshire where he was employed as the station master at Damems railway station, on the Worth Valley line. Around the time of the Second World War, John was transferred to Leeds City railway station where he served as an inspector until his retirement.

Following the death of his wife in 1972, John William Taylor passed away at Leeds in August 1976, aged eighty-one years.

John's brothers Herbert and Joseph Henry Taylor are also on the Roll of Honour, as is his brother-in-law, George Andrew Hughes.

TAYLOR, Gunner – Joseph Henry ✝

Royal Field Artillery

Joseph was born in 1898 at Darley Dale, a son of railway porter Herbert Taylor and his wife Hannah. In 1911 Joseph was a thirteen-year-old farm servant at Bury Hill Farm, Alderwasley. He entered France in October 1915 and was killed in July 1917 aged nineteen. He was buried at Dickebusch New Military Cemetery Extension near Ypres. At the time his parents were living at Crich Carr.

Derbyshire Times: 25th August 1917

The sad news was received last week by Mr and Mrs Taylor of Mill Cottage, Whatstandwell, that their son Gunner J. H. Taylor was killed in action. Gunner Taylor was 19 years of age, and previous to enlisting was employed in farm work. Major Paul wrote as follows to Mrs Taylor: – "It is with deep regret that I have to announce to you the death of your son, Gunner J. H. Taylor, who was killed in action at the battery on July 21st. During the last few months he has been in this battery he has always worked well and kept cheerful, and I feel the loss of this boy greatly. The body was brought down from the gun line, and he was buried by a military chaplain in a British Cemetery behind the lines."

He is remembered on the Alderwasley War Memorial (see page 235).

TAYLOR, Driver – Maurice

Royal Engineers

Maurice was born at Crich in about 1895 and was raised by his grandparents John and Sarah Heappey. He attested at Buxton in March 1915 aged twenty, an unmarried quarryman. He went into Connaught Hospital with asthma in November 1915 and January 1916, when it was decided that he was permanently unfit for military service and he was discharged. Four of his uncles, Andrew, Ernest, Jesse and Lot Heappey, are also on the Roll of Honour.

TAYLOR, Driver – Samuel

Royal Field Artillery

Photo Aileen Taylor

Samuel was born in about 1892 at Crich, the son of John and Margaret Taylor. John died in 1895 aged thirty-two when Samuel was three years old. The family lived at Rose Cottage, Whatstandwell and Samuel worked as a warehouse hand. He enlisted in January 1915 at Derby aged twenty-three, an unmarried wire-dresser of Yews Cottage, Crich and a Baptist. He entered France in March 1917 and the following year, March 1918, he was wounded but remained on duty. He was demobbed in February 1919.

On the original Crich Roll of Honour he appears twice. He was originally recorded as a Private but the family objected to this as his rank was "Driver", so he was added again with this corrected.

TAYLOR, Driver – William ✝

Royal Engineers

Photo Simon Johnson

William Taylor was born at his mother's native Ashover in 1878. He was the oldest of the eleven children of Samuel Taylor and Elizabeth Wilson.

William was raised at Plaistow Green on the outskirts of the parish of Crich, where his father plied his trade as a cattle dealer. William followed his father into this trade and spent most of his adult life working as a calf dealer. William never married, and had no children.

As a young man he was part of the 2nd Volunteer Battalion of the Sherwood Foresters, which was based at Chesterfield. Volunteer battalions were precursors of the modern-day Territorial Army. British losses suffered during the Second Boer War in South Africa in December 1899 led to a call for more troops. Accordingly, on 2nd January 1900, a special Army Order was issued calling upon the volunteers to furnish their contingent of trained men to reinforce the army in the field. William Taylor was one of the first men to be attested as part of the 1st Volunteer Company of the Sherwood Foresters. He arrived in South Africa on 23rd February 1900, where the service companies of the volunteer battalions took part in the campaign with great credit. William remained in South Africa until his honourable discharge on 29th April 1901. He received the Queen's South Africa Medal, which was awarded to all military personnel who served in the Second Boer War in South Africa. This medal survives with William's nephew in Derbyshire. Various clasps were added to the medal to indicate each action and campaign of the war. William's medal has four clasps which indicate his service in Johannesburg, Cape Colony, Orange Free State and Diamond Hill.

Following his military service in South Africa, William returned to his family at Plaistow Green, returning to his trade as a calf dealer. After his father's death in 1908, William and his family briefly moved to live at Ashover Hay before moving to the hamlet of Wheatcroft, on the outskirts of the parish of Crich. Prior to his service in the army during the First World War, William had also been employed at Oakerthorpe Colliery.

During the early stages of the First World War, as an experienced former soldier, the call to arms found William ready to respond. He was attested for service with the Royal Engineers at Chesterfield on 1st February 1915, with the rank of Driver. Shortly afterwards he was attached to the 84th Field Company which served as part of the 20th (Light) Division and embarked for France as part of the British Expeditionary Force on 23 July 1915. The Division spent the duration of the war in action on the

Western Front, taking part in many of the significant actions, including phases of the Battles of the Somme in 1916 and the Third Battle of Ypres in 1917.

William was wounded in action during the Battle of Cambrai on 28th November 1917 when he received a gunshot wound to the abdomen. He was moved to the Casualty Clearing Station but his wound was so severe that he passed away shortly after admission. He was thirty-nine years old. William was laid to rest in Rocquigny-Equancourt Road British Cemetery, which lies in countryside east of Amiens in the Somme region of France. After his death his personal effects of pipe and pencil were returned to his mother.

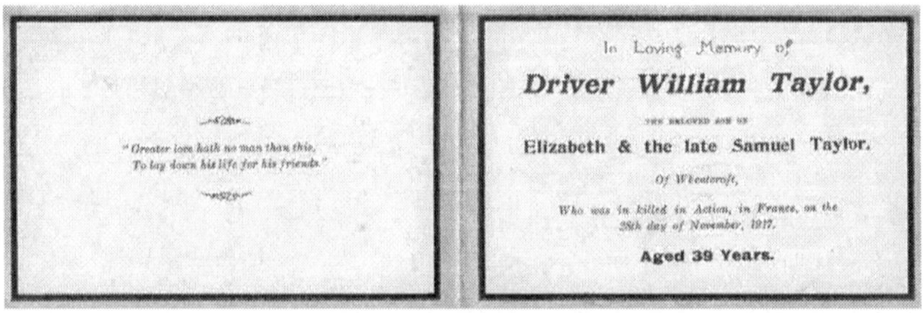

*"Greater love hath no man than this,
To lay down his life for his friends."*

In Loving Memory of

Driver William Taylor,

THE BELOVED SON OF

Elizabeth & the late Samuel Taylor.

Of Wheatcroft,

Who was in killed in Action, in France, on the 28th day of November, 1917.

Aged 39 Years.

Derbyshire Times: 22nd December 1917

Mrs Taylor, Wheatcroft, Crich, has received news that her only son, Driver William Taylor, has been killed in action. The news was conveyed in the following letter from the matron of the Casualty Clearing Station, France, dated November 28th: – "It is with great regret I have to tell you of the death this day of your son, Driver W. Taylor, from wounds received in action. He came to us this morning so severely wounded in the abdomen that all we could do for him was of no avail, for he succumbed to his injuries shortly after admission. His end was peaceful and free from pain. It may be of some little comfort to you to know he did not suffer. With sincere sympathy".

Driver Taylor, who was 39 years of age and single, served with the Sherwood Foresters for three years during the South African war. In February, 1915, he joined the Royal Engineers, and six months afterwards was sent to France. He formerly worked at the Oakerthorpe Colliery and is well known in the Crich and Ashover district.

THORPE, Gunner – Wilfrid

Royal Garrison Artillery

Photo Hilda Turner

Wilfrid, born in 1897 was the son of Thomas and Mary Thorpe who farmed at Plaistow Hall, near Wheatcroft, Crich. Although named Wilfrid most official documents record him incorrectly as Wilfred. His father built the Wheatcroft Institute, a wooden structure used for meetings and entertainments in Wheatcroft hamlet. At some time during the war Wilfrid was wounded.

Undated newspaper report

> Letters explaining the nature of Gunner Wilfred Thorpe's wounds have been received by his parents, Mr and Mrs Thomas Thorpe, Plaistow Hall, Crich. Gunner Thorpe, along with several chums, was in a dug-out, and Fritz was strafing with his long range shells, one of which dropped just over them. Gunner Thorpe and several chums were wounded. He was hit in the leg and arm. He was moved to the base hospital, and later to England. He is now at a military hospital at Leicester. Enlisting fourteen months ago, Gunner Thorpe went to France with the Royal Garrison Artillery in May. He is the youngest son of Mr and Mrs T. Thorpe.

TOMLINSON, Private – Arthur Noble Blanche ◊

Sherwood Foresters (Nottinghamshire and Derbyshire Regiment)

Noble was born in 1890 and raised in Crich by his uncle and aunt George and Clara Twigg. He worked as a door machinist before joining the Sherwood Foresters in October 1914. He is on the Crich recruits photographs on page 237. Noble entered France in June 1915 and was discharged through sickness in October 1916; he was awarded the Silver War Badge.

TOWNSEND, Private – Ezra

Regiment unknown

Ezra was born in Exton, Rutland during 1884, the son of Amos and Margaret Townsend. By 1911 he had moved to work as an agricultural labourer in Wingerworth, then in 1912 he married Alice Housley from Crich. His brothers-in-law, William and George Housley, are also on the Roll of Honour.

WAIN, Driver – Charles ✝

Royal Field Artillery
Royal Horse Artillery

Charles was born in 1883 at Hilton, the son of Joseph and Agnes Wain. After living in the Etwall area of Derby the family moved to Ambergate where Charles worked as an engine driver in the Johnson and Nephew wireworks. In April 1914 he married Constance Gertrude Daniel at Ripley. Aged twenty-one, Charles enlisted in the Royal Field Artillery at Uttoxeter in January 1906. He was in Connaught Hospital, Aldershot during February 1907 with contusion of the knee, and in January 1908 he gained his first good conduct badge. In January 1909 he was transferred to the Army Reserve until August 1914, when he was mobilised at Athlone and in the September was posted to France. On 8th August 1918 he was killed in action, aged thirty-four, and was buried at the Corbie Communal Cemetery Extension near Amiens.

His wife, Constance, was sent Charles' property of metal chain and whistle, three discs, belt, ribbon, knife, wound stripes, pipe, badge, comb, wallet, cards, photo, letters, two Old Testaments and a sprig of heather. She was awarded a pension of 29s 7d per week for herself and their three children.

Derbyshire Times 24 August 1918

WHATSTANDWELL SOLDIER'S FATAL WOUNDS

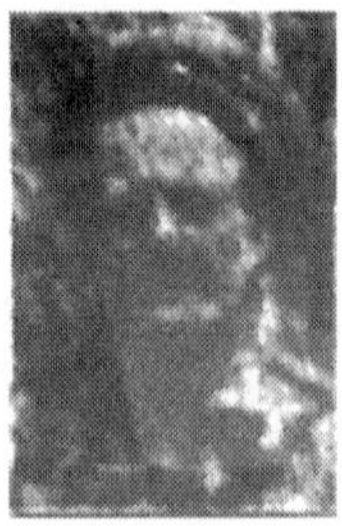

The sad news was received by Mrs Wain, of Whatstandwell, at the end of last week, that her husband Driver Charles Wain of the Royal Horse Artillery had died from the effects of wounds received in action in France on the 8th inst. He was born at Milton Cotton about 34 years ago and later on his parents came to Ambergate where they still are. Previous to enlisting some years ago he was employed at the Ambergate Wireworks. When the war broke out he was amongst the first to be called up. He leaves a widow and three children, the eldest being four years and the youngest five months.

Charles is also remembered on the Alderwasley Memorial (see page 235).

WALKER, Driver – John Thomas

Sherwood Foresters (Nottinghamshire and Derbyshire Regiment)

John was born in about 1886 at Heage and was raised by his widowed grandmother Hannah Walker. He married Ada Mellows, of Crich, in 1905 and they moved to live in Ironville. He was one of the first to sign up to the Sherwood Foresters in October 1914 and can be seen on the recruits photograph on page 237. He is recorded as having the rank of driver on the Church Roll of Honour so it is presumed that he may have changed regiments during the course of the war.

WALKER, Lance Corporal – Percy Travis ◊

East Yorkshire Regiment

Labour Corps

Percy was born at South Normanton in about 1891 and was raised by John and Hannah Travis, his uncle and aunt. In 1914 he married Edith May Brown of Crich. He enlisted in December 1915 and served overseas; he was discharged, aged twenty-seven, in October 1919 with a Silver War Badge.

WALTERS, Air Mechanic – James William

Royal Air Force

Born at Crich in 1899, James was the son of Charles and Rosannah Walters.

WASS BROTHERS

Ernest and Frank were the sons of Robert and Susannah Wass who lived at Whatstandwell. Their father was a superintendent in the grit quarry who was killed on the Midland Railway in 1895.

WASS, Sapper – Ernest

Royal Engineers

Ernest was born at Crich in 1881. He worked as a stonemason before joining the Royal Engineers. His brother Frank is also on the Roll of Honour.

WASS, Private – Frank

Regiment unknown

Frank was born in 1878 at Crich and worked as a stonemason. He married Mary Adams in 1901 and he died in 1939 aged sixty. His brother Ernest is also on the Roll of Honour.

WASS, Corporal – Robert Walter William

Machine Gun Corps

Robert was the son of William and Jane Wass, born at Crich Carr in 1899.

WATTS, Private – George Ernest

Regiment unknown

Photo Jean Smith (née Maskrey)

Ernest Watts in later life

In 1886 George Ernest Watts, known as Ernest, was born at Brampton, on the outskirts of Chesterfield. He was the son of William Watts and Eliza Dawson. By 1911 he was working as a butcher's assistant while living with relatives in Brampton. At this time his widowed father was living with his daughter at the hamlet of Sawmills, just outside the boundary of the parish of Crich.

Ernest served in the army during the war, with the rank of Private. Unfortunately his service records have not survived, and it hasn't been possible to identify his regiment. After he was discharged from the army, he returned to his occupation as a butcher and by 1923 was living in the Derbyshire village of Holloway, close to Crich. Ernest remained a resident of Holloway for the rest of his life. He was later employed at the Mill Close lead works at Darley Dale and in 1923 he married a widow named Beatrice Ethel Maskrey (née Woodward).

George Ernest Watts was killed in a road accident near High Peak Junction at Cromford on 28th August 1941, aged fifty-five years. At the time he was a pillion passenger on a colleague's motorbike, returning home from work at Darley Dale. The motorbike had been involved in a collision with another vehicle, which subsequently disappeared from the scene of the accident. Both Ernest and his colleague were killed in the accident.

WETTON, Corporal – Walter E. ◊
Labour Corps

On the original Roll of Honour he is recorded as Walker Wetton. This name cannot be found in the census, the Birth, Marriage and Death indices nor in the army records.

Making the assumption that it should be Walter Wetton, we know that Walter was born in Crich about 1893 and was brought up by his uncle and aunt Samuel and Martha Killer at Wirksworth. He enlisted in August 1914 and was discharged in April 1919 with the Silver War Badge, on account of wounds received.

WHAWELL, Gunner – James William
Royal Field Artillery

Born in 1891 at Ambergrove, James' parents were Charles and Emily Whawell. Both James and his father worked at the Ambergate wireworks. He attested in January 1915 at Derby aged twenty-four and entered France in October 1915. In March 1916 it was discovered that he suffered from trench foot and was admitted to Boscombe Hospital. In August 1918 he was admitted to the Canadian General Hospital, Le Treport with an abscess on his thigh before being sent back to the UK aboard the hospital ship HS *Carisbrook Castle* for treatment at Glasgow Hospital. He was demobbed in February 1919. His Army Record had a note that he had been admitted at various times to Stanley Hospital Rouen, 2nd Canadian Hospital, VAD at Craigs Head, Bournemouth and 3rd Scotland Hospital in Glasgow.

HS *Carisbrook Castle on which James travelled to England*

WHITE, Lance Corporal – John ✝

Sherwood Foresters (Nottinghamshire and Derbyshire Regiment)

Photo Cliff Housley

John was born in 1896 at Crich, the son of Amos and Eliza White. His father worked on Cromford Canal. He attested in June 1915 aged nineteen, an unmarried collier who was living at Buckland Hollow. On 4th August 1917 he died of his wounds and is buried at Dozinghem Military Cemetery. He is remembered on the Sawmills Memorials; see page 231.

WHITEHEAD, Driver – Fred ◊

Royal Engineers

Born in about 1889, Fred attested for the Royal Engineers in October 1915, aged twenty-six; he was a married quarryman who lived near the Cross at Crich. He had married Elsie Crowder in 1912. While serving in France he was treated at Rouen Hospital for a cut finger and in November 1918 was discharged as being no longer physically fit. He was awarded the Silver War Badge.

WHITEHURST, Private – Albert ✝

Royal Fusiliers (City of London Regiment)

Born at Crich Carr in 1887, Albert was the son of gamekeeper Joseph Whitehurst and his wife Ann. Albert also became a gamekeeper and married Lilian Davies in 1913; they went to live at Brailsford. He died 28 March 1918 after being twice wounded on previous occasions. He is remembered at the Arras Memorial.

WILKINSON BROTHERS

Daniel and David were the sons of David Wilkinson and his wife Mary. In 1894, after their father's death, their mother married his brother, Henry Wilkinson, a herbalist who lived at Crich Carr. So, Henry was both their uncle and step-father.

WILKINSON, Private – Daniel Broadhurst ◊

York and Lancaster Regiment

Daniel was born at Crich in 1879 and worked as stonemason. He enlisted in the Army in December 1915 but was badly wounded; his leg had to be amputated, and consequently he was discharged on 10th January 1919 with the Silver War Badge when he was aged forty. He had married Alice Madeleine Pitt at Birkenhead during 1916.

Photo Irene Wilkinson

WILKINSON, Sergeant – David Harold

Royal Army Medical Corps

David was born in 1889 at Crich, and worked as a chemist. He joined the Royal Army Medical Corps and entered France in April 1915. He married Dorothy Murfin in Nottingham in 1926. They lived in Chapel Street, Ripley, working in the family herbalist shop, D. Wilkinson and Sons. Later they owned and ran the garage on Derby Road which subsequently became the Ripley Co-op's garage.

Photo Irene Wilkinson

WILLIAMS, Corporal – Albert **MM**
Royal Field Artillery

Photo Margaret Suddes

Albert, born in Birmingham in about 1895, was the son of George and Louisa Williams who lived at Sawmills before they moved to Cromford Road, Crich. Before he joined the Royal Field Artillery he worked at Ambergate Wireworks. He enlisted at Derby in January 1915 and entered France in the July of that year. He was awarded the Military Medal in April 1918 before being demobbed in February 1919.

Albert's Military Medal

Military Medal for Bravery in the Field

Letter dated 4.4.18; 20th Division No. A/9473

O/C D.A.C.

I have much pleasure in bringing to your notice No. 84055 Cpl. A. Williams, No. 3 Section D.A.C.

This N.C.O. was in charge of a complete sub-section during the whole of the recent operations, between St. Quentin and Domart-Sur-La-Luce, and kept the entire front line supplied with S.A.A. Ammunition, Lewis and Vickers Guns, Belts and Drums.

He carried out his duties in a conspicuously gallant manner and materially aided the Battalions holding the line under very critical circumstances; he worked untiringly day and night, setting a splendid example to those under him.

I should be very grateful if he may officially informed of our appreciation.

(signed) H. Muller, Lieut:Colonel

A.A. & Q.M.G. 20th Division

DAC was the Divisional Ammunition Column of the Royal Field Artillery.

The following memorabilia and photographs are courtesy of Margaret Suddes.

Albert received a commendation certificate which read:

20th (Light) Division.

The Major-General Commanding 20th (Light) Division has received a report of the gallant conduct of 84055, Corpl. A. Williams, No. 3 Section, 20th D.A.C. from 21st March to 1st April between ST. QUENTIN and DOMART-SUR-LA-LUCE, in working untiringly day and night during the whole of this period keeping units in the fighting line supplied with small arms ammunition, setting a splendid example to those under him and he wishes to congratulate him on his fine behaviour.

GG Slaney Major General

Commanding 20th (Light) Division

20th (Light) Division.

The Major-General Commanding 20th Light Division has received a report of the gallant conduct

and he wishes to congratulate him on his fine behaviour.

Major-General
Commanding 20th Light Division

Albert wanted to receive his Military Medal at his place of work, Johnson and Nephew Wireworks, Ambergate.

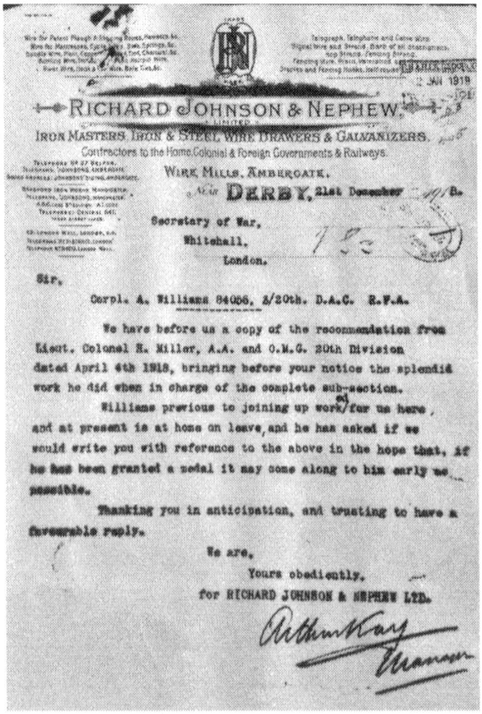

RICHARD JOHNSON & NEPHEW, LIMITED

IRON MASTERS, IRON & STEEL WIRE DRAWERS & GALVANIZERS.

Contractors to the Home, Colonial & Foreign Governments & Railways.

WIRE MILLS, AMBERGATE,

Near DERBY, 21st December 1918.

Secretary of War,
Whitehall,
London.

Sir,

Corpl. A. Williams 84056, 2/20th. D.A.C. R.F.A.

We have before us a copy of the recommendation from Lieut. Colonel H. Miller, A.A. and Q.M.G. 20th Division dated April 4th 1918, bringing before your notice the splendid work he did when in charge of the complete sub-section.

Williams previous to joining up worked for us here, and at present is at home on leave, and he has asked if we would write you with reference to the above in the hope that, if he has been granted a medal it may come along to him early as possible.

Thanking you in anticipation, and trusting to have a favourable reply.

We are,
Yours obediently,
for RICHARD JOHNSON & NEPHEW LTD.

Arthur Kay
Manager

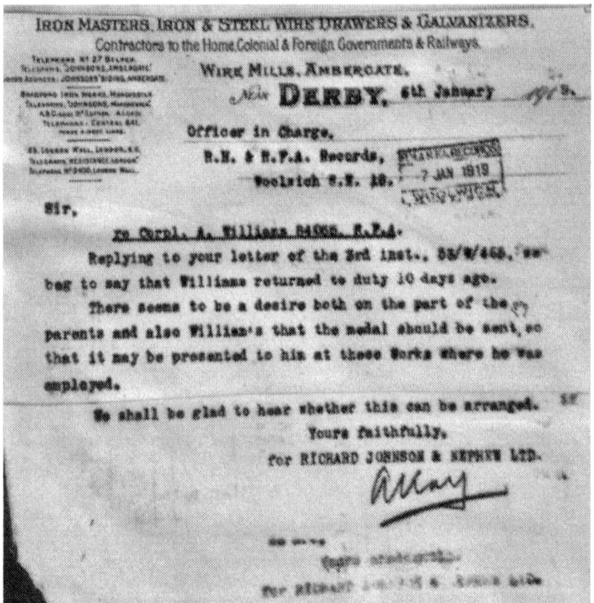

IRON MASTERS, IRON & STEEL WIRE DRAWERS & GALVANIZERS.

Contractors to the Home, Colonial & Foreign Governments & Railways.

WIRE MILLS, AMBERGATE,

Near DERBY, 6th January 1919.

Officer in Charge,
R.H. & R.F.A. Records,
Woolwich S.E. 18.

Sir,

re Corpl. A. Williams 84056, R.F.A.

Replying to your letter of the 3rd inst., 33/W/463, we beg to say that Williams returned to duty 10 days ago.

There seems to be a desire both on the part of the parents and also William's that the medal should be sent, so that it may be presented to him at these Works where he was employed.

We shall be glad to hear whether this can be arranged.

Yours faithfully,
for RICHARD JOHNSON & NEPHEW LTD.

A Kay

Unknown newspaper cutting

MILITARY MEDALLISTS

Corpl. Albert Williams, D.A.C., third son of Mr and Mrs George Williams, Saw Mills, Ambergate, has been awarded the Military Medal for gallant conduct in the field. On the first day of the big offensive and for nine consecutive days Corpl Williams worked day and night in supplying the guns with ammunition. In civil life he was employed as a wire drawer at the Ambergate Wire Mills, voluntarily enlisting in January 1915, and went to France in July of the same year. Up to the present he has come through scathless (sic). Corpl. Williams is 24 years of age.

Like many servicemen Albert sent home cards, many of which were sentimental and beautifully created.

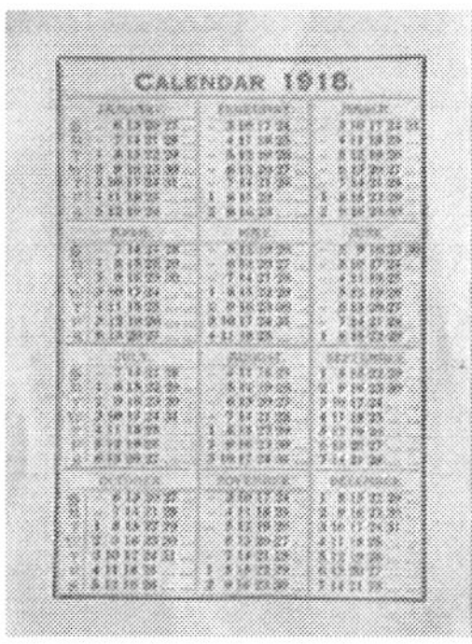

The photographs below show Albert as a Private and with Myra Hayes, whom he married in June 1920.

After the war Albert was very heavily involved with village activities. He died on 4th June 1970 aged seventy-six and his obituary summed up his life.

Unknown cutting June 1970

A FORGOTTEN HERO PASSES ON

On Tuesday, last week was laid to rest the late Albert Williams, M.M. of 10 Cromford Road, Crich. Although he was born in Birmingham his parents came to reside at Ambergate when he was three years of age and later came to reside at Moseley Street, Ripley, during the first Great World War 1914-18.

The late Corporal Williams volunteered for active service early on and was sent to the Maryhill Barracks Glasgow. He saw service in many of the epic wars at Arras, Cambrai, the Somme, Ypres, and St Quentin. It was in 1918 that he gained his military medal.

The citation re the winning of this medal reads as follows: "20th Light Division. Gallant conduct of 84055 Corporal A. Williams, No. 3 Section 20th D.A.C. from 21st of March to 1st April, 1918, between St Quentin and Domart Sur-La-Luce in working untiringly day and night during the whole of this period setting a splendid example to those under him." It was the proud boast of the late Albert Williams, that during the whole of his active service he never lost a man who was under his command.

After the war Corporal A. Williams married Myra Hayes of Crich and they settled down in Crich, where Albert Williams was a legendary figure. He took an active part in all the carnivals organised to raise funds for the hospitals. He represented Crich on the Belper Rural District Council with distinction for a number of years. He was also a prominent member of Crich Parish Council and its chairman.

For a number of years he was a prominent member of Crich schools and chairman of the Evergreen Club. In this time Albert Williams played many parts and his aim was to be of service to his fellow man. This modest hero will long be remembered and revered by those who had the privilege to know him.

After the death of his wife he was well cared for by Miss Emma Greenhough, his son Clarence, and his daughters Lorna and Janet. Many of his friends came to pay him tribute at Crich Parish Cemetery. In his passing, we have lost a great hero, a staunch Labour supporter and a loyal comrade. We salute his memory and deeply mourn his passing.

WM. H. EMMAS-WILLIAMS

WILLIAMS, Captain – James

Chaplain to the Forces

James Williams with his wifeMary Ann

James Williams was born at the Welsh village of Llanddewi Brefi, Cardiganshire, on 13 April 1879. He was the seventh of the nine children of David and Anne Williams, with five brothers and three sisters. James was raised in the family farmhouse, Pant-gwyn, on the Llanfair Mountain.

In 1963, the Reverend David Williams, a near neighbour and colleague of members of James's family, published a local history book titled Y Wladfa Fach Fynyddig. In the book, Reverend Williams provided information about James's family, and recalled that 'James [Williams]… after working in the coal mines in south Wales for a few years, became a student at Lampeter Grammar School and eventually became an Anglican minister.' Crockford's Clerical Directory of 1932 confirms that James studied at St David's College in Lampeter and graduated with a Licentiate in Divinity in 1910. He was ordained as a deacon in 1911 and as a priest in 1912. James subsequently served as curate of the church in Llandybie between 1911 and 1914 before moving to Derbyshire to become curate at St Mary's Church at Crich between 1914 and 1922. By 1918 James was living on The Common at Crich with his wife, Mary Ann. They do not appear to have had any children.

His entry in Crockford's Clerical Directory also shows that, during his time at Crich, James served as a Temporary Chaplain to the Forces in 1918-1919. Army chaplains are the only British Army officers who do not carry standard officer ranks. They are officially designated 'Chaplain to the Forces' (CF), though they do have grades which equate to the standard ranks and wear the insignia of the equivalent rank. Chaplains were usually addressed as 'Padre', never by their nominal military rank. A Chaplain to the Forces 4th Class (the lowest class) equated to the nominal military rank of Captain. Although no service records have been located for James, it can therefore be assumed that this nominal rank of Captain was used when his name was listed on the Roll of Honour inside St Mary's Church at Crich.

After his war service ended, James returned to his post as curate at St Mary's Church at Crich before becoming the vicar of Christ Church at Wessington in 1922. After the Benefices of Wessington and Brackenfield were united in 1923, James also assumed responsibility for Holy Trinity Church at Brackenfield. It has been suggested that James remained in this latter post until his retirement, whereupon he appears to have returned to Wales with his wife.

The Reverend James Williams passed away at Swansea on 19 September 1957, aged seventy-eight years. He was laid to rest in the village of Pontyberem in Carmarthenshire.

As James's parents were still living in the family farmhouse at Llanddewi Brefi at the time of the First World War, he was also commemorated on the Roll of Honour inside St Mary's Church in the neighbouring village of Llanfair Clydogau, which was the church James's family attended. Unfortunately this Roll was badly water-damaged a number of years ago, and has subsequently been lost after it was sent for renovation.

WILLIAMSON BROTHERS

Arthur and George were the sons of William and Mary Williamson. Although their parents were not Crich-born they lived most of their married life in the village. Their father was a police constable in Crich before becoming a farmer in later life.

WILLIAMSON, Lance Corporal – Arthur Ernest ✞
West Riding Regiment (Duke of Wellington's)

Arthur was born at Crich in 1890, and before the start of the war he worked as a husbandsman in Huddersfield, where he enlisted in August 1914. He entered France in July 1915 and was killed in action shortly after on 2nd March 1916 aged twenty-three. He is remembered on the Ypres (Menin Gate) Memorial. His death was reported in the Derbyshire Times as follows:

Derbyshire Times 18 March 1916

FRITCHLEY MAN KILLED

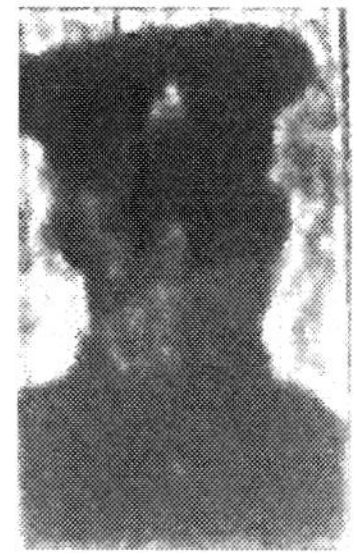

On Friday last week Mr and Mrs Wm. Williamson, farmers at Fritchley, received a letter informing them that their son Lance-Corpl. Signaller Arthur Ernest Williamson of the 9th Duke of Wellington had fallen in action, although this has not yet been confirmed by the War Office. He was 23 years of age, single and was educated at Fritchley School. About twelve years ago he went to work at the farm of the late Mr John Sadler in Yorkshire. Later he worked at a brickyard, also in Yorkshire. He attended evening classes and was successful in winning a scholarship for the Leeds University. Just prior to enlisting he obtained a post connected with cattle diseases at Heanor. He paid a visit to his home in December last on eight days furlough. He enlisted on the 31st August 1914 and had nine months training, after which he went to Flanders, being there eight months altogether. He was killed by a shell in the trenches. He was held in high esteem by his comrades and officers as can be seen by the following and other letters which have been received by his parents:– "Dear Mrs Williamson, it is with the deepest sorrow and regrets that I write this letter to inform you of the very sad news of your son's death, which occurred on Thursday, March 2nd during a heavy bombardment by the enemy. We all miss him very much as he was always so cheerful and willing. As for his work, I cannot praise it enough. His courage and fearlessness in the presence of great danger were a fine example to the other men. I may also add that he was on the verge of getting full corporal's stripes and I shall have the greatest difficulty in replacing him. Please accept my deepest sympathy in your very sad bereavement – Yours sincerely, R Dawes, 2nd Lieut. 9th Duke of Wellington's Regiment."

WILLIAMSON, Gunner – George Henry

Regiment unknown

George was born at Fritchley in 1894. Before joining the Army he worked as a gardener.

WILSON BROTHERS

George and James were the sons of George and Eliza Wilson. Their father was a limestone quarryman and the family lived at the Hat Factory, between Crich and Fritchley.

WILSON, Rifleman – George

Regiment unknown

George was born in 1898 and worked as a draper's assistant before he joined the army.

WILSON, Sergeant – George James **DCM, MM**

Sherwood Foresters (Nottinghamshire and Derbyshire Regiment)

Photo Cliff Housley

George was born in 1889 at Crich, the son of William and Mary Ann Wilson. He enlisted in the Sherwood Foresters in March 1908 at Belper, aged eighteen, a waggoner by trade. In 1911 he was serving as a private at Plympton St. Mary. He was one of the first to enter France in September 1914 and was discharged from Egypt in November 1921. He had a distinguished service, earning the Distinguished Conduct Medal, the Military Medal, the 14 Star (with clasp and roses), the British War Medal and the Victory Medal.

London Gazette 1 January 1919

> For gallantry and devotion to duty. On the night of the 21st/22nd March, 1918, near Vaux Wood, this N.C.O., who was in charge of the ration limbers, went forward by himself to find the Battalion, and then returned to guide up the ration limbers under very heavy shell fire. Throughout the night he behaved with great coolness and disregard of danger. On several other occasions when the battalion was in front of Dranoutre, in April, 1918, he displayed great courage and tenacity in leading his ration limbers to the company headquarters under heavy shell fire and machine gun fire. His work at all times has been excellent.

WILSON, Stoker – James (Jim)

Royal Navy

Born in 1891, Jim was a colliery engine driver before enrolling in the Royal Navy in July 1911, for a period of twelve years. During his service he went from Stoker to Leading Stoker. During the war years he served aboard HMS *Zealandia*, *Victory II*, *Vernon* and *Agincourt*. *Victory II* and *Vernon* were shore-based postings. He left the service in June 1921 with the report that his conduct had been very good.

WITHERS, Lance Corporal – George

Regiment unknown

George was born in the London area in about 1896, the son of Evan and Sophia Withers. In some records Evan is recorded as Esau. During 1911 the family were living at the Hat Factory, Crich where his father was a foreman in the limestone quarry. At that time George was working as a labourer.

The Hat Factory is in the centre of the photograph

WOOD, Private – John Thomas

Regiment unknown

John Thomas was born about 1873 at Cloughfold in Lancashire. His parents were born in the Belper area. When he married Agnes Hannah Holmes in 1901 they lived at Milford before moving to Crich, from where John Thomas worked at the Ambergate wireworks.

WOODLAND, Signaller – Joseph Edgar

Royal Navy

He was known as Edgar. He was born in 1888 at Derby, the son of Joseph and Fanny Woodland. His father was a railway inspector and Edgar became a clerk for the railway company. He joined the Navy in November 1915, and his record noted that he was a clerk, C of E and a swimmer. In February 1916 he passed out of signal school and was posted to the Royal Naval Barracks at Chatham. He left the service in May 1919. He married Margaret (Maggie) Puttock in 1919 and they lived at Fritchley.

Edgar sent Maggie photographs and postcards from the various places he was stationed. He served in the Mediterranean.

Photos Jim Walker

Edgar with shoulder flash of telegraphist and wearing Mediterranean uniform, 1916

Two Maltese seamen and Margaret Puttock, his wife-to-be

Card from Edgar to Maggie from Greece dated 1916

Postcard sent to Margaret dated 18 December 1917

Undated postcard on which Edgar asks Maggie what she thinks of the ship

WOOLLEY BROTHERS

Charles, John Isaac and William were the sons of William and Elizabeth Ann Woolley. William was a lead miner some forty years older than Elizabeth. After William died she remarried to John Martin and the family then lived near to St Mary's Church.

WOOLLEY (WALTERS), Lance Corporal – Charles

Regiment unknown

Charles was born in 1883, the son of Elizabeth Ann Walters, before she married William Woolley. Charles was known both as Walters and Woolley. Nothing is known of his service record.

WOOLLEY, Sergeant – John Isaac (Ike)

Sherwood Foresters (Nottinghamshire and Derbyshire Regiment)

King's Shropshire Light Infantry

Photo Peter Woolley

Ike was born at Crich in 1898 and worked for the Butterley Company before joining the Sherwood Foresters. He enlisted in March 1916 aged nineteen and became a signaller. He was posted to the King's Shropshire Light Infantry in April 1917. At Gommecourt in September 1918 he was gassed and severely wounded by a gunshot to his left thigh, injuring the sciatic nerve. His knee movement was limited to an angle of 45° and could not be fully extended and also his ankle was not freely flexible and there was great muscular wasting. He spent time in the South African General Hospital at Abbeville, France, the 15th Canadian Hospital in Taplow, Buckinghamshire, the War Hospital at Reading, the Military Hospital, Edmonton. Eventually he had to have his leg amputated.

In 1923 he became the first warden of Crich Memorial Tower which was dedicated to the men of the Sherwood Foresters (see page 295); he retired in 1970. During the Second World war he was commander of Crich Home Guard. Ike died on 7th April 1980 aged eighty-two.

WOOLLEY, Private – William (Bill)

Regiment unknown

Bill was born in about 1891 at Crich and worked on the railway.

WRAGG BROTHERS

George and John were the sons of Edward and Rebecca Wragg, who in 1911 were living at Thurlow Booth, Whatstandwell. Edward worked in the limestone quarry.

John and Samuel were the sons of William and Eliza Wragg who lived at Town End, Crich. Their father, William, worked in the limestone quarry.

John Thomas and Luke were the sons of John and Zilla Wragg.

WRAGG (RODGERS), Private – Frederick ✝
Grenadier Guards

Born in 1886, Frederick worked as a quarryman before enlisting in the Grenadier Guards at Derby. He entered France in December 1915 and died of his wounds on 18th August 1916 aged thirty after being transferred back to the UK. He is buried in Crich Churchyard. It is possible that he is the F. Rodgers on the Sawmills Memorial. His mother Harriet Wragg married William Rodgers and his half-brothers Amos, George and James are on the Roll of Honour. In 1911 Frederick was recorded in the census as Frederick Rodgers.

WRAGG, Private – George
Sherwood Foresters (Nottinghamshire and Derbyshire Regiment)

George was born in about 1898 at Crich. While serving with the Foresters he was reported as being wounded in France and his whereabouts became a mystery. Earlier in the war, during 1915, his brother John Edward had also been wounded

Derbyshire Times 19 May 1917

> Mr and Mrs Edward Wragg, "The Tors", Crich, late of Thurlow Booth Whatstandwell, would be grateful to receive further information as to the whereabouts and condition of their son, Pte George Wragg, No. 70545, Sherwood Foresters, "C" Co., 12th Platoon, B.E. France, who was reported as wounded on the 9th April last. They received a letter from his officer, but have heard nothing since.

George's brother John Edward is also on the Roll of Honour.

WRAGG, Driver – John

Royal Field Artillery

Born in 1892, John worked in the limestone quarry, as did his father. He enlisted at Ripley in September 1914 (at the same time as his brother Samuel) aged twenty-two, living at Folds Yard in Crich. Both brothers were in the Royal Field Artillery. He entered France in December 1914 and in May 1917 he was posted to Salonika. He was demobbed in March 1919, described as being sober, reliable and intelligent.

John's brother Samuel is also on the Roll of Honour.

WRAGG, Lance Corporal – John Edward

Northamptonshire Regiment

John was born in 1891, and like his father he worked in the limestone quarry. He married Emily Townsend in 1912. He entered France in July 1915 and the following October, was wounded.

Derbyshire Times 9 October 1915

WHATSTANDWELL MAN WOUNDED

Mr and Mrs Edward Wragg, of Hollow Booth, Whatstandwell, have received a note from their son Pte. Jno. Ed. Wragg, now in the 2nd Northants, who is now in hospital at Sunderland having been wounded in the recent great battle. He is 25 years of age, and has a wife and two children, who reside at Ripley. Mr Wragg, who also has another son (George) in the Sherwood Foresters is himself only 50 years of age, and has been in indifferent health for over a year, and during which time he has been unable to follow his occupation as a quarryman. He had a younger son (Tom) killed last year at the Oakerthorpe Colliery, Wingfield. The letter says: – "I landed here on Tuesday. I got wounded in the shoulder, and had a piece of shrapnel taken out on Friday, while I was in France. I got knocked out on the second day; it was dreadful. I did not see the charge but should have liked to have been in it; there are hundreds over here with me, who were in it."

About eighteen months later his brother George was also wounded.

George and John's brother-in-law was Charles Russell, who worked as a gardener at Alderwasley Hall. Charles Russell was awarded the Military Medal.

WRAGG, Private – John (Jack) Thomas ✝

Duke of Cornwall's Light Infantry

Born in 1893, Jack worked as a quarryman before joining the army. He entered France in July 1915 and was killed in action on 16th August 1917, aged twenty-one; he is remembered on the Tyne Cot Memorial.

Derbyshire Times 25 August 1917

ANOTHER CRICH LOSS

> On Friday news was received by Mr and Mrs John Wragg of Crich, that their son John Wragg (21), Duke of Cornwall's Light Infantry had been killed in action. Gunner Wragg had been on ten days leave during this month, and he looked quite happy and cheerful amongst his old Crich friends, who mourn his loss. He enlisted soon after the war began.

John is also remembered on the Memorial Tablet in the Wesleyan Chapel, Crich (see page 228).

WRAGG, Gunner – Luke

Royal Garrison Artillery

Born in about 1898, Luke was named after his grandfather. Before the war he worked as a farm labourer.

WRAGG, Driver – Samuel

Royal Field Artillery

Born in 1895, Samuel enlisted at Ripley in September 1914 with his brother John, both joining the Royal Field Artillery. He entered France in December 1914 and then was posted to Salonika in February 1916. In January 1919 he was hospitalised with amoebic dysentery and spent two months at the Northern General Hospital and Brighton Military Hospital. He was demobbed in March 1919.

Samuel's brother John is also on the Roll of Honour.

WRIGHT, Driver – Samuel

Regiment unknown

Born in 1879 at Bonsall, Samuel was the son of Samuel and Selina Wright. His mother died when he was an infant. In 1905 he married Alice Ethel Farnsworth of Crich Carr and they went to live at Whatstandwell, where he worked at a carter.

WYLES, Cadet – George

Royal Air Force

Photo Grace Mary Wyles

George, born in July 1900, was a son of the Crich Police Sergeant Robert John Wyles and his wife Elizabeth Amy. They lived at the police-house on the Common, Crich. On his service record it shows that he joined the RAF in July 1918 and was recorded as being fit for observer or pilot.

The photo was taken in 1911 with Sergeant Robert John Wyles standing at the front. Probably George is third from the left

YATES BROTHERS

George and John were the sons of were George and Mary Yates who lived at Plaistow Green, Crich.

YATES, Private – George

Regiment unknown

George born in about 1895 and was a labourer in a woodyard.

YATES, Private – John

Regiment unknown

John was born in about 1896.

YEOMANS, Private – Ernest

Sherwood Foresters (Nottinghamshire and Derbyshire Regiment)

Ernest was born in about 1886. He lived with his grandparents Anthony and Elizabeth Yeomans in Holloway for most of his life. As a young man he moved to live in Alfreton and married Rose Mackley on 21 July 1914 at Belper. He attested on 10 December 1915 and was with the Army Reserve until mobilized on 13 June 1916. However, his service life was short because he was discharged on medical grounds on 29 June 1916.

Appendices

Memorials around the parish to men who are on the Roll of Honour

Crich Roll of Honour 1923

Inside St. Mary's Church, Crich is a Roll of Honour to all the men who served. There are three hundred and ninety-five names on the Roll, of whom sixty-two were killed or died.

The criteria for being named on the Roll is unknown. Obviously men who were born or lived in the Parish of Crich are included, but there are some names with what appear to be tenuous links with the area and some where we have found no link at all.

There are several omissions and errors on this Roll, which hopefully have been corrected in this Memorial Book and on the new Roll of Honour which has been created for the 2014 centenary of the start of World War One.

Memorial Plaque

In St Mary's Church, Crich is a memorial plaque to sixty-two men who lost their lives in the Great War.

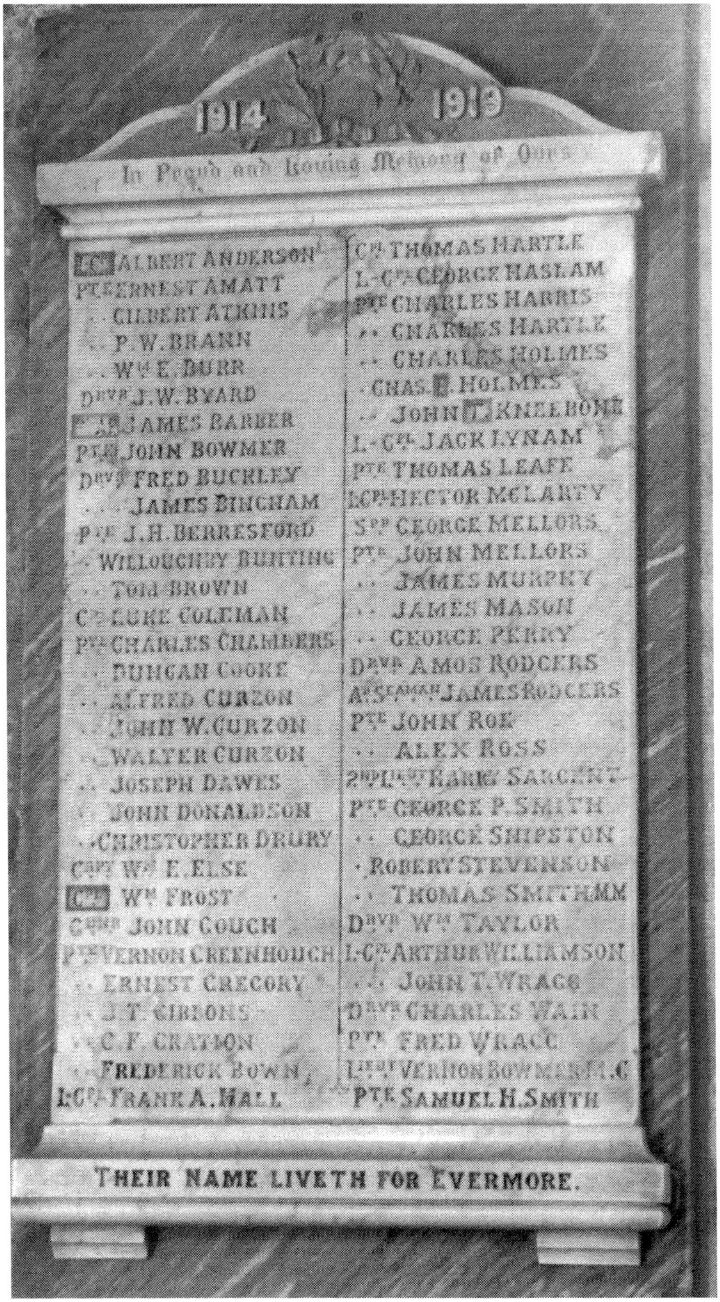

There are omissions on this plaque.

Dedication of the Memorial Plaque 21 March 1920

Programme David Smith

The Parish Church.
CRICH.

UNVEILING and DEDICATION
OF THE
Roll of Honour

Presented in memory of the Crich men who made the supreme Sacrifice in the Great War, 1914-1919.

To be Unveiled and Dedicated by the Right Reverend The
Bishop of Derby, D.D.,
at 10.30 a.m., on
Sunday, 21st March, 1920.

In Proud and Loving Memory of

Albert Anderson
Ernest Amatt
Gilbert Atkins
P. W. Brann
Wm. E. Burr
J. W. Byard
James Barber
John Bowmer
Fred Buckley
James Bingham
J. H. Berresford
Willoughby Bunting
Tom Brown
Luke Coleman
Charles Chambers
Duncan Cooke
Alfred Curzon
John W. Curzon
Walter Curzon
Joseph Dawes
John Donaldson
Christopher Drury
Wm. E. Bliss
Wm. Frost
John Gough
Vernon Greenhough
Ernest Gregory
J. T. Gibbons
G. F. Gratton
Frederick Bown
Thomas Hartle
George Haslam
Charles Harris
Charles Hartle
Charles Holmes
Chas. F. Holmes
John T. Knowbone
Jack Lynam
Thomas Leafe
Hector McClarty
George Mellows
John Mellows
James Murphy
James Mason
George Perry
Amos Rodgers
James Rodgers
John T. Roe
Alex. Ross
Harry Sargent
George Smith
George Shipston
Robert Stevenson
Thomas Smith
Wm. Taylor
Arthur Williamson
John T. Wragg
Charles Wain
Fred Wragg
Vernon Bowmer
Frank A. Hall
Samuel H. Smith

"Gone West."

When toil is ended, and the daylight dies,
A glory lingers in the western skies,
And whispers, "Rest!"
And, with a splendour, so divinely bright,
That Heaven and earth seem mingled in its light,
The Sun goes West.

Call him not "dead," who fell at Duty's feet,
And passed thro' Light, where earth and Heaven meet,
To radiant rest:
Call him not dead—thy fallen soldier-son,
But say: "The warfare waged—the victory won—
He has gone West!

But not to sleep in never-dawning dark,
With but a Cross, or withered flower, to mark
His shrine of rest:
Nay; but to wear the Victor's crown he won,
And rise again in glory, like the Sun,
He has gone West!"

SAMUEL K. COWAN, M.A.

The framed Roll of Honour in the church names all those who served.

Dedication of Crich War Memorial

Photo Colleen Hardwick

Masons Walter Fanton (left) and Isaac Coleman (right) working on the memorial

Photo Joyce Denton

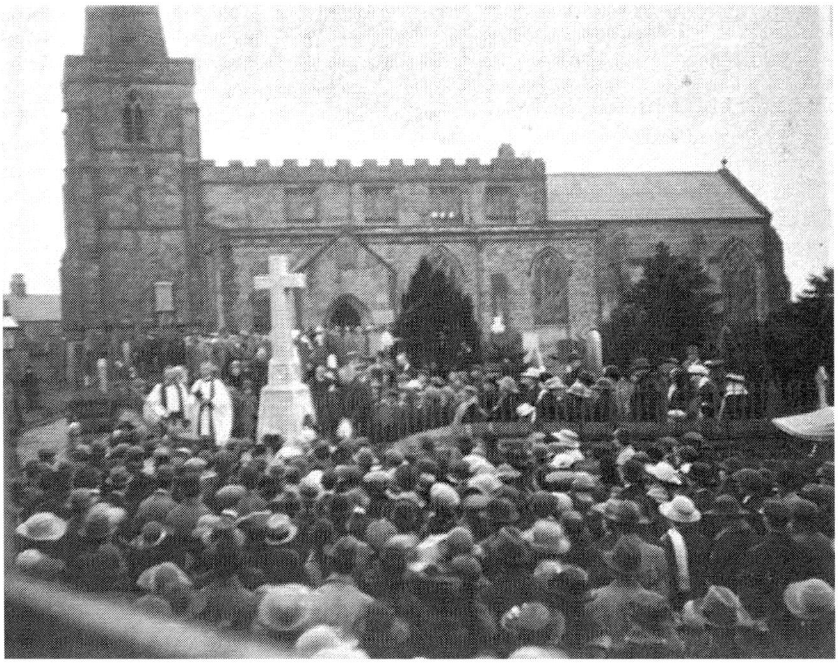

Service to dedicate the War Memorial outside St Mary's Church, Crich, c. 1920

Crich War Memorial

The War Memorial stands by the church gates.

There are sixty-three names on the Memorial.

Corporal W.L. Croft appears here but not on the plaque or the Roll of Honour inside the church.

Front Face

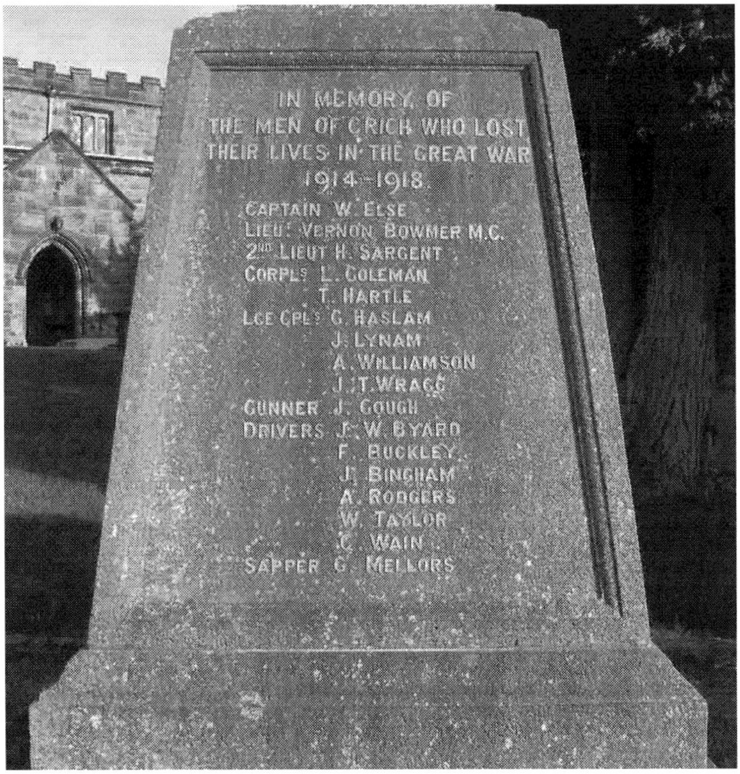

Captain	W. Else	Gunner	J. Gough
Lieut	Vernon Bowmer M.C.	Drivers	J.W. Byard
2nd Lieut	H. Sargent		F. Buckley
Corpls	L. Coleman		J. Bingham
	T. Hartle		A. Rodgers
Lce Cpls	G. Haslam		W. Taylor
	J. Lynam		C. Wain
	A. Williamson	Sapper	G. Mellors
	J.T. Wragg		

South-facing Panel

Privates	E Gregory	Privates	J. Mason
	J.T. Gibbons		G. Perry
	G.F. Gration		J. Roe
	C. Harris		A. Ross
	C. Hartle		G. P. Smith
	C. Holmes		G. Shipston
	C. Holmes		R. Stevenson
	J.T. Kneebone		T. Smith M.M.
	T. Leafe		F. Wragg
	H. McLarty		S.H. Smith
	J. Mellors	L. Cprl	F.A. Hall
	J. Murphy		

North-facing Panel

Seaman	J. Rodgers	Privates	C. Chambers
Lce. Cpl.	A. Anderson		D. Cooke
Privates	E. Amatt		A. Curzon
	G. Atkins		J.W. Curzon
	P.W. Brann		W. Curzon
	W. E. Burr *		J. Dawes
	J. Barber		J. Donaldson
	J. Bowmer		C. Drury
	F. Bown	Cpl.	W. Frost
	J.H. Berresford	Pte.	W. Greenhough
	W. Bunting	Cpl.	W.L. Croft
	T. Brown		

* William Burr did not die during the war, he was reported as "Missing in Action" but was later found to be a Prisoner of War in Germany.

Memorial Tablet
Wesleyan Chapel, Crich

James Mason
Alex Ross
Duncan Cook (Cooke)
Charles Hartle
Thomas Hartle
John Wragg
George Mellows (Mellors)

Wesleyan Chapel, Crich

Baptist Roll of Honour

There used to be a Roll of Honour in the Baptist Chapel in Crich Market Place. This was installed in February 1916 and contained the names of twenty-two of the scholars who were serving King and country. Sadly, the Roll has since disappeared.

Derby Daily Telegraph

14 February 1916

INTERESTING GATHERING AT CRICH

An event of unusual importance in connection with the Baptist Church and Sunday School at Crich which took place on Saturday, this being the presentation of a roll of honour, generously given by a prominent Derby Baptist member. Prior to the gift being transferred to the church and school, an excellent tea was partaken of at the Council School, this also being provided by the same gentleman, and his invitation to the members of the church and congregation was widely accepted.

After tea the company adjourned to the Baptist Church, and Mr S. Walker, of Derby, presided over a large gathering. Here the roll of honour was presented, this containing the names of 22 scholars who were serving King and country, being handed over by the chairman. Mr Walker complimented the church and school on the splendid response made by it to the country's call, and it was highly creditable, not only to the denomination, but to the village. He hoped the roll of honour will revive many happy associations of the past, and that the members would prepare to give, on return, a loyal and faithful welcome to our soldiers. Short addresses were given by Messrs. T. Ashton and G. Lander, representing the church, and Messrs. H. Dyson and A. Haslam on behalf of the Sunday School, after which a sincere vote of thanks was conveyed to the gentleman presenting the roll of honour. Mr A. Morgan, of Derby, in a brief address, complimented the Ladies Committee on the excellent spread they had provided. During the evening the choir rendered the anthem "The House of the Lord", "Wellingborough," and "The Banner of Christ." In replying to a vote of thanks for the president Mr Walker expressed the meeting's appreciation of Mr W. Henry Cowlishaw for preparing the roll of honour.

Memorial Plaque outside Lea Mills

IN MEMORY OF THE MEN WHO WENT FROM LEA MILLS
AND DIED FOR THEIR COUNTRY IN THE GREAT WAR 1914 – 1918

L/Cpl Hubert Petts 10th Sherwood Foresters St Eloi March 3rd 1916

Pte Arthur Brown 1/6th Sherwood Foresters Neuville St Eloi April 17th 1916

L/Cpl Wilfred Keeling 10th Sherwood Foresters Contalmaison July 7th 1916

Sergt Fred Fox 5th Dorsets Arras Aug 5th 1916

Pte Josiah Fletcher 1/6th Sherwood Foresters Doullens Sept 3rd 1916

Pte Bertram Sheldon 1/6th Sherwood Foresters St Eloi Oct 8th 1916

Pte Harry Alfred Thorpe 1/6th Sherwood Foresters Thiepval Oct 9th 1916

Pte John William Poyser 6th York & Lancasters Beaumont Hamel Jan 17th 1917

Pte Charles Francis Holmes 10th K O Yorks L Inf Tincourt Feb 6th 1918

Pte Fred Gregory 18th Welsh Regt Aire Dec 1918

"They were a wall unto us both by night and by day"

Sawmills War Memorial

The memorial was moved from the old Sawmills Chapel and re-sited in Sawmills Village Hall in December 2013 when it was also rededicated.

Some of the names are also on the Crich Roll of Honour and War Memorial.

Harry Boden
Ebenezer Boden
Arthur Cecil Hinton
James Murphy
Frederick Rodgers (Wragg?)
H. Rodgers (Amos Rodgers?)
James Rodgers
Charles Wain
John White

It is believed that F. Rodgers is Frederick Wragg, half-brother to Amos and James Rodgers.

The following are also on the Crich Roll of Honour.

James Murphy (page 140); Amos Rodgers (page 157); James Rodgers (page 157);
Frederick Rodgers – recorded as Frederick Wragg (page 213);
Charles Wain (page 194); John White (page 198)

Harry Boden, Ebenezer Boden and Arthur Cecil Hinton are not on the Crich Roll of Honour.

BODEN BROTHERS

Ebenezer and Harry were the sons of George and Annie Boden, who lived at Bullbridge and Sawmills. Their mother Annie who was born in Crich, died in 1901. Both brothers are also remembered on the Wingfield Park War Memorial (see page 233).

BODEN, Rifleman – Ebenezer James ✝

King's Royal Rifle Corps

Ebenezer enlisted at Derby in March 1915, aged twenty-nine, a coal miner of Sawmills. He died of his wounds on 18th August 1916 and is remembered on the Thiepval Memorial.

BODEN, Private – Harry ✝

Sherwood Rangers Yeomanry

Sherwood Foresters (Nottinghamshire and Derbyshire Regiment)

Harry enlisted in March 1917 aged eighteen, while working as a winder. He lived at Meadow Cottage, Sawmills. Originally he was with the Sherwood Rangers Yeomanry before being posted to the Sherwood Foresters. He was reported missing on 21st March 1918 and is remembered on the Arras Memorial. It was noted in the records that he was the brother of George Boden of Meadow Cottage, Sawmills.

HINTON, Private – Arthur Cecil ✝

Sherwood Foresters (Nottinghamshire and Derbyshire Regiment)

Arthur was born at Staveley in about 1895; his parents were Joseph and Elizabeth Hinton. In 1911 he was working on William Flint's farm at Wingfield Park, Fritchley; William was his grandfather. He enlisted in August 1914 at Derby aged twenty and entered France in September 1915. In June 1917 he was wounded by a shell which fractured his leg, and on 7th February 1918, he was killed and is buried in Grevillers British Cemetery. His personal effects of cigarette case, cap badge and belt were sent to his mother. He is also remembered on the Wingfield Park War Memorial (see page 233).

Smith's Cemetery, Wingfield Park

In Wingfield Park, between Fritchley and South Wingfield, is a small private cemetery. Within the cemetery there is a War Memorial to men who died during the two World Wars. Some of the Great War names are also on the Crich and Sawmills memorials.

HONOUR WITHOUT STAIN

1914 – 1918

CAPT. BERNARD RIDLEY WINTHROP SMITH

PTE. WILLIAM BINNIE

PTE. ROBERT HARRISON

PTE. ARTHUR CECIL HINTON

PTE. ROBERT STEVENSON

SGT. JOHN TAYLOR

PTE. EBENEZER JAMES BODEN

PTE. HARRY BODEN

PTE. HAROLD COOPER

"GREATER LOVE HATH NO MAN THAN THIS,

THAT A MAN LAY DOWN HIS LIFE

FOR HIS FRIENDS."

Sir Francis Nicholas Smith, of South Wingfield Hall, left a legacy for the upkeep of this beautiful cemetery. One family member buried there is Bernard Ridley Winthrop-Smith who was killed during WWI.

He was born in 1882 at Duffield and was educated at Carters, Farnborough, Eton and Trinity College, Cambridge. He took part in the 1905 Oxford-Cambridge boat race before joining the Scots Guards as a Second Lieutenant. He became a full Lieutenant in 1910.

Bernard R. W. Smith.

In 1913 he was seconded to the Colonial Office in the East African Protectorates, but he returned home on the commencement of hostilities and was one of the first to enter France in 1914. During the November of that year, at Ypres with his platoon, he attacked a German trench and while on open ground was struck by shrapnel which fractured his skull.

While receiving treatment at Boulogne Military Hospital, with his parents at his bedside, he died without regaining consciousness on 15 November 1914. On the day of his death he was made up to the rank of Captain.

His body was returned to England and buried in the private cemetery in Wingfield Park.

Alderwasley War Memorial

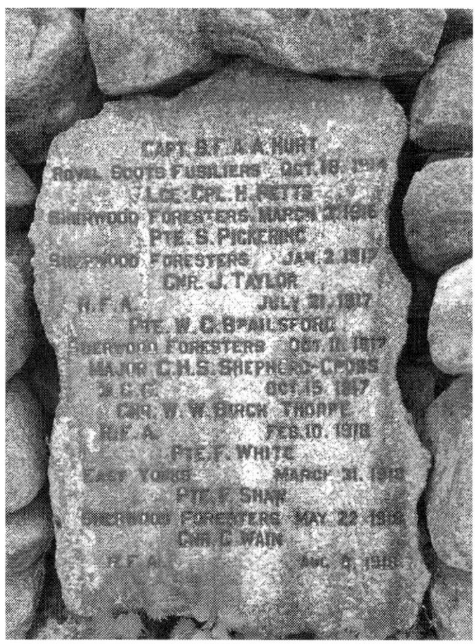

Capt S. F. A. A. Hurt
Royal Scots Fusiliers Oct. 18. 1914

Lce. Cpl. H. Petts *
Sherwood Foresters. March 3.1916

Pte. S. Pickering
Sherwood Foresters. Jan. 2. 1917

Gnr. J. Taylor *
R.F.A. July 21. 1917

Pte. W. C. Brailsford
Sherwood Foresters. Oct. 11. 1917

Major C. H. S. Shepherd-Cross
M.G.C. Oct. 15.1917

Gnr. W. W. Birch Thorpe
R.F.A. Feb 10.1918

Pte. F. White
East Yorks March 31. 1918

Pte. F. Shaw
Sherwood Foresters. May 22. 1918

Gnr. C. Wain *
R.F.A. Aug 8. 1918

* On the Crich Roll of Honour

Group photographs which include men who are on the Roll of Honour

Crich Sherwood Foresters Recruits 19 October 1914

Taken in the garden of *Roskeen,* home of Dr Macdonald, whose son Ian is the officer on the photograph.

Photo Crich Heritage Partnership

Ian P. Macdonald; William Burr; William Curzon; John Walker; Nelson Martin; Jack Kneebone; William Frost; Walter (Wammy) Mellors; Jack Cauldwell; Jack Porter; George Perry; Noble Tomlinson

Nelson Martin was underage at this time. Later he enlisted with the Seaforth Highlanders.

Crich Sherwood Foresters Recruits
30 October 1914

Uniformed Crich recruits in the grounds of *Roskeen* on Surgery Lane, Crich.

Photo Crich Heritage Partnership

Included with these recruits are: Ian Macdonald; Billy Curzon; Jack Porter; Walter (Wammy) Mellors; Jack Kneebone; Billy Burr; Noble Tomlinson; Tom Coleman; Billy Frost; Luke Coleman; Jack Cauldwell; George Perry. It is believed that John Roe, brothers Herbert and Steven Bollington (and possibly John) are also amongst this group.

Alderwasley Cricket Club 1910

Several of the players went off to war and are on the Roll of Honour.

Photo Miss E.D. Bunting

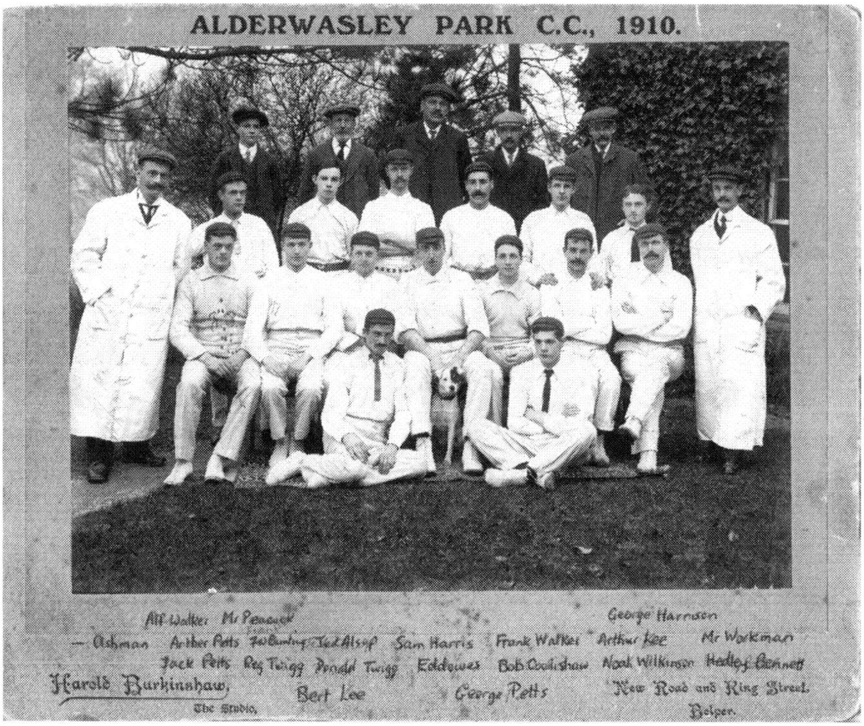

Back Row – Alf Walker, Mr Peacock, George Harrison, (two unknown)

Standing – ? Ashman, Arthur Petts, Frank Bunting, Ted Alsop, Sam Harris, Frank Walker, Arthur Lee, Mr Workman

Seated – Jack Petts, Reg Twigg, Donald Twigg, ? Eddowes, Bob Cowlishaw, Noah Wilkinson, Hedley Bennett

Front – Bert Lee, George Petts

Brass Bands

Crich Brass Band, just before WWI c.1910

Several of the men who served played with Crich Brass Band before and after the war. Sadly no names were recorded on this photograph, but it is presumed that it contains some of the men who went into the forces.

Whatstandwell Brass Band c. 1920

Arthur Mason is third from the left on the font row

Similarly some of the men played with the Whatstandwell Brass Band.

Crich Football Club c. 1912

Taken outside the Cliff Inn.

Several of the players are on the Roll of Honour.

Photo: Sue Worboys

Back row: John Bowmer, Alfred Bowmer, ?, Fred Brown (Jottie), Blucher Bowmer, Charlie Harper, Jim Wragg (goalie), Donald Hawkes, George Booker, ?, Don Nadin, ?,

Front row: Vernon Bowmer, Cyril Booth, Harry Lynam, ? Harrison

Crich Football Club 1912 – 13

Many of the players went off to war.

Photo Terry Daniels

W. R. CLAYTON S. BERRISFORD F. DAWES S. HOLMES T. BOWMER J. BOWMER W. SMITH S. BOWMER J. BUCKLEY J. WETTON
V. BOWMER P. S. SMITH D. P. HAWKES (CHAIRMAN) J. LEAFE (CAPTAIN) G. S. HOUSLEY (HON. SEC.) J. BOWMER G. BOLLINGTON
H. HARRISON F. H. BRUMWELL (VICE-CAPTAIN) CAVENDISH CUP J. C. HARTSHORNE H. HOLMES
CAVENDISH CUP MEDALS DERBYSHIRE CUP MEDALS (RUNNERS UP)

CRICH FOOTBALL CLUB
1912-13

Cavendish Cup

Back Row: W.R. Clayton, S. Berrisford, F. Dawes, S. Holmes, T. Bowmer, J. Bowmer, W. Smith, S. Bowmer, J. Buckley, J. Wetton

Seated: V. Bowmer, P.S. Smith, D.P. Hawkes (Chairman), J. Leafe (Captain), G.S. Housley (Hon. Sec.), J. Bowmer, G. Bollington

Front: H. Harrison, F.H. Brumwell (Vice Captain), J.C. Hartshorne, H. Holmes

Whatstandwell Football Club 1922-23

Photo Simon Johnson

The Whatstandwell Football Team of 1923 contained many of the men who served in the war and are on the Roll of Honour.

Back row (from the left) – J. Roe (Treasurer); B. Flint (Captain); J. Lee; A. Shaw; R. Carlisle; C. Greenough

Middle Row – M. Jackson; J. Bowmer; H. Taylor; S. Cowlishaw: A. Mason; J. Worthy; A. Walker; G. Cowlishaw

Front Row – F. Cowlishaw; J. Mountney; H. Ludlam; J. Batterley; J. Byard; G. Bollington; R. Barber; H. Cowlishaw; F. Fearn (Secretary)

Lea Mills Postcard 1

A set of three postcards (without names) was produced by Lea Mills showing employees who enlisted early in the war. We have tried to identify every one of them.

Lea Mills Postcard 2

Lea Mills Postcard 3

Belgian Refugees

Photo from a private album

Belgian refugees outside the Jovial Dutchman c. 1915.

It is known that the De Ridder and Maes families lived in the village and that their children attended school there. Two of the men from these families are on the Crich Roll of Honour – they were possibly Belgian Agents.

Fritchley also had Belgian refugees including Francis Schonken, who made and sold highly decorated and carved furniture.

Advert from the Crich Illustrated Guide c. 1915

Recruitment

Pay

Propaganda

Medals

Fund-raising

Home Support

Recruitment in WWI

1914: FIRST VOLUNTEERS

At the start of the war the Army consisted of the Regular Army, a Territorial Force and the Special Reserve. There was no conscription – joining the army was entirely voluntary. Recruitment during August 1914 was high and this gained even more momentum in early September following the British retreat at the Battle of Mons. By January 1915 about a million men had volunteered. These men could choose which regiment they would like to join.

1915: VOLUNTEER ARMY

Men volunteered for a variety of reasons: unemployment; some employers "encouraged" men to sign up; Poor Law Guardians would occasionally refuse to support fit military-aged men; and many who thought it their patriotic duty.

In 1915 the number of men of military age was five-and-a-half million; with about half-a-million men reaching military age each year. By September 1915 two-and-a-quarter million men were in the forces and one-and-a-half million were in reserved occupations. Of the remaining men, two in five were of such poor health that they were unsuitable for military service.

After the Dardanelles Expedition the number of volunteers fell off alarmingly. This is when the huge recruitment poster campaign began. Public meetings and newspapers recounted German atrocities, and men were put under the threat of "public shame". Members of the women's suffrage movement were encouraged to give out white feathers, as a sign of cowardice to men of military age in their community – hoping to shame them into enlisting. This is the reason the Silver War Badge was introduced, to protect men who were ineligible or had been discharged.

Lord Derby was very active in encouraging volunteers through the "Pals Battalions" where men from the same factory, community, club, or similar joined and served together. Sadly, this meant a community could lose all its military-aged men in a single day. It was promised that bachelors would be called up before married men.

1916-1918 CONSCRIPTION

The Lord Derby scheme had too few bachelors volunteering, so in January 1916 a Military Service Bill was introduced conscripting unmarried or widowed men aged between eighteen and forty-one into the armed forces. In May 1916 conscription was extended to include married men.

Even with conscription the numbers of men enlisting was not enough owing to the men required for essential work at home and those who were in poor health. During the period from 1917 to 1918 about 35% of men examined were unfit for military service. In 1918 the British Army had fewer men than in 1917, and about half the infantry was aged nineteen or younger.

EXEMPTIONS

Men who had been "called up" could appeal against their conscription at a local Military Services Tribunal. These appeals could be based on work of national importance, business or domestic hardship, medical unfitness, and conscientious objection. By the end of June 1916 about three quarters of a million men had applied for exemption. Occasionally the tribunals granted temporary exemptions which were reviewed regularly.

A common misconception is that most of those seeking exemption were conscientious objectors; in fact, only around 2% were appealing on grounds of conscience. Around seven thousand conscientious objectors were granted non-combatant duties, about three thousand had to work in special work camps and around six thousand were imprisoned.

RECRUITMENT POSTERS

Public announcements

High Peak News

22 August 1914

THE KING'S MESSAGE TO THE ARMY

The following message was issued by King George V to the army on the departure to the front:–

BUCKINGHAM PALACE

Aug. 9, 1914

> You are leaving home to fight for the safety and honour of my Empire.
>
> Belgium, whose country we are pledged to defend, has been attacked, and France is about to be invaded by the same powerful foe.
>
> I have implicit confidence in you, my soldiers. Duty is your watchword, and I know your duty will be nobly done.
>
> I shall follow your every movement with deepest interest, and mark with eager satisfaction your daily progress; indeed your welfare will never be absent from my thoughts.
>
> I pray God to bless you and guard you and bring you back victorious.

GEORGE R. I.

LORD KITCHENER'S ADVICE TO SOLDIERS

In a remarkably frank memorandum to our troops Lord Kitchener warns them against excesses, and to exercise courtesy and kindness towards the peoples amongst whom they are to campaign. He concludes with the words, "Do your duty bravely. Fear God, and Honour the King."

Soldiers' pay

Derbyshire Times 19 Sept 1914

NEW PAY FOR SOLDIERS' WIVES

Prime Minister's Statement

Speaking in the House of Commons on Tuesday, the Prime Minister said that with regard to soldiers' separation allowances the Government had decided during the continuance of the war to adopt a scale based on a minimum allowance of 12s 6d a week, as against 11s 6d now. On that basis a wife with one child would receive 15s as compared with 12s 10d under the old scale; with two children 17s 6d against 14s 7d; with three children 20s against 16s 4d; and four children 22s against 17s 6d. The special allowance for London of 3s 6d would remain unaltered.

They also proposed to pay a separation allowance in the case of relatives – mothers and sisters. Where the soldier made an allotment the State subsidy would be proportionate and on the scale he had just mentioned.

As regards the Navy, it had been decided to grant separation allowance to wives and children and details of the scheme would be announced as soon as possible. In both cases the allowance would be paid weekly through the Post Office. The question of pensions was still under consideration.

Mr Austen Chamberlain asked whether the Government would consider the suggestion of continuing to the widow for a certain period after the decease of her husband the allowance she was entitled to as a wife.

The Prime Minister said that would be considered sympathetically.

Mr John Ward asked whether these facts would be circulated among all the recruiting committees.

The Prime Minister said he would undertake to circulate the information among the army and navy the exact list of scales the existing ones being placed side by side. The new scales would date from October 1st.

Note: 1s (one shilling) = 5p

6d (six pence) = 2½p

War Service for Women

Derbyshire Times 27 March 1915

WAR SERVICE FOR WOMEN

In order to meet both the present and the future needs of national industry during the war, the Government wish to obtain particulars of the women available, with or without previous training, for paid employment. Accordingly, they invite all women who are prepared if needed to take paid employment of any kind – industrial, agricultural, clerical, etc. – to enter themselves upon the Register of Women for War Service, which is being prepared by the Board of Trade Labour Exchanges.

Any woman living in a town where there is a Labour Exchange can register by going there in person. If she is not near a Labour Exchange she can get a form of registration from the Local Agency of the Unemployment Fund.

The object of registration is to find out what reserve force of women's labour, trained or untrained, can be available if required.

Any woman who by working helps to release a man or to equip a man for fighting does national war service.

WWI Medals

Men from the parish who served in the war were often awarded medals. The medals were for bravery and service to their country. The following medals were awarded.

MILITARY CROSS MC

The Military Cross is awarded to officers and is the third-level military decoration. It is granted in recognition of an act, or acts, of exemplary gallantry during active operations against the enemy on land.

The award dates from 28 December 1914 and is for commissioned officers of the substantive rank of Captain or below, and for Warrant Officers.

DISTINGUISHED CONDUCT MEDAL DCM

The Distinguished Conduct Medal is a high level award for bravery. It is a second-level military decoration awarded to other ranks of the British Army.

MILITARY MEDAL MM

The Military Medal was awarded to the Army and other services, below commissioned rank, for bravery in battle on land.

The award dates from 25 March 1916. It was the 'other ranks' equivalent to the Military Cross, which was only awarded to commissioned officers. The medal ranked below the Distinguished Conduct Medal.

CAMPAIGN MEDALS

These were the 1914 Star, the 1914–15 Star, the British War Medal and the Victory Medal.

The most frequent combinations are "trios" and "pairs". Trios are made up of one or other of the 1914 or 1914-15 Stars (they could not be awarded together), the British War Medal and the Victory Medal. The three-medal combination was usually referred to as "Pip, Squeak and Wilfred". Pairs were generally for servicemen who joined the war after 1915, and are the British War Medal with the Victory Medal, commonly known as "Mutt and Jeff". If only one medal was issued it would be the British War Medal. "Pip Squeak and Wilfred" were Daily Mirror cartoon characters and "Mutt and Jeff" were from the San Francisco Chronicle.

1914 STAR

The 1914 Star, sometimes called the Mons Star, was issued to officers and men of the British forces who served in France or Belgium between 5 August and midnight of 22/23 November 1914. The first date is the day after Britain's declaration of war and the second date marks the end of the First Battle of Ypres.

1914 STAR WITH CLASP

This was often known as Clasp and Roses. The Clasp was awarded to those who had operated within range of enemy mobile artillery between 5 August and midnight of 22/23 November 1914.

When the ribbon bar was worn alone, recipients of the clasp to the medal wore a small silver rosette on the ribbon bar.

1914-15 STAR

This medal was issued to officers and men who served in any theatre of the war between 5 August 1914 and 31 December 1915 (other than those who had already qualified for the 1914 Star).

Recipients also received the British War Medal and Victory Medal – this medal was never awarded singly.

The soldier's regiment and number are inscribed on the flat rear face of the Star.

If a man did not qualify for a 1914 or 1914–15 Star, he did not see service in a theatre of war before 1916.

BRITISH WAR MEDAL

The medal was awarded to any member of the fighting forces who left the UK while on service. It did not matter whether they entered a theatre of war or not.

All men who served in the main theatres of war qualified for this medal, as did those who left the UK for service in places such as India and Palestine.

VICTORY MEDAL

This medal was awarded to all those who entered a theatre of war, so that every recipient of the Victory Medal also qualified for the British War Medal, but not the other way round. For example, if a soldier served in India he would get the British War Medal but not the Victory Medal. All three armed services were eligible.

SILVER WAR BADGE

The Silver War Badge was issued to those who had been honourably discharged due to wounds or sickness during the war. The recipient need not have served abroad. The badge was first issued in September 1916, and came with an official certificate of entitlement.

The sterling silver badge was to be worn on the right breast while in civilian dress; it was forbidden to wear it on a military uniform. It had been the practice of some women to present white feathers to apparently able-bodied young men who were not wearing the King's uniform. The badge indicated that the wearer had served their country.

Non-UK medals which men from Crich were awarded included:

MEDALIA BARBATIE SI CREDINTA

During the war Roumania was associated with the Allied powers and this award was also given to British non-commissioned officers for acts of bravery in the Eastern Theatre of War. It was awarded in three classes – 1st class in gold, 2nd class in silver and 3rd class in bronze. For military service the medal was awarded with crossed swords.

The words 'Barbatie Si Credinta' have a literal translation of "Manhood and Faith". In the context of this award "Manhood" means courage and bravery and "Faith" means faith in God.

Prince of Wales National Relief Fund

With so many of its men serving in the forces it was little wonder that the community was active in fund-raising. The Prince of Wales National Relief Fund was one of the charities which was well supported.

The Times, 7th August 1914

> Buckingham Palace - all must realise that the present time of deep anxiety will be followed by one of considerable distress among the people of this country least able to bear it. We must earnestly pray that their suffering may be neither long nor bitter, but we cannot wait until the need presses heavily upon us. The means of relief must be ready in our hands. To allay anxiety will go some way to stay distress. A National Fund has been founded, and I am proud to act as its Treasurer. My first duty is to ask for generous and ready support, and I know that I shall not ask in vain. At such a moment we all stand by one another, and it is to the heart of the British people that I confidently make this earnest appeal.
>
> Edward, Prince of Wales

This appeal, made in the first days of the war, was necessary as a result of the rapid mobilisation of the British Army following Germany's invasion of Belgium. The Army was well below war strength and army reservists were quickly called back to the 'colours' at extremely short notice. This caught thousands of families totally unaware and often created significant difficulties for dependants. Other areas of the population faced extreme hardship, especially those involved in trade with Germany who lost their employment overnight, the many mill workers placed on short time and the East Coast fishing industry. Sylvia Pankhurst wrote at the time:

> *There was terrible confusion, masses of women did not know how or where to apply for their allowances, and waited long and vainly for them to come through automatically.*
>
> *The purchasing power of large sections of the people had dwindled to zero; to be work-less then meant literal starvation. The small unemployment benefit obtainable under the national insurance applied only to a few trades. It was an axiom of the poor law practice that relief, save the shelter of the workhouse, must not be granted to the "able-bodied" and their dependents. Even had poor law procedure allowed it, the guardians had not the funds to cope with this great wave of unemployment.*

There was no extra government funding to help those in distress the whole burden fell on the public via the Prince of Wales Fund.

On the 8th August 1914 the Times reported that the Fund would be used *"both for the distress arising from the war among the families of soldiers and sailors ... as well as from industrial distress."* Within a week the Fund had raised a million pounds (equivalent to over £50,000,000 in today's money).

In August 1914 Fritchley Friends gathered together in the Meeting House to consider how far they could assist in relief work in connection with the Prince of Wales Fund. They wrote the following letter –

Fritchley, 10th of eighth month, 1914

The following Friends give in their names to assist in the relief work about to be undertaken in connection with the "Prince of Wales National Relief Fund" provided that the organization having control of the same is not under military direction and that our doing so is not to be understood as being in any way a substitute for military service or as an 'alternative service', an expression in the circular asking us to undertake such work, we regret our services are tendered simply with the desire to meet an unusual degree of distress regardless of its cause. One or two of our members have had to bear a little hard judgement from some of our neighbours because of being obliged to refuse to take part in the 'Red Cross' work. We feel that the Red Cross Society working under military direction is a direct help to military operations. We desire earnestly to do all we can to relieve suffering wherever it is, but feel restrained from in any way acting in conjunction with the military authorities.

It was at this time that a number of young men from Crich, who opposed the attitude of the local Quakers, damaged the shop of Thomas Davidson, a minister of Fritchley Quakers, and they verbally abused several members of the Meeting. On the whole, the position of Friends regarding the war was not understood by the villagers, but it was accepted as yet another part of the make-up of this respected but uniquely religious body who were prepared to carry their beliefs into their daily life and to take the consequences.

Ref: "The Quakers of Fritchley" by Walter Lowndes (1986)

Workers at local factories and mills supported the fund.

Belper News 25 January 1915

AMBERGATE

£60 FOR THE WAR FUND

In company with the employees of most industries in the country when war broke out, the employees of the Ambergate Wire Works agreed to the deduction of a weekly contribution from their wages on behalf of the Prince of Wales' National Relief Fund, and up to the end of last year the sum of £60 had been contributed.

Official postcards were sold, a halfpenny going to the Fund for each card sold

National Egg Collection

Crich Parish, along with other parishes, was very supportive of its serving men. Crich Knitting Guild sent postcards and postal orders to the men, and the community supported fund-raising activities both locally and nationally. One call for help enabled a large number of residents, both adults and children, to support wounded servicemen. That was the *National Egg Collection* appeal which was started in August 1915. It was estimated that 200,000 eggs per week were needed nationally for the wounded servicemen. The local organiser was Miss Olive Marden-Smedley, of Lea Green, whose father was the Managing Director of Lea Mills. Sub-depots were set up in all the parishes, including Crich, to aid their collection with the intention of collecting a million eggs a month for the wounded.

Derby Daily Telegraph Friday, 30 April 1915

> The National Egg Collection for Wounded Soldiers and Sailors is developing on a scale which the promoters can scarcely have anticipated. Something like 200,000 new-laid eggs are being contributed every week by well-disposed people at home, and distributed among wounded and invalid soldiers. About ten thousand per day are being shipped to the base hospitals in France, and the War Office, needless to say, have expressed their full approval and warm appreciation of what is being done.

Derby Daily Telegraph Thursday, 6 May 1915

DERBYSHIRE ROYAL INFIRMARY

> The work of the Infirmary was constantly growing. This year they had received nearly 400 wounded soldiers, and if there was one single object which demanded our charity at the present time it was the care of the wounded soldiers.
>
> The Mayor, in thanking the ladies, said they were pleased to do what they could for the infirmary. The Mayoress and himself were determined that it should be a record year. He hoped the ladies would secure even the smallest donation, and instanced the value of little things, the success of the egg collection, whereby 2,168 had been obtained on three Fridays for the Infirmary and other institutions.

During February 1917 there was a special 'Children's Week' when 300,000 eggs were collected. This was at a time when the weather was very bad and eggs were scarce. At times a lack of food for the poultry created problems and hens were slaughtered.

Derby Daily Telegraph Thursday, 7 June 1917

NO NEED FOR SLAUGHTERING HENS

> The National Egg Collection for the Wounded have received from Captain Charles Bathurst, M.P., of the Ministry of Food, the following statement: –
>
> There is no sufficient justification for the wholesale slaughtering of laying hens, although no doubt there is room for a large reduction in the head of male stock. A certain amount of cereal food of an inferior kind and quality ought still to be available for laying hens, as well as a large amount of garden and other refuse which is now wasted.

By January 1918 the scheme had sent over seven million eggs to UK hospitals and over twenty-five million to hospitals abroad. However, there was a national egg shortage which had become serious because people had become panicked by orders coming from the Food Controller and the Board of Agriculture, and had disposed of their chickens. The War Office asked for a further quarter of a million eggs per month over and above the existing supplies. An appeal was launched to reach a target of forty million eggs. People were asked to sacrifice their own eggs for the wounded soldiers and sailors. Poultry farmers could despatch the eggs for free to the Central London Depot, or to one of the local depots. People who had their own chickens were asked to give a tenth of their eggs each week and those without chickens were encouraged to give money so that eggs could be bought.

Derby Daily Telegraph Thursday, 26 September 1918

> Forty million new laid eggs for the wounded have been collected in Great Britain and Ireland by the National Egg Collection through its various depots now numbering 2,100.

Tobacco Fund

Parcels were regularly sent out to the serving men from their families, the parish, employers, local and national organisations. The contents of the parcels were very varied and wide-ranging, but one item seemed to be most welcomed and that was tobacco.

The Duke of Devonshire, in his capacity as Lord Lieutenant of the County, together with the mayors of Derby, Chesterfield and Ilkeston set up a fund to send a mixed Christmas parcel containing food, candles, boracic ointment, vaseline, dubbin, shaving soap and other items to each Derbyshire man serving in the Royal Navy or regiments at the Front. Before the end of November despatches of the parcels, each worth 5s 6d, had been made to the men serving in the Dardanelles and in the eastern theatre of war. Separate funds were organised by local communities to send Christmas boxes to their own fighting men.

The *Derbyshire Times* was quick to point out that the Derbyshire Christmas boxes did not contain any tobacco and urged its readers not to forget its Tobacco Fund. They wrote:

> There are many reasons why our Soldiers should be kept well supplied with smokes. The first is because nothing comforts them so. Nothing soothes their nerves in the same way, and nothing they enjoy so much. There are, however, other reasons that could be given such as from a hygienic point of view. A trench cannot be the sweetest place imaginable, even with the greatest care for cleanliness, and the smell of tobacco helps. Remember we are trying to help our readers in this duty of keeping our soldiers supplied. We have arranged that all tobacco and cigarettes sent through our Fund goes duty free, and further-more we save all the trouble and cost of package and postage. You must allow for a little delay in your contribution reaching its destination, as the order has to go through Guernsey.
>
> Contributors can make their choice of any of the following parcels: –
>
> (501) – 70 Wills "Woodbines" Cigarettes
>
> (502) – 50 Martins "Arf-a-Mo" Cigarettes
>
> (503) – 40 Wills "Gold Flake" Cigarettes
>
> (504) – 30 Martins "Glory Boys"
>
> (505) – 25 Cigarettes, in a nice slide pocket case
>
> (506) – 6 short "Panatella" Cigars in case
>
> (507) – 4 Ounces Tobacco
>
> If you sent any of these "smokes" to the Front yourself, the postage alone would cost you 1s. Through our Fund the shilling covers both the cost of the "smokes" and the postage. But it does more than this, as out of every shilling subscribed

by our readers, we will set aside one penny, with which we will send parcels of "smokes" to British Prisoners of War in Germany, who are sadly in need of comforts.

Readers can send in any amount in advance for shilling parcels to be sent every week to their friends. Thus, if 10s were sent, it would provide 70 "Woodbines" every week by post and thus give the soldier 10 cigarettes every day for ten weeks, in addition to which some lonely prisoner in Germany would benefit to the extent of one penny for every shilling subscribed.

There will be no sixpenny personal parcels but readers can send any number of sixpences to our General Fund, for our local regiments as hitherto.

In sending subscriptions for personal parcels, please give fullest particulars, including name and number, rank, Company, Battalion and Regiment. Say which parcel you prefer by giving the reference number, 501, 502, 503, 504, 505, 506, or 507 according to the list.

Our General Fund is continued and the six-penny parcels, with the post-cards, are sent for as our general distributions will permit.

The newspapers regularly carried letters from local soldiers at the front requesting not only cigarettes but also mouth organs, footballs, playing cards, batteries for electric pocket lamps and even someone to send them letters. Many of the appeals cited boredom when out of the front line as the reason. Letters were also published from sincerely grateful soldiers when their appeals were met. The receipt of local newspapers from home was always very welcome and *The High Peak News* assisted this by printing in the masthead of the front page the words "A Piece of String and a Stamp will carry this to a Friend in the Trenches". There were printed dotted lines for the sender to fill in the name of the serviceman, his Company, Regiment and whether he was a member of the British or Mediterranean Expeditionary Forces.

OUT OF ACTION

WOUNDS

ILLNESS

PRISONERS

Voluntary Aid Detachment

Many of the wounded men on the Crich Roll of Honour had a period of convalescence at a Voluntary Aid Detachment (VAD) Hospital, although this was not necessarily close to home. During WWI there were about three thousand such hospitals set up in large houses, school buildings, church halls, institutes and other large buildings. The area around Crich had several VAD hospitals which were supported by the community. They were at South Wingfield, Belper, Cromford, Matlock and Darley Dale. Derbyshire had thirty-seven such hospitals established throughout the war.

These auxiliary hospitals were attached to central military hospitals – the patients remained under military control while convalescing. They were administered by Red Cross county directors and usually staffed by:

- a commandant, who was in charge of the hospital (except for medical and nursing services)
- a quartermaster, who was responsible for the receipt, custody and issue of articles in the provision store
- a matron, who directed the work of the nursing staff
- members of the local voluntary aid detachment, who were trained in first aid and home nursing

Members of the VAD who had received training in first aid and nursing came to the fore. They cleaned and prepared the rooms which were to become hospital wards. Local doctors provided the medical care and the VADs were supervised by one or more registered nurses.

British Red Cross Museum and Archives

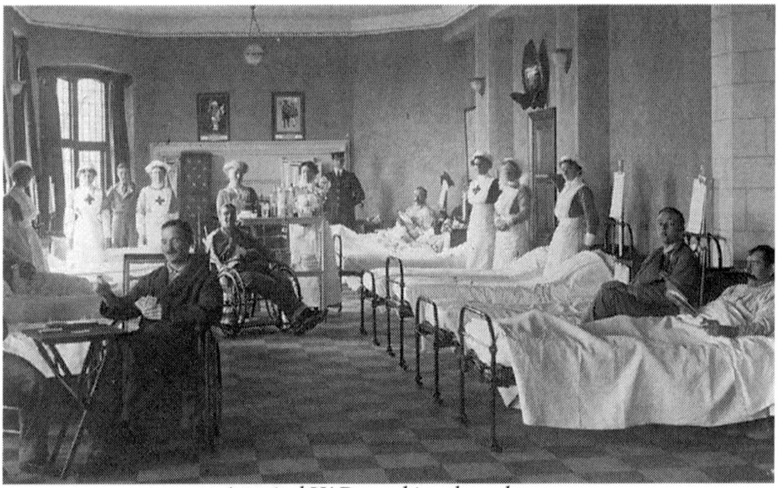

A typical VAD ward in a large house

SOUTH WINGFIELD RED CROSS VAD HOSPITAL

Photographs courtesy of the South Wingfield Local History Society

In South Wingfield the VAD Hospital was situated at Mill House opposite the school on Church Lane. It was owned by the Bower family, owners of the local mills.

The Country Branches: Their organisation and work during the first months of the war, vol. 1 (1917): British Red Cross Publication

Name of hospital: South Wingfield VAD

Officer in charge: Mrs Francis Smith

No. of beds: 12

No. of patients received: 88

No. of months open: 14

Grants received: None

Mill House, South Wingfield

Matron, Doozy Thompson, with nurses and soldiers in 1916

Soldiers and nurses at Mill House in 1916

Soldiers and nurses at Mill House, date unknown

BELPER RED CROSS VAD HOSPITAL

In Belper the Strutt family provided Green Hall, which was at the top of King Street, opposite the Belper Memorial Garden, as a VAD hospital. The hospital began receiving wounded men in December 1914; it had forty beds and an up-to-date operating theatre, all financed by George Herbert Strutt. Over three thousand men were cared for there throughout the war. The matron was Nurse Crump (who was awarded the Royal Red Cross in 1918) and the Commandant was Mrs Herbert Strutt (who was awarded the OBE for services to the Red Cross).

Green Hall, Belper Red Cross VAD Hospital

Belper News 23 April 1915

VOLUNTARY NURSES WANTED

In anticipation of the numbers of wounded who are expected shortly to arrive in this country, the War Office desire about 3000 members of Voluntary Aid Detachments to offer themselves for Special Service in Military Hospitals. As the whole of this number can hardly be spared from Detachments that are already hard at work, women holding both the First Aid and Nursing Certificates are allowed to join V.A.D.s for a week or two to satisfy the Commandant as to their capabilities, so that he or she may recommend them for this Special Service. If anyone should offer herself who does not hold both "First Aid" and "Nursing" Certificates, but who has had any hospital training, she cannot be admitted under this scheme, but the County Director will be glad to submit her offer to the War Office for the case to be considered on its merits.

The demand for this Special Service is very urgent and we are asked to state that anyone wishing to offer themselves should apply to their local Red Cross Township Leader for further particulars and the necessary forms.

Belper residents were advised to stop providing the wounded servicemen with alcoholic drink as they were still under military discipline – although this was sometimes ignored and the penalty paid!

Derby Telegraph, 31 August 1916

SUPPLYING WOUNDED SOLDIERS WITH DRINK

WOMAN SENT TO PRISON AT BELPER

At Belper Petty Sessions to-day (Thursday), before Ald. R. Waite and other magistrates, Martha E. Jewkes, married woman, Belper, and Rhoda M. Thorpe, Whatstandwell, were charged with procuring liquor for wounded soldiers at Belper. Sergeant Buxton said that on the 10th August he went to Jewkes' house and told her that soldiers had gone into the Red Cross Hospital drunk. She admitted that beer had been fetched for the soldiers. A soldier said he was invited, with two others, to this house. Thorpe fetched all the beer, four or five pints. The money was found among the soldiers, and they were at the house about an hour and a half.

Supt. Vardy said he saw the two women, and Jewkes admitted fetching two pints of beer, and the other defendant acknowledged getting four pints. Thorpe was a woman of very doubtful character. He was satisfied that the landlady of the house did not know the liquor was for soldiers. The magistrate reprimanded Jewkes, who was fined £1, and Thorpe was ordered one month without the option.

The British Journal of Nursing

13 July 1918, pages 23 & 24

THE ROYAL RED CROSS

The King conferred the decoration of the Royal Red Cross upon the following ladies at Buckingham Palace, on July 3rd, as follows:–

SECOND CLASS

CRUMP, Miss E.M. Matron, Red Cross Hospl., Belper, Derbyshire

Derby Daily Telegraph, 25th November 1918

WAR SERVICES IN HOSPITALS

LIST OF LOCAL MENTIONS

A communique has been issued giving a list of names of those brought to the notice of the Secretary of State for War by the Chairman of the Joint War Committee of the British Red Cross Society and Order of St. John of Jerusalem in England for valuable services rendered in connection with the war.

The Derbyshire names are:– Mrs F. Harber, Red Cross VAD Hospital, Belper; [*with others*]

WILLERSLEY CASTLE VAD HOSPITAL, CROMFORD

The home of the Arkwright family in Cromford was offered to the military authorities as a potential hospital.

Derby Daily Telegraph, 7th August 1914

MR ARKWRIGHT OFFERS WILLERSLEY CASTLE AS HOSPITAL

Mr F. C. Arkwright, Deputy Lieutenant for Derbyshire, has placed Willersley Castle, Cromford, at the disposal of the military authorities to be used, if necessary, as a hospital. Willersley is a fine mansion 15 miles from Derby. Mr Arkwright has reserved only two rooms for himself and his family.

Willersley Castle, VAD Hospital in WWI

High Peak News, 27 March 1915

WOUNDED SOLDIERS IN HOSPITAL AT WILLERSLEY.

By the kindness of Mr. F. C. Arkwright, D.L., J.P.

Derby Daily Telegraph, 15th March 1918

THE ROLL OF HONOUR

LOCAL NURSES MENTIONED

The names of the under mentioned have been brought to the notice of the Secretary of State for War for valuable nursing services rendered in connection with the war:–

Sister Mrs K.R. Bonham Carter, Willersley Auxiliary Hospital, Cromford

Nurse Miss W. Elin, Willersley Auxiliary Hospital, Cromford

Nurse Miss M. Wright, Willersley Auxiliary Hospital, Cromford

WHITWORTH INSTITUTE VAD HOSPITAL, DARLEY DALE

High Peak News 22 May 1915

DARLEY DALE

THE WHITWORTH INSTITUTE WOUNDED

AN IDEAL HOSPITAL

This Hospital is now doing excellent work for all wounded men sent home from the fighting lines in France and Belgium.

The Voluntary Aid Detachments in Darley Dale and Matlock have combined in order to equip about forty beds. Half of these are now occupied, the men having arrived by motor ambulances last Monday week. During the two weeks they have been at Darley they have all made excellent progress, and several of them are now sufficiently well for discharge.

The Institute has proved itself an ideal building for the purpose, and the work of the two Women's Detachments has demonstrated the value of the First Aid and Nursing training they have undergone during the past two years in preparation for this most useful work. The Red Cross Society has sent fully trained Hospital

Sisters, who superintend the willing helpers V.A.D.

> The Hospital is under the CONTROL OF THE TWO COMMANDANTS, Dr Marie Goodwin Orme (Matlock) and Dr Cecil Sharp (Darley Dale). The kitchen department is in the hands of Mrs Boycott, and the improved condition of the men is in no small degree due to her efficient work in preparing excellent meals for them. For the maintenance of the Hospital a subsistence allowance for the men is made by the War Office, but that is insufficient to cover the cost of working the Hospital, and an appeal is made for contributions in money or in kind.
>
> Owners of motor-cars would be rendering service to the Hospital and a great pleasure and benefit to the men if they would occasionally take some of the convalescents for drives. Arrangements can be made with the Quarter-master or the Sister in charge, so that suitable patients may be selected. Provisions of all sorts, fruit, vegetables, milk, butter, eggs, jams, pickles, biscuits, cakes, etc. are urgently needed. Mineral waters, tobacco, cigarettes, plants, flowers, stationery, games, cards, gramophone records will also be very acceptable. Gifts may be sent to the Whitworth Institute, Darley Dale, addressed to the quartermaster.

The Red Cross records for Whitworth Red Cross VAD Hospital show that in 1916 there were fifty-five beds but by 1918 this had risen to eighty-eight. Patients treated in 1916 totalled four hundred and twenty-nine, which rose to six hundred and twenty-eight in 1918. Around two thousand soldiers were treated here during the war period.

Derby Daily Telegraph, 9th June 1915

DUCHESS OF DEVONSHIRE VISITS WOUNDED

The Duchess of Devonshire paid a surprise visit yesterday to the British wounded at the Whitworth Institute, which has been handed over to the Red Cross Society. Her Grace was accompanied by Lady Maud Cavendish, and she was quite pleased with the arrangements which are made for the accommodation of the wounded by the Matlock and Darley Dale Red Cross Societies, of which Dr Sharpe and Dr Marie Orme are the Commandants.

Photo Sharon Hibbitt

MATLOCK AUXILIARY HOSPITAL, DARLEY DALE

Whitworth Hospital, Darley Dale

Reference to this hospital was made in a newspaper report of 1917.

Derby Daily Telegraph, 16th August 1917

RED CROSS AND DERBYSHIRE SOLDIERS' COMFORTS

MEETING OF THE JOINT COUNTY COMMITTEES

A joint meeting of the County Committee of the Derbyshire branch of the British Red Cross Society and the Derbyshire Soldiers' Comforts Association was held at Derbys Infirmary.

[General information on attendees and comment from the Deputy President]

The County Director (Mr Cecil H. Armitage) presented his report, which contained the following:–

"We have now in Derbyshire 16 Red Cross VAD hospitals and wards with 656 beds, 5 St John VAD hospitals and wards with 165 beds, 6 Red Cross private hospitals with 216 beds, and 6 Red Cross civil hospitals with 387 beds – a total of 1,424 beds. ...

In consequence of orders received that auxiliary hospitals of less than ten beds are no longer to be used, I have written to the Whitworth Cottage Hospital, Darley Dale , notifying them and thanking them for all their kind help. ...

Special grants had been made to Willersley Red Cross Hospital, Bakewell Red Cross VAD Hospital, Derby Infirmary, Darley Dale Red Cross VAD Hospital, in each case for an open shelter, which are very much appreciated by the men, and considerably expedite their recovery.

The *High Peak News* on 9th February 1918 reported honours for Dr Marie Orme at Red Cross VAD Hospital at Darley Dale, Mrs Ella Smith at Red Cross VAD Hospital in South Wingfield and Mrs Emily Strutt at Red Cross VAD at Belper.

Commonwealth Prisoners of War in Germany during the First World War

Between the outbreak of war in August 1914 and the Armistice of November 1918, the German forces captured almost 300,000 Commonwealth servicemen on the Western Front. Approximately one third of these prisoners were held in German occupied territory in France and Belgium, but most were transported to camps located throughout Germany. In common with the other belligerent states, Germany was poorly equipped to house, feed and clothe large numbers of enemy troops, but prisoners of war had been granted certain rights under international agreements established at Geneva in 1864 and The Hague in 1899 and 1907. The Red Cross also monitored conditions in the camps and ensured that food, clothing, and personal correspondence sent from Britain were safely delivered to prisoners. In June 1917, and again in July 1918, the British and German governments agreed to exchange prisoners who were too badly wounded to fight again, and hundreds of prisoners were repatriated through the Netherlands. Finally, the fear that the thousands of German prisoners in Britain and France would be mistreated in retaliation meant that Allied POWs often enjoyed quite humane treatment. This was especially the case for officer prisoners, who were segregated into separate camps and not forced to work.

Despite these various checks on the mistreatment of prisoners, conditions in German camps varied widely and as many as 12,000 Commonwealth servicemen died in captivity. Some of these men were badly wounded when taken prisoner and died shortly after arriving in Germany. Some prisoners also died as a result of violence perpetrated by their captors, but although violence was common, particularly during the first year of the war, the killing of prisoners was rare. Non-commissioned officers and privates were often forced to work and some died of exhaustion or accidents while labouring in coalmines, stone quarries or steel works. However, by far the most common cause of prisoner death in wartime Germany was disease. Prisoners weakened by wounds, poor diet or fatigue were particularly susceptible to the effects of disease and an outbreak of typhus in 1915 and the influenza epidemic of 1918 had a devastating effect on the Allied prisoner population.

Ref: Commonwealth War Graves Commission website: *http://www.cwgc.org*

German Prisoners of War in Crich

Photo: Graham Swift

The building to the right of the bakery was used to house German prisoners of war. It was in this upper room that the German prisoners slept during the winter months, exercising in the large room below. In the summer months they were housed in tents close to Hilts Quarry where they worked. Three of the prisoners died and were buried in Crich churchyard where Fred Walker (the Church Warden) tended the graves and was paid a small fee by the War Graves Commission for doing so. Between the wars the bodies were repatriated back to Germany. The three were Otto Gehrhardt, aged twenty-three, Franj Kaminski ,aged twenty-eight and Franz Koyub, aged thirty-one.

While the prisoners were working in Hilts Quarry they were treated kindly by the locals, in particular by Henry and Lily Holtham. Henry was a foreman engine driver at the quarry. Lily Holtham would bake for them and Henry provided extra rations from his allotment.

The Military Service Act 1916

Traditionally all members of the British armed forces signed up voluntarily, so during 1914 and 1915 the whole army were volunteers. They could choose their regiment, and were accepted up to the age of forty-five. After accepting the "Kings Shilling" and swearing an oath to serve King and Country (called the attestation) they awaited joining-up instructions.

Then came the 1916 Military Services Act. On 27th Jan 1916, voluntary enlistment stopped. All men between eighteen and forty-one, unmarried or widower were conscripted. There was no choice of service, regiment or unit. This was extended to include married men on 25th May 1916. The act brought conscription into effect for the first time in the war. It placed Britain on a "total war" footing and stated the following:

Every British male subject who, on 15th August 1915 was ordinarily resident in Great Britain and who had attained the age of nineteen but was not yet forty-one and on 2nd November 1915 was unmarried or a widower without dependent children unless he met certain exceptions or had met the age of forty-one before the appointed date, was deemed to have enlisted for general service with the colours or in the reserve and was forthwith transferred to the reserve. He now came under the controls specified in the Army Act. This was as of Thursday 2nd March 1916.

Provision was made under Section 20 of the Reserve Forces Act 1882 for information being obtained from the man with regard to his preference for service in the Navy. The Admiralty had the first right of call on men who expressed this preference.

Men were encouraged to voluntarily enlist under the Group System (called the Derby Scheme, after Lord Derby) before the Act came into place.

Schedule of Exceptions (categories of men who were not deemed to have enlisted)

1. Men ordinarily resident in the Dominions abroad, or resident in Britain only for the purpose of their education or some other special purpose.
2. Existing members of the regular or reserve forces or of the Territorial Force who are liable for foreign service or who are, in the opinion of the Army Council, not suitable for foreign service.
3. Men serving in the Navy or Royal Marines or who are recommended for exception by the Admiralty.
4. Men in Holy Orders or regular ministers of any religious denomination.
5. Men who had served with the military or Navy and been discharged on grounds of ill-health or termination of service.
6. Men who hold a certificate of exemption or who have offered themselves for enlistment since 4 August 1914 but been rejected.

Claiming exemption from military service

An application may be made before the appointed date to a Local Tribunal for the issue of a certificate of exemption. There were four grounds for exemption:

1. If it is expedient in the national interests that he should be engaged in other work, or, if he is being educated or trained for any other work, that he should continue.
2. If serious hardship would ensue owing to his exceptional financial or business obligations or domestic position.
3. Ill health or infirmity.
4. Conscientious objection to the undertaking of combatant service.

A certificate could be absolute, conditional or temporary. Exemptions for continued education or training and those on financial hardship grounds could only be temporary. If the conditions under which an exemption was granted changed, it was the duty of the person to inform the authorities. A fine of up to £50 could be applied if he did not do so. False statements or misrepresentation at the time of application for exemption could lead to imprisonment with hard labour for up to six months.

A system of Local, Appeal and Central Tribunals was arranged. Each registration district as defined in the National Registration Act 1915 would have a Local Tribunal or Tribunals consisting of between 5 and 25 members each. A Tribunal could work through a committee that it could appoint. There would also be Appeal and Central Tribunals with members appointed by the Crown. Any person aggrieved by the decision of a Local Tribunal could make an appeal.

Classes

Men were allocated into a Class, which was connected with the year of their birth, and were notified that they would be called up by Class.

Class 1 was for those born in 1897. They were 18 years old. They were told they would not be called up until they were aged 19. Class 2 was for those born in 1896, Class 3 for 1895 and so on up to Class 23 for those born in 1875.

A Public Proclamation was placed in prominent spots, advising the public the date on which a particular Class would begin call-up. This was deemed to be sufficient notice, but in additional generally each man received an individual notice. It was the individual's responsibility to be alert to such notices and to report himself for duty. There were penalties for not reporting and for inducing or assisting a reservist to absent himself.

Ref: The Long, Long Trail (*www.1914-1918.net*)

Conscientious Objectors (COs)

In 1914, after 20,000 casualties had been recorded in the first two weeks of the war, compulsory call-up for British men looked increasingly likely. Pacifist members of the No-Conscription Fellowship, set up in 1915, successfully campaigned to secure 'the conscience clause' in the 1916 Conscription Act: the right to claim exemption from military service.

Over 16,000 men made that claim. They were required to attend a tribunal (an interviewing panel with legal authority) to have the sincerity of their claims assessed. The government meant well; these tribunals were intended to be humane and fair, but it was left to local councils to choose the people who actually sat on the panels, and they often selected themselves. They were a mixed bunch: businessmen, shopkeepers, landowners, retired military officers, civil servants and the like, most of them too old to be called up. Most were also strongly patriotic and therefore prejudiced against anyone who they thought was not. Often they were people 'of not very great depth of vision or understanding', genuinely confused about their task and its complicated guidelines. A few tribunal members were women, who seemed particularly incensed by the conscientious objectors' (COs') point of view. Another hazard for COs was that each tribunal panel contained one army-selected member, attending every hearing and with the right to cross-examine each applicant. These 'military representatives' had a common aim: to get as many men as possible into the army to fill the gaps left by the dead.

The COs came from all walks of life, and varied widely in their ability to cope with often rude and aggressive interviewers. Some didn't get a chance to say a word, others embarked on well-prepared arguments. Whatever they said, the result was the same: only a handful received full exemption, and many were denied any form of exemption at all.

The COs fell into three categories, all representing difficult choices for them to make:

1. Some were 'absolutists', opposed to conscription as well as war, upholders of civil liberty and the freedom of the individual – values that were thought to be respected in Britain. Absolutists (most of whom were committed pacifists) believed that any alternative service supported the war effort and in effect supported the immoral practice of conscription as well. The tribunals had the power to give these men complete and unconditional exemption.
2. Some were 'alternativists', prepared to undertake alternative civilian work not under any military control. Tribunals had the power to exempt them from military service on condition that they actually did this work.
3. Some were 'non-combatants' who were prepared to accept call-up into the army,

but not to be trained to use weapons, or indeed have anything to do with weapons at all. Tribunals had the power to put these men on the military register on this basis.

However, the tribunals didn't use their powers with much judgement or sympathy. Not only did they rarely grant unconditional exemption, they also often allocated absolutists or alternativists to non-combatant duties. In many cases applications were turned down altogether, which meant that the men were liable for call-up as ordinary soldiers. These unwilling conscripts could be arrested and handed over to the military; if they disobeyed military orders they would be court-martialled and sent to prison.

Even in prison, choices created dilemmas. Some apparently innocent prison tasks turned out to be part of the war effort, and had to be resisted. Those who refused to do any work at all were punished with solitary confinement and bread-and-water diets for long periods.

Prisons in those days were still run on inhumane systems inherited from the nineteenth century. The silence rule was particularly harsh: it was almost impossible to keep, yet it provoked severe punishment when broken.

Ref: Peace Pledge Union Project (*www.coproject.org.uk*)

After the 1916 Military Services Act 750,000 men applied for exemption nationally but only about 2% of the applications were on grounds of conscientious objection.

7,000 were granted non combatant status

3,000 were sent to work camps

6,000 were imprisoned

The 'no military connected' activity for some objectors added extra "hardship" and controversy. They gave no support to Red Cross activities, the Prince of Wales Fund came under close scrutiny, and, when in prison, if the "hard labour" was considered military-based then refusal would lead to solitary confinement and a bread-and-water diet.

FRITCHLEY QUAKERS

Fritchley was the centre of a strong Quaker community and as such contained several conscientious objectors. This caused friction in the parish, and several Quaker businesses and personalities suffered attack and abuse.

FRITCHLEY CONSCIENTIOUS OBJECTORS

THOMAS DAVIDSON

Thomas Davidson reported to the Friends that he had paid several visits to young men imprisoned at Normanton Barracks, Derby for objecting to bearing arms. He was in general treated with consideration by the Captain in charge, Captain Clymo, who very readily accorded him permission to see them.

GEORGE WILLIAM DAVIDSON

In March 1917 George W. Davidson's exemption had been renewed for six months, as a farmer, but in June it was withdrawn when he was charged with assisting an absentee to avoid arrest and had to appear before the Local Tribunal again, which only gave him Non Combatant Service.

It was reported in the Ripley & Heanor News on 13 July 1917 that:

> "Among the cases dealt with by the Derbyshire Appeals Tribunal at Derby on Monday was that of G. W. Davidson, grocer and farmer, of Fritchley, who appealed, on business grounds and as a conscientious objector, against the withdrawal of his exemption by the Belper Rural Tribunal. On it being suggested to him that he found work for conscientious objectors, he replied that the only ones he employed were those sent to him by the Army to be engaged in agricultural occupations. He also had a nurse of German nationality, who came to him direct from Lord Lansdowne's service and on that nobleman's personal recommendation. The Court granted exemption conditionally upon [him] undertaking agricultural work to their satisfaction."

This he could not accept and appealed to the County Appeal Committee. After a good deal of difficulty he was allowed to take a farm elsewhere, on condition that it must be at least twenty miles from Fritchley. He moved to a farm at Seagrave in Leicestershire with his family in November 1917 and his exemption was not further called into question.

ARTHUR H. LUDLOW AND ARTHUR B. WATKINS

When the second Military Service Act came into force conscripting young married men, George William Davidson, Arthur H. Ludlow and Arthur B. Watkins appeared before the Belper Tribunal, and as farmers George W. Davidson and Arthur B. Watkins were granted conditional exemption; the latter was required to work part-time for other farmers, which he did and his exemption was continued from time to time until the end of the war.

Arthur H. Ludlow, who was in the employment of the Midland Railway Company in their offices at Derby, was pressed very strongly to attest before he was liable to be called up but he steadily refused, and lost his situation in consequence. He was arrested on the 17th May 1917 and court martialled at Derby, where he was sentenced to one hundred and twelve days imprisonment and removed to Wormwood Scrubs prison. After the completion of his sentence he was taken under escort to Sunderland, court martialled again and sentenced to eighteen months hard labour. His health was much impaired and he was urged by a sympathetic officer, who knew the family, to accept clerical work under the Military for a time, with the promise of early discharge. Bravely supported by his wife, he steadily refused even though he was told he would not be able to live through his sentence. As a result of urgent appeals on his behalf to the War Office he was eventually discharged from the Army on health grounds.

HENRY SMITH

Henry Smith was arrested in August 1916 and appeared before the Belper Branch of Magistrates with a view to his being handed over to the military authorities.

After the military representative who appeared to prosecute had stated his case, Henry Smith was invited to reply and divided his defence into three heads:-

i. As to point of fact: I submit that I cannot be an absentee from something I have never joined.
ii. As to point of law: I submit that I am a conscientious objector recognised by the Tribunal, and as such ought to be totally exempted. (I explained to the Tribunal that Non Combatant service did not meet the case.)
iii. Finally, gentlemen, my last defence is on religious grounds. I believe that Christianity is opposed to warfare.

After a few minutes' deliberation, the decision to decline the order was announced by the Chairman:

> *The Bench are satisfied that Henry Smith is a bona-fide conscientious objector, holding the principles of the Society of Friends. The Bench is aware there is a Friends Ambulance Corps and hope the defendant will volunteer for that.*

The military representative was dissatisfied with the decision and requested permission to take the matter further and this was granted.

Henry Smith was court-martialled three times and was finally released from prison in March 1919 on health grounds. It had been three years since his first appeal to the County Appeal Tribunal.

Respect for the peace-loving Quakers of Fritchley led in some measure to the fact that Fritchley Meeting House was not commandeered by the military.

Harassment included the sending of postcards ridiculing the conscientious objector.

Friends Meeting House, Fritchley

Crich pacifist trouble

A clear indication of ordinary Derbyshire people's feelings towards pacifists was shown graphically at Crich on the evening of Saturday 30th June 1916. The previous week, leaflets had been distributed saying that a great demonstration would be held at Crich under the auspices of the Derby and District Independent Labour Party. The leaflets had asked: "*Is it really necessary to go on? Are we by continuing the war, actually preparing for that world without war, which we all long to see? Are we rather not multiplying evil and planting the seeds of bitterness which can never bear the fruit of peace?*"

The reason for selecting Crich as a venue is unknown, but it was a community from which a large number of men had enlisted voluntarily, some of whom had been killed, wounded or taken prisoner.

After tea at the Mount Tabor Chapel, the large number of delegates repaired to the Market Place and from the beginning it was clear that things were going to be lively. The Derbyshire Times correspondent reported the events:

> A large crowd – several hundreds strong – quickly assembled, and although the first speaker managed to say a few words, he very quickly had to give up the attempt. Tin-cans, grass-ends, etc., were requisitioned by the loyal and patriotic populace, who also vociferously sang patriotic songs, the result being that speaking was utterly impossible. For about two hours the pacifists tried to "convert" the audience, but eventually had to beat an undignified retreat. Several of them retired in the direction of Fritchley, at which place they received a reception, if anything, more warm than at Crich. Amongst the "booty" was a hat which belonged to one of the speakers, which at the time of writing adorned the lamp-post in the centre of the Market Place, the spike on the top of the post having perforated the hat, making it look like a German helmet.
>
> When it is considered the sacrifices people of the Crich parish made in connection with the war, it speaks volumes for their pluck and endurance that they so emphatically rejected the apostles of "peace-at-any-price."

Mount Tabor Chapel
Bowns Hill, Crich

PHOTOGRAPHS

Local men with their regiments. Snapshots of the soldier's life in the Great War.

The following album shows regimental photographs which include parish men as well as photographs from the personal collections of parish men who served. The photographs include images of themselves, their friends or fellow soldiers. Sadly, most of these do not have names ascribed but as they have been saved all these years they must have some importance or significance to the men or their families. They provide a snapshot of life serving in the forces during the Great War.

In the research for this Memorial Book many photos were received showing local men as part of a group.

Photo Ken Pykett

Local men assembling at Ripley before setting off for war, August 1914

Photo Ken Pykett

5th Battalion Sherwood Foresters marching from Ripley Drill Hall on Shirley Road. Recalled from Filey Training Camp and mobilised the next day, 4th August 1914

Photo Tony Holmes

E Company, 6th Battalion of the Sherwood Foresters on August 6th 1914 marching through Matlock Bath en route to Chesterfield.

Photo Frank Priestley

Sherwood Foresters at home preparing for war

Photo Margery Whitham

Sherwood Foresters at home preparing for war

Photo Adam Lancashire

North Staffordshire soldiers

Herbert Spencer of Ripley and other local men are on this photograph

Photo Rosemary Hall

Taken at Crich, showing officers enjoying a pint before going off to their units

Photo Keith Fretwell

Wilfred Martin seated

Soldiers on Ambergate Station

Photo Margaret Suddes

Cooking duties

Photo Joyce Denton

Regimental Band of King's Own Yorkshire Light Infantry

Photo Roger Worthy

Mass burial service

Photos Michael Porter

From the collection of Jack Porter who was in the Sherwood Foresters

Photo David and Liz Houlden

Pioneers, all with unlit cigarettes. Job Hopkinson is second left.

Photo Nellie Brumwell

VAD nurse with wounded soldiers

WAR ENDS

CELEBRATION AND REMEMBRANCE

CRICH MEMORIAL TOWER

Peace Day Remembrance and Celebration Crich 1918

Victory Parade at the top of Bowns Hill, Crich

Photo Sue Worboys

Floral Tribute 1918

Photo Sue Worboys

Crich Market Place remembrance event 1918

Crich Stand
A memorial to the Sherwood Foresters

Crich Memorial Tower was opened on Monday 6th August 1923 at 4 p.m. by General Sir Horace L. Smith-Dorrien, Colonel of the Sherwood Foresters. It was built on the site of an earlier tower constructed by the Hurt family of Alderwasley.

Opening ceremony of the Memorial Stand, Monday 6 August 1923

1930, Crich Market Place on Stand Sunday before the march to the Memorial Tower

Stand Sunday is the first Sunday in July, when there is the annual pilgrimage from Crich village to the Memorial Stand for a Service of Remembrance.

The Sherwood Foresters
Nottinghamshire and Derbyshire Regiment.

✠

OPENING
of the
Memorial Tower
at
Crich, Derbyshire,
Monday, 6th August, 1923, at 4 p.m.
by
General Sir Horace L. Smith-Dorrien
G.C.B., G.C.M.G., D.S.O.,
Colonel of the Regiment

DEDICATION
by The Rt. Revd.
The Lord Bishop of Southwell, D.D.

Chairman:
His Grace The Duke of Portland, K.G., G.C.V.O.
(Lord Lieutenant of Nottinghamshire),
supported by
His Grace The Duke of Devonshire,
K.G., G.C.M.G., G.C.V.O.
(Lord Lieutenant of Derbyshire).

The Great War : 1914 - 1919.

Battle Honours:

France and Flanders		
Gallipoli	...	1915-1916
Italy	...	1918
Aisne	...	1914-1918
Neuve Chapelle		
Loos		
Somme	...	1916-1918
Ypres	...	1915-1917-1918
St. Quentin Canal		
Cambrai	...	1917-1918

Inscription on the Tower

"To the memory of 11,409 men of all ranks of the Sherwood Foresters (Nottinghamshire and Derbyshire Regiment) who gave their lives for their King and their Country in the Great War, 1914-1919, and in honour of 140,000 of their Comrades who served during the War in Thirty-two Battalions of the Regiment, this Monument is gratefully erected by the People of the Counties of Nottingham and Derby."

To remind us of their sacrifice
and our duty.

The Service.

Hymn.

The Supreme Sacrifice
by John S. Arkwright.

Band of the 1st Battalion The Sherwood Foresters.

O valiant Hearts, who to your glory came
Through dust of conflict and through battle-flame;
Tranquil you lie, your knightly virtue proved,
Your memory hallowed in the Land you loved.

Proudly you gathered, rank on rank to war,
As who had heard God's message from afar;
All you had hoped for, all you had, you gave
To save Mankind—yourselves you scorned to save.

Splendid you passed, the great surrender made,
Into the light that nevermore shall fade;
Deep your contentment in that blest abode,
Who wait the last clear trumpet-call of God.

These were His servants, in His steps they trod,
Following through death the martyr'd Son of God:
Victor He rose, victorious too shall rise
They who have drunk His cup of Sacrifice.

O risen Lord, O Shepherd of our Dead,
Whose Cross has bought them and whose Staff has led—
In glorious hope their proud and sorrowing Land
Commits her Children to Thy gracious hand. *Amen.*

The Lesson.

Revelations, chap. xxi., verses 1—7 inclusive.

The Revd. A. Stanley Bishop,
Hon. Chaplain to the Forces.

3

Opening of The Tower
by
General Sir Horace L. Smith-Dorrien,
G.C.B., G.C.M.G., D.S.O.,
Colonel of the Regiment.

Dedication
by the
Rt. Revd. The Lord Bishop of Southwell,
D.D.

Prayers.

Let us remember before God all those who died for the Empire's Cause.

O, ALMIGHTY Lord, the God of the spirits of all flesh, we praise Thy Name for the valour and the sacrifice of all who for our King, our Country and our Empire, laid down their lives for us. Grant them, O Lord, eternal rest, and may light perpetual shine upon them, through Jesus Christ our Lord. *Amen.*

And for our Comrades, who died the Death of Honour, let us make our prayers in love and hope.

REMEMBER in Thy Kingdom those who in the cause of Truth and Freedom were found faithful unto death. Grant that we, being encouraged by their example and their fellowship, may contend valiantly for Thy Truth and do Thy Will with steadfast faith; so that at the last we may with them enter into the joy of Thy eternal kingdom, to Whom, with the Father and the Holy Spirit, One God of Love, be praise and glory for ever. *Amen.*

GRANT, O Lord, we beseech Thee, that the course of this world may be so peacefully ordered by Thy governance, that Thy Church may joyfully serve Thee in all godly quietness, through Jesus Christ our Lord. *Amen.*

O GOD, Who art a most strong Tower to all them that put their trust in Thee, whose only beloved Son did suffer and die for us, accept at our hands this Memorial, wherewith we commemorate the sacrifice which our brothers made; and grant that they who shall look upon it from afar may ever be mindful of the price that has been paid for their redemption, and may learn to live unto Him who died for them, Our Lord and Saviour, Jesus Christ. *Amen.*

TO the honour and glory of Almighty God and in memory of our Brothers who laid down their lives for us, and those Sherwood Foresters who served in the Great War, we dedicate this Memorial in the name of the Father, and of the Son, and of the Holy Ghost. Pour Thy blessing, O Lord, on all who pass by or dwell around this hallowed Memorial. Grant that now and in the days to come they may be taught freely to give as these their brothers did; call them to Thy service and make them worthy of Thy calling, through Jesus Christ our Lord. *Amen.*

Let us pray that we may be worthy of those who have given their lives for their country.

ALMIGHTY God, who hast made us citizens of this realm, enable us who now remain in the safety of our homes to be worthy of those who died for us. Grant us with a willing spirit to do our duty, with gladness to bear each others burdens; with undaunted faith to shed abroad in the hearts of the people both courage and good cheer that by active service we may ever be found faithful, through Jesus Christ our Lord. *Amen.*

COMFORT, O Lord, we pray Thee, all who are mourning the loss of those near and dear to them. Be with them in their sorrows; support and cheer them with Thy love; teach them to rest and lean upon Thee; give them faith to look beyond the trouble of this present time, and to know that neither life nor death can separate us from the Love of God, which is in Christ Jesus our Lord, to whom with the Father and the Holy Ghost be all honour and glory, now and ever. *Amen.*

OUR Father, which art in heaven, Hallowed be thy Name. Thy kingdom come. Thy will be done in earth, As it is in heaven. Give us this day our daily bread. And forgive us our trespasses, as we forgive them that trespass against us. And lead us not into temptation; but deliver us from evil: For thine is the kingdom, the power, and the glory, For ever and ever. *Amen.*

The Last Post.

Buglers of 1st Battalion The Sherwood Foresters.

HYMN.

Band of the 1st Battalion The Sherwood Foresters.

O GOD, our help in ages past,
Our hope for years to come,
Our shelter from the stormy blast,
And our eternal home;

Beneath the shadow of Thy Throne
Thy Saints have dwelt secure;
Sufficient is Thine arm alone,
And our defence is sure.

Before the hills in order stood,
Or earth received her frame,
From everlasting Thou art God,
To endless years the Same.

A thousand ages in Thy sight
Are like an evening gone;
Short as the watch that ends the night
Before the rising sun.

Time, like an ever-rolling stream,
Bears all its sons away;
They fly forgotten, as a dream
Dies at the opening day.

O God, our help in ages past,
Our hope for years to come,
Be Thou our guard while troubles last,
And our eternal home. *Amen.*

THE BLESSING.

Reveille.

Buglers of the 1st Battalion The Sherwood Foresters

HIS GRACE THE DUKE OF PORTLAND, K.G., G.C.V.O.
will ask
GENERAL SIR HORACE L. SMITH-DORRIEN,
G.C.B., B.C.M.G.,
to address the meeting.

Address by

General Sir Horace L. Smith-Dorrien,

G.C.B., B.C.M.G., D.S.O.

HIS GRACE THE DUKE OF DEVONSHIRE,
K.G., G.C.M.G., G.C.V.O.,
will thank him on behalf of the two Counties.

Wreaths of Remembrance

Will be placed at the Foot of the Memorial by
THE SHERWOOD FORESTERS
OLD COMRADES ASSOCIATION
and all UNITS that fought in THE GREAT WAR.

God Save The King.

Over the door to the Stand is inscribed:

TO THE MEMORY OF 11,409 MEN OF ALL RANKS OF THE SHERWOOD FORESTERS (NOTTINGHAMSHIRE AND DERBYSHIRE REGIMENT) WHO GAVE THEIR LIVES FOR THEIR KING AND THEIR COUNTRY IN THE GREAT WAR 1914–1919 AND IN HONOUR OF 140,000 OF THEIR COMRADES WHO SERVED DURING THE WAR IN THIRTY-TWO BATTALIONS OF THE REGIMENT THIS MONUMENT IS GRATEFULLY ERECTED BY THE PEOPLE OF THE COUNTIES OF NOTTINGHAM AND DERBY.

TO REMIND US OF THEIR SACRIFICE AND OUR DUTY.

The Memorial Plaque in front to the Stand reads:
"GENTLEMEN WE WILL STAND AND FIGHT"
(Le Cateau 1915)
TO THE EVER GLORIOUS MEMORY OF
THAT GREAT SOLDIER AND GENTLEMAN
GENERAL
SIR HORACE LOCKWOOD SMITH DORRIEN
G.C.B. G.C.M.G. D.S.O.
COLONEL OF THE SHERWOOD FORESTERS
(NOTTINGHAMSHIRE AND DERBYSHIRE REGIMENT)
1905–1930
ERECTED AS A TOKEN OF LOVE
AND ESTEEM BY HIS COMRADES
OF THE REGIMENT IN WHICH
HE SERVED SO MANY YEARS. WHOEVER LEADS SUCH A LIFE
NEED NOT CARE UPON
HOW SHORT WARNING
IT BE TAKEN FROM HIM

FINAL RESTING PLACES

WHERE THE MEN WHO GAVE THEIR LIVES ARE REMEMBERED AND BURIED

The following information is taken from the website of the Commonwealth War Graves Commission (*www.cwgc.org*).

Abbeville Communal Cemetery Extension

Somme, France

1992 Casualties

For much of the First World War, Abbeville was the headquarters of the Commonwealth lines of communication and several Stationary Hospitals were located there variously from October 1914 to January 1920. The communal cemetery was used for burials from November 1914 to September 1916. The extension was begun in September 1916.

Crich Roll of Honour name –

Charles Hartle

Albert Communal Cemetery Extension

Somme, France

867 Casualties

Albert was held by French forces against the German advance on the Somme in September 1914. It passed into British hands in the summer of 1915 and the first fighting in July 1916 is known as the Battle of Albert, 1916. It was captured by the Germans on the 26th April 1918, and before its recapture by the 8th East Surreys on the following 22nd August (in the Battle of Albert, 1918) it had been completely destroyed by artillery fire. The extension was used by fighting units and Field Ambulances from August 1915 to November 1916, and more particularly in and after September 1916, when Field Ambulances were concentrated at Albert.

Crich Roll of Honour name –

Henry Westbury Sargent

Anneux British Cemetery

Nord, France

554 Casualties

The original cemetery was made by the 57th Division Burial Officer and by various units in October 1918. At the Armistice it contained 131 graves but was then greatly increased when graves were brought in from the surrounding battlefields and small cemeteries in the area.

Crich Roll of Honour name –

Ernest Gregory

Arras Memorial

Pas de Calais, France

34,782 Casualties

This memorial commemorates almost 35,000 servicemen from the United Kingdom, South Africa and New Zealand who died in the Arras sector between the spring of 1916 and 7 August 1918, the eve of the Advance to Victory, and who have no known grave. The most conspicuous events of this period were the Arras offensive of April–May 1917, and the German attack in the spring of 1918.

Crich Roll of Honour names –

Joseph Dawes

Christopher Durie

John Mellows (Mellors)

John Henry Perry

Alexander Ross

George Parkinson Smith

Albert Whitehurst

Basra Memorial

Iraq

40682 Casualties

Until 1997 the Basra Memorial was located on the main quay of the naval dockyard at Maqil, on the west bank of the Shatt-al-Arab, about eight kilometres north of Basra. Because of the sensitivity of the site, the Memorial was moved by presidential decree. The move, carried out by the authorities in Iraq, involved a considerable amount of manpower, transport costs and sheer engineering on their part, and the Memorial has been re-erected in its entirety.

The Basra Memorial is now located thirty-two kilometres along the road to Nasiriyah, in the middle of what was a major battleground during the first Gulf War.

Crich Roll of Honour name –

Charles Chambers

Becourt Military Cemetery, Becordel-Becourt

Somme, France

705 Casualties

The Military Cemetery was begun in August 1915, by the 51st (Highland) Division, and carried on by the 18th and other Divisions in the line until the Battle of the Somme, 1916. It continued in use, chiefly by Field Ambulances, until April 1917 and Plot II was made by the 18th Division at the end of August 1918.

Crich Roll of Honour name –

Fred Buckley

Bienvillers Military Cemetery

Pas de Calais, France

1196 Casualties

The cemetery was begun in September 1915 and used until March 1917, then reopened from March to September 1918, when the village was again near the front line. It was completed in 1922–1924 when a number of graves, mainly from 1916, were brought in from the battlefields of the Ancre.

Crich Roll of Honour name –

Joseph Ernest Amatt

Bucquoy Road Cemetery, Ficheux

Pas de Calais, France

1844 Casualties

In November 1916, the village of Ficheux was behind the German front line, but by April 1917 the German withdrawal had taken the line considerably east of the village and in April and May the VII Corps Main Dressing Station was posted here for the Battle of Arras. It was followed by Casualty Clearing Station, which remained at Boisleux-au-Mont until March 1918, and continued to use the Bucquoy Road Cemetery begun by the Field Ambulances. From early April to early August 1918 the cemetery was not used, but in September and October more Casualty Clearing Stations came to Boisleux-au-Mont and extended it. By the date of the Armistice, it contained 1,166 burials but was greatly increased when graves were brought in from the surrounding battlefields and from small cemeteries in the neighbourhood.

Crich Roll of Honour names –

John Gough

Robert Stevenson

Cambrin Military Cemetery

Pas de Calais, France

815 Casualties

The Cemetery is often called Cambrin Chateau Cemetery. It was begun in February 1915 and used as a front line cemetery until December 1918. It contains many graves from the Battle of Loos

Crich Roll of Honour name –

Harry Griffin

Cologne Southern Cemetery

Cologne, Nordrhein-Westfal, Germany

2590 Casualties

More than one thousand Allied prisoners and dozens of German servicemen were buried in Cologne Southern Cemetery during the First World War. Commonwealth forces entered Cologne on 6 December 1918, less than a month after the Armistice, and the city was occupied under the terms of the Treaty of Versailles until January 1926. During this period the cemetery was used by the occupying garrison. In 1922 it was decided that the graves of Commonwealth servicemen who had died all over Germany should be brought together into four permanent cemeteries at Kassel, Berlin, Hamburg and Cologne. Over the course of the following year, graves were transferred to Cologne Southern Cemetery from over one hundred and eighty different burial grounds in Hanover, Hessen, the Rhine and Westphalia.

Crich Roll of Honour name –

James Barber

Contay British Cemetery, Contay

Somme, France

1130 Casualties

The site was chosen in August 1916 for burials from the 49th Casualty Clearing Station (CCS), which arrived at Contay at the end of August. It was joined by the 9th CCS in September. Most of the burials were made from these two clearing stations.

Crich Roll of Honour name –

John Thomas Lynam

Corbie Communal Cemetery Extension

Somme, France

915 Casualties

Corbie was about twenty kilometres behind the front when Commonwealth forces took over the line from Berles-au-Bois southward to the Somme in July 1915. The town immediately became a medical centre, with Nos. 5 and 21 Casualty Clearing Stations based at La Neuville (the suburb across the Ancre) until October 1916 and April 1917 respectively. The communal cemetery was used for burials until May 1916, when the plot set aside was filled and the extension opened. The majority of the graves in the extension are those of officers and men who died of wounds received in the 1916 Battle of the Somme. The remainder relate to the fighting of 1918.

Crich Roll of Honour name –

Charles Wain

Daours Communal Cemetery Extension

Somme, France

1,225 Casualties

The preparations for the Somme offensive of July 1916 brought a group of casualty clearing stations to Daours. The extension to the communal cemetery was opened and the first burials made between June and November 1916. The Allied advance in the spring of 1917 took the hospitals with it, and no further burials were made in the cemetery until April 1918, when the Germans recovered the ground they had lost. From April to the middle of August 1918 the extension was almost a front line cemetery. In August and September 1918 the casualty clearing stations came forward again, but in September the cemetery was closed.

Crich Roll of Honour name –

Thomas Samuel Brown

Dickebusch New Military Cemetery Extension

Ieper, West-Vlaanderen, Belgium

542 Casualties

The New Military Cemetery was begun in February 1915 and was used until May 1917 by fighting units and Field Ambulances, with a few further burials taking place in March and April 1918. The Extension was used from May 1917 to January 1918.

Crich Roll of Honour name –

Joseph Henry Taylor

Dozinghem Military Cemetery

Poperinge, West-Vlaanderen, Belgium

3,240 Casualties

Westvleteren was outside the front held by Commonwealth forces in Belgium during the First World War, but in July 1917, in readiness for the forthcoming offensive, groups of casualty clearing stations were placed at three positions called by the troops Mendinghem, Dozinghem and Bandaghem. The cemetery at Dozinghem was used by Casualty Clearing Stations until early in 1918.

Crich Roll of Honour names –

Willoughby Bunting

John Thomas Roe

John White

Duhallow A.D.S. Cemetery

Ieper, West-Vlaanderen, Belgium

1314 Casualties

Duhallow Advanced Dressing Station, believed to have been named after a southern Irish hunt, was a medical post just north of Ypres (now Ieper). The cemetery was begun in July 1917 and in October and November 1918, it was used by the 11th, 36th and 44th Casualty Clearing Stations. The cemetery contains many graves of the artillery and engineers and forty-one men of the 13th Company Labour Corps, killed when a German aircraft dropped a bomb on an ammunition truck in January 1918. After the Armistice, the cemetery was enlarged when graves were brought into this cemetery from isolated sites and a number of small cemeteries on the battlefields around Ypres.

Crich Roll of Honour name –

George Shipston

Etaples Military Cemetery

Pas de Calais, France

10,816 Casualties

During the First World War the area around Etaples was the scene of immense concentrations of Commonwealth reinforcement camps and hospitals. It was remote from attack, except by aircraft, and was accessible by railway from both the northern or the southern battlefields. In 1917, 100,000 troops were camped among the sand dunes and the hospitals, which included eleven general, one stationary, four Red Cross hospitals and a convalescent depot. In total they could deal with 22,000 wounded or sick.

Crich Roll of Honour name –

Walter Lucas Croft

Faubourg D'Amiens Cemetery, Arras

Pas de Calais, France

2647 Casualties

The Commonwealth section of the cemetery was begun in March 1916, behind the French military cemetery established earlier. It continued to be used by Field Ambulances and fighting units until November 1918. The cemetery was enlarged after the Armistice when graves were brought in from the battlefields and from two smaller cemeteries in the vicinity.

Crich Roll of Honour name –

Harry Sylvester Hartle

Five Points Cemetery, Lechelle

Pas de Calais, France

97 Casualties

Lechelle was captured for the second time early in September, 1918 and the cemetery was made by the 53rd Field Ambulance and the 18th Casualty Clearing Station, which were posted near the site. (The origin of the name is not known with certainty.) It was used until the following month.

Crich Roll of Honour name –

Hector McLarty

Foncquevillers Military Cemetery

Pas de Calais, France

600 Casualties

In 1915 and 1916 the Allied front line ran between Foncquevillers and Gommecourt. The cemetery was begun by French troops, and taken over by Commonwealth forces. It remained in use by units and field ambulances until March 1917, the burials in July 1916 (particularly in Plot I, Row L) being especially numerous. The cemetery was used again from March to August 1918, when the German offensive brought the front line back to nearly the old position. Seventy-four graves were brought in after the Armistice from the battlefields of 1916 and 1918 to the east of the village.

The village of Foncquevillers was "adopted" by the town of Derby.

Crich Roll of Honour name –

Percy William Brann

Fouquieres Churchyard Extension

Pas de Calais, France

412 Casualties

Many of the burials from May 1915 to April 1918 and between April and October 1918 took place from Field Ambulances stationed in the village. The great majority of the graves are those of Territorial soldiers, 249 of them from the 46th (North Midland) Division, which spent three years in the neighbourhood and based its transport at Fouquieres.

Crich Roll of Honour name –

James William Mason

Gommecourt Wood New Cemetery, Foncquevillers

Pas de Calais, France

284 Casualties

Gommecourt Wood New Cemetery was made after the Armistice, when graves were brought in from the battlefields of July 1916, March 1917, and March, April and August 1918, and from certain smaller burial grounds.

Crich Roll of Honour names –

Luke Coleman

John Maurice Gibson

Haringhe (Bandaghem) Military Cemetery

Poperinge, West-Vlaanderen, Belgium

769 Casualties

Bandaghem, like Dozinghem and Mendinghem, were the popular names given by the troops to groups of casualty clearing stations posted to this area during the First World War. The cemetery site was chosen in July 1917 for the 62nd and 63rd Casualty Clearing Stations and burials from these and other hospitals (notably the 36th Casualty Clearing Station in 1918) continued until October 1918.

Crich Roll of Honour name –

Thomas Smith

Houchin British Cemetery

Pas de Calais, France

700 Casualties

The cemetery was opened in March 1918 when the 6th Casualty Clearing Station came to Houchin. From April to September the German advance made Houchin unsafe for hospitals, and the cemetery was used by the 55th (West Lancashire) Division. In September 1918 the 6th Casualty Clearing Station returned to Houchin and was joined by the 15th Casualty Clearing Station in October.

Crich Roll of Honour name –

Samuel Smith

Iwuy Communal Cemetery

Nord, France

132 Casualties

Iwuy was occupied by British troops in the middle of October 1918. The Iwuy Communal Cemetery was extended by German troops during their occupation, but the Extension was acquired by the commune after the Armistice, and the German military graves (with twenty-one French) were removed to other cemeteries.

The British Plot was made by the 51st (Highland) Division in October 1918 and eleven British graves were brought in from among the German graves after the Armistice.

Crich Roll of Honour name –

Walter Curzon

Kut War Cemetery

Iraq

410 Casualties

In April 1915 the Indian Expeditionary Force, which had landed at Fao the previous November, began its advance inland with the intention of clearing Turkish forces out of south-west Iraq. Amara was occupied in early June and the advance continued along the line of the Euphrates to Nasiriya and along the Tigris to Kut, which was taken on 29 September. The advance to Baghdad was resumed on 11 November, but was brought to a standstill against the strong Turkish defences at Ctesiphon on 22–24 November. By 3 December the force, comprising chiefly the 6th (Poona) Division of the Indian Army, was back in its entrenched camp at Kut, where they were besieged by Turkish forces. Heavy casualties were suffered in desperate but unsuccessful attempts to reach the town and raise the siege in January, March and April. The garrison was forced to capitulate on 29 April 1916 and nearly 12,000 men were taken prisoner, many of whom later died in captivity. The town was reoccupied by Commonwealth forces in February 1917 and at the end of June it became an administrative, railway and hospital centre.

Kut War Cemetery was made by the 6th (Poona) Division between October 1915 and May 1916 and was increased in size when graves were brought in from other sites after the Armistice.

This cemetery has suffered neglect owing to the troubles in this region of the world.

Crich Roll of Honour name –

Thomas Hartle

Le Grand Beaumart British Cemetery, Steenwerck

Nord, France

301 Casualties

Steenwerck remained untouched for much of the First World War, but on 10 April 1918 it was captured during the German advance and remained in their hands until the beginning of October.

The original cemetery was made by fighting units and Field Ambulances in April and October 1918. It was increased after the Armistice when graves were brought in from the battlefields of Steenwerck, Nieppe and Armentieres.

Crich Roll of Honour name –

Thomas Edwin Leafe

Le Touret Military Cemetery, Richebourg-L'avoue

Pas de Calais, France

908 Casualties

The cemetery was begun by the Indian Corps (and in particular by the 2nd Leicesters) in November, 1914 and it was used continuously by Field Ambulances and fighting units until March 1918. It passed into German hands in April 1918, and after its recapture a few further burials were made during September and October.

Crich Roll of Honour name –

John Thomas Duggan

Metz-En-Couture Communal Cemetery British Extension

Pas de Calais, France

430 Casualties

The Communal Cemetery was used by the enemy for the burial of German soldiers. The British Extension was begun in April 1917, and used until March 1918.

The village was noted for its extensive system of underground cellars. It was later "adopted" by the County Borough of Halifax.

Crich Roll of Honour name –

John William Byard

Ploegsteert Memorial

Comines-Warneton, Hainault, Belgium

11,385 Casualties

The memorial commemorates more than 11,000 servicemen of the United Kingdom and South African forces who died in this sector during the War and who have no known grave.

Most of those commemorated by the memorial did not die in major offensives, such as those which took place around Ypres to the north or Loos to the south. Most were killed in the course of the day-to-day trench warfare which characterised this part of the line, or in small scale set engagements, usually carried out in support of the major attacks taking place elsewhere.

Crich Roll of Honour names –

John Stanley Harrison Berresford

John Donaldson

Rocquigny-Equancourt Road British Cemetery, Manancourt

Somme, France

1817 Casualties

The cemetery was begun in 1917 and used until March 1918, mainly by the 21st and 48th Casualty Clearing Stations posted at Ypres, and to a small extent by the Germans, who knew it as "Etricourt Old English Cemetery".

Crich Roll of Honour names –

William Frost

William Taylor

St Sever Cemetery Extension, Rouen

Seine-Maritime, France

8647 Casualties

During the First World War, Commonwealth camps and hospitals were stationed on the southern outskirts of Rouen. Almost all of the hospitals at Rouen remained there for practically the whole of the war. They included eight general, five stationary, one British Red Cross and one labour hospital, and No. 2 Convalescent Depot. A number of the dead from these hospitals were buried in other cemeteries, but the great majority were taken to the city cemetery of St Sever. In September 1916, it was found necessary to begin an extension, where the last burial took place in April 1920.

Crich Roll of Honour name –

Duncan Cooke

Struma Military Cemetery

Greece

896 Casualties

The Struma River flows through Bulgaria southward to the Greek frontier, then south-east into the Aegean Sea. From the Allied base at Salonika a road ran north-east across the river to Seres, and it was this road that the right wing of the Allied army used for the movements of troops and supplies to the Struma front during the Salonika Campaign. In the autumn of 1916 the 40th Casualty Clearing Station was established and the cemetery made for it was originally called Kilo 71 Military Cemetery.

Crich Roll of Honour name –

Amos Rodgers

Thiepval Memorial

Somme, France

72,198 Casualties

The Thiepval Memorial, the Memorial to the Missing of the Somme, bears the names of more than 72,000 officers and men of the United Kingdom and South African forces who died in the Somme sector before 20 March 1918 and who have no known grave. Over 90% of those commemorated died between July and November 1916.

Crich Roll of Honour names –

John Bowmer

Alfred Curzon

James Crowder Murphy

Tincourt New British Cemetery

Somme, France

1736 Casualties

The villages of Tincourt and Boucly were occupied by British troops in March 1917, during the German retreat to the Hindenburg Line. From the following May until March 1918 Tincourt became a centre for Casualty Clearing Stations. On the 23rd March 1918 the villages were evacuated and they were recovered, in a ruined condition, about the 6th September. From that month to December 1918 Casualty Clearing Stations were again posted to Tincourt. The cemetery was begun in June 1917 and used until September 1919. After the Armistice it was used for the reburial of soldiers found on the battlefield, or who had been buried in small French or German cemeteries.

Crich Roll of Honour name –

Charles Francis Holmes

Tyne Cot Memorial

Zonnebeke, West-Vlaanderen, Belgium
34,950 Casualties

The Tyne Cot Memorial now bears the names of almost 35,000 officers and men whose graves are not known; it is one of four memorials to the missing in Belgian Flanders in an area known as the Ypres Salient.

Crich Roll of Honour names –

Albert Anderson

Vernon Greenhough

George Haslam

John (Jack) Kneebone

George Perry

John Thomas (Jack) Wragg

Unicorn Cemetery, Vendhuile

Aisne, France

599 Casualties

Vendhuile was very nearly reached in the Battle of Cambrai 1917. It was taken by the 27th and 30th American Divisions at the end of September 1918, and cleared by the 12th and 18th Divisions on 30 September. After the fight, men of the 18th Division were buried by the 50th (Northumbrian) Division in the Unicorn Cemetery (the name is taken from the Divisional mark of the 50th Division). The rest of the cemetery was formed after the Armistice when graves were brought in from the surrounding battlefields, isolated sites and from the later small cemeteries of 1917 and 1918.

Crich Roll of Honour name –

Charles Holmes

Vlamertinghe New Military Cemetery

leper, West-Vlaanderen, Belgium

1802 Casualties

For much of the First World War Vlamertinghe was just outside the normal range of German shell fire and the village was used both by artillery units and Field Ambulances. Burials were made in the original Military Cemetery until June 1917, when the New Military Cemetery was begun in anticipation of the Allied offensive launched on this part of the front in July. Although the cemetery continued in use until October 1918, most of the burials are from July to December 1917.

Crich Roll of Honour name –

William Edwin Else

Windmill British Cemetery, Monchy-Le-Preux

Pas de Calais, France

367 Casualties

On 23 April 1917, in the Second Battle of the Scarpe, Infantry Hill and Guemappe were captured by Commonwealth troops. Guemappe was lost the same day but was retaken almost at once, and further progress was made in the following days. In May, the 29th Division began this cemetery and buried in it a number of the dead from 23 April. It continued in use until March 1918, and was used again from August to October 1918.

Crich Roll of Honour name –

John William Curzon

Ypres (Menin Gate) Memorial

Ieper, West-Vlaanderen, Belgium

54,406

The site of the Menin Gate was chosen because of the hundreds of thousands of men who passed through it on their way to the battlefields. It commemorates casualties from the forces of Australia, Canada, India, South Africa and the United Kingdom who died in the Salient. In the case of United Kingdom casualties, only those prior to 16 August 1917 are remembered here (with some exceptions). United Kingdom and New Zealand servicemen who died after that date are named on the memorial at Tyne Cot, a site which marks the furthest point reached by Commonwealth forces in Belgium until nearly the end of the war.

Crich Roll of Honour names –

Hubert (Bert) Petts

Samuel Henry Smith

Arthur Ernest Williamson

Plymouth Naval Memorial

Devon, UK

23,211 Casualties

After the First World War, an appropriate way had to be found of commemorating those members of the Royal Navy who had no known grave, the majority of deaths having occurred at sea where no permanent memorial could be provided.

An Admiralty committee recommended that the three manning ports in Great Britain – Chatham, Plymouth and Portsmouth – should each have an identical memorial of unmistakable naval form, an obelisk, which would serve as a leading mark for shipping. The memorials were designed by Sir Robert Lorimer, who had already carried out a considerable amount of work for the Commission, with sculpture by Henry Poole. The Plymouth Naval Memorial was unveiled by HRH Prince George on 29 July 1924.

Crich Roll of Honour name –

James Rodgers

Ten men on the Roll of Honour were buried in UK churchyards.

St Margaret's Churchyard

Cley-Next-The-Sea, Norfolk

7 Casualties

Crich Roll of Honour name –

George Mellors

St Mary's Churchyard

Crich, Derbyshire

8 Casualties

Eight servicemen were buried in the Crich Parish churchyard of St Mary's.

Also interred in the churchyard were three German prisoners of war who died while imprisoned in Crich War Camp. They were Otto Gehrhardt (23), Franj Kaminski (28) and Franz Koyub (31). Their bodies were returned to Germany after the war.

Crich Roll of Honour names –

Gilbert Atkins

James Hunt Bingham

Vernon Bowmer

Frederick Charles Bown

John Turner Gibbons

George Frederick Gration

Frank Arthur Hall

Frederick Wragg (Rodgers)

St. Woolos Cemetery

Newport, Monmouthshire

265 Casualties

Crich Roll of Honour name –

Charles Harris